I0829917

Deconstructed Screen Printing

The Beauty of the Organic Line

By Susan Brooks

© Copyright 2024 Susan Brooks

ALL RIGHTS RESERVED
No part of this book may be reproduced in any manner
without the express written consent of the author except
in the case of brief excerpts in critical reviews and articles.

All inquiries should be addressed to the contact information listed on
this website: www.susanbrookstextileartist.com

ISBN: #978-1-7331956-1-4

Susan Brooks
Louisville, Colorado

Developmental Editor: Janice Brewster Weiser,
www.creativegirlfriendspress.com
Cover and Book Designer: Karen Sulmonetti,
www.sulmonettidesign.com

Dedication

To the unseen women, students and lovers of art who continue to pursue their passion in their homes and studios.

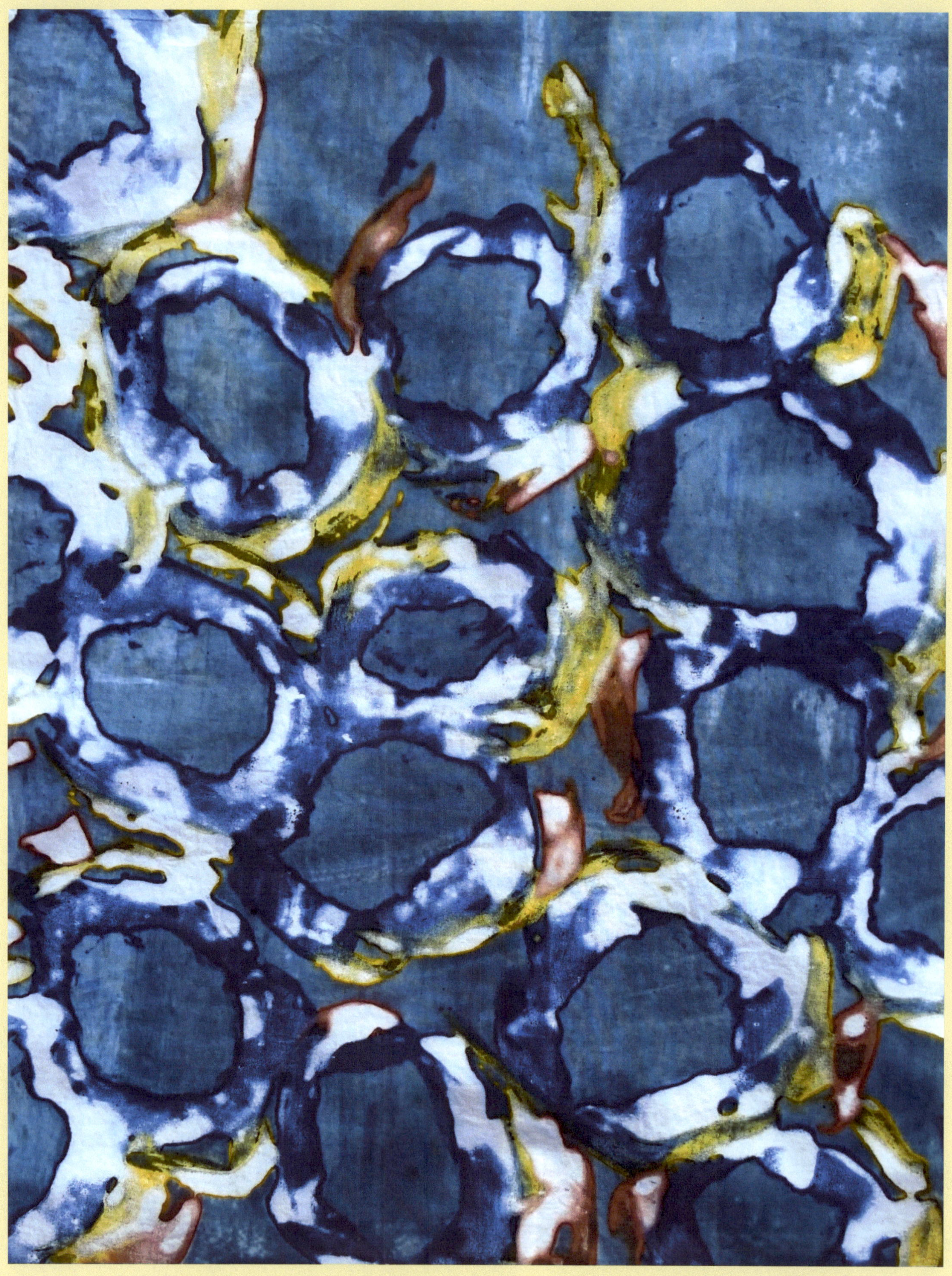

Table of Contents

Left: The design on this print was made using paper resist.
Read more about this technique on page 76.

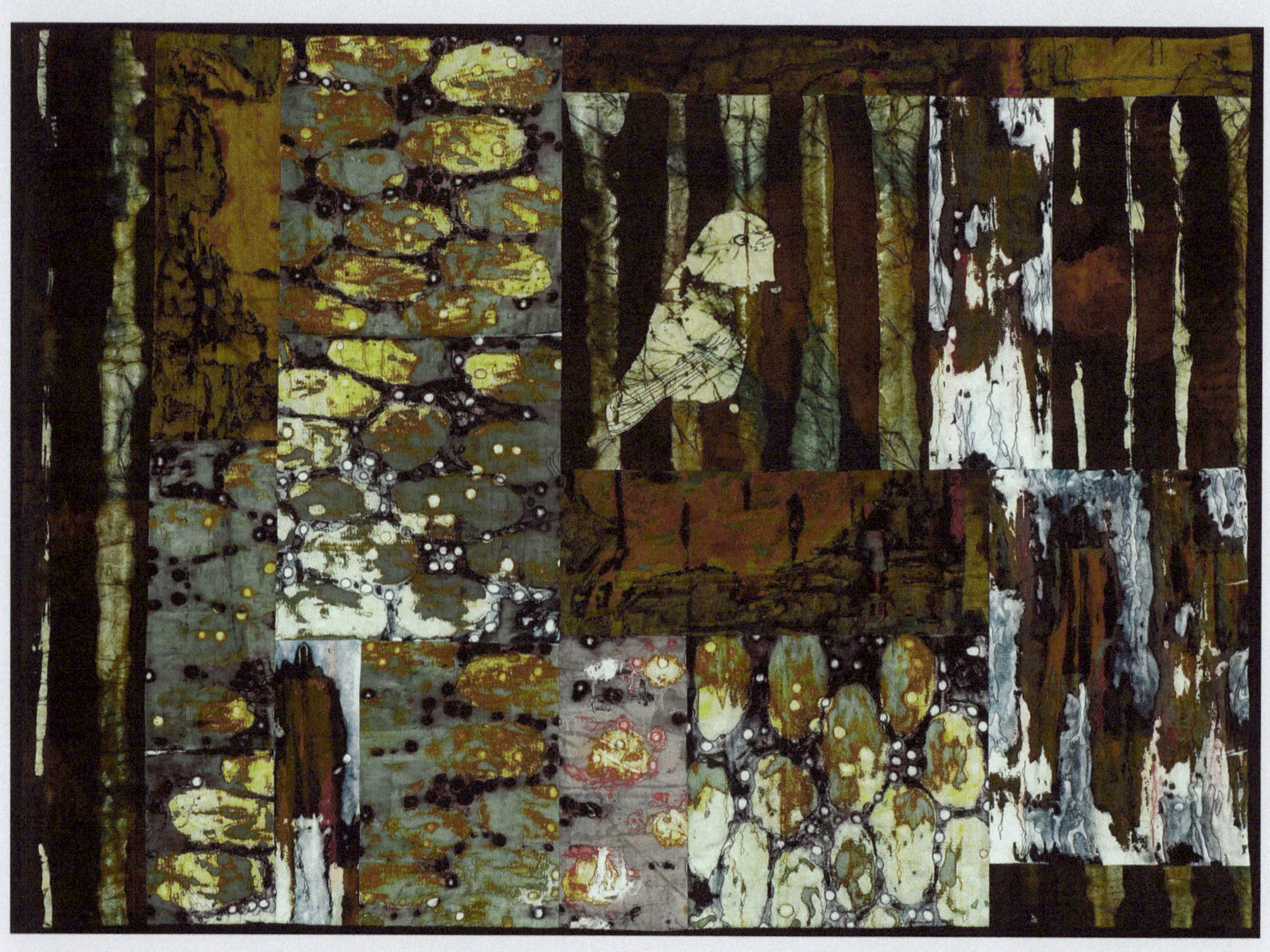

"Little Bird" (40" x 29") by Susan Brooks, featuring a variety of screen prints on cotton fabric.

  Deconstructed Screen Printing: The Beauty of the Organic Line

Deconstructed
Screen Printing

My gift to the reader is to pass on my love of fabric, as well as the techniques and ability to replicate and produce images inspired by nature, color and your own stories. This is my companion book to *Eco-Dyed Art Journals: Using Nature's Imprints*, where we explore using plant-based dyes to create organic images. Deconstructed screen printing is another way to create these organic, nature-based lines and shapes using Procion dyes.

Fiber is used in our everyday living; to provide comfort and safety from the elements, as clothing, to build shelters and to sleep under, as bedding and quilts.

Fabric is also used to create art: wall art, wearable art, gifts, journals and timeless heirlooms to be given to family and friends. Deconstructed screen printing is an exciting way to add one-of-a-kind patterns and designs to fabric.

THE PROCESS

Deconstructed screen printing, also known as breakdown printing, is a process that creates organic images of complexity, layering and texture. The basic process follows these steps:

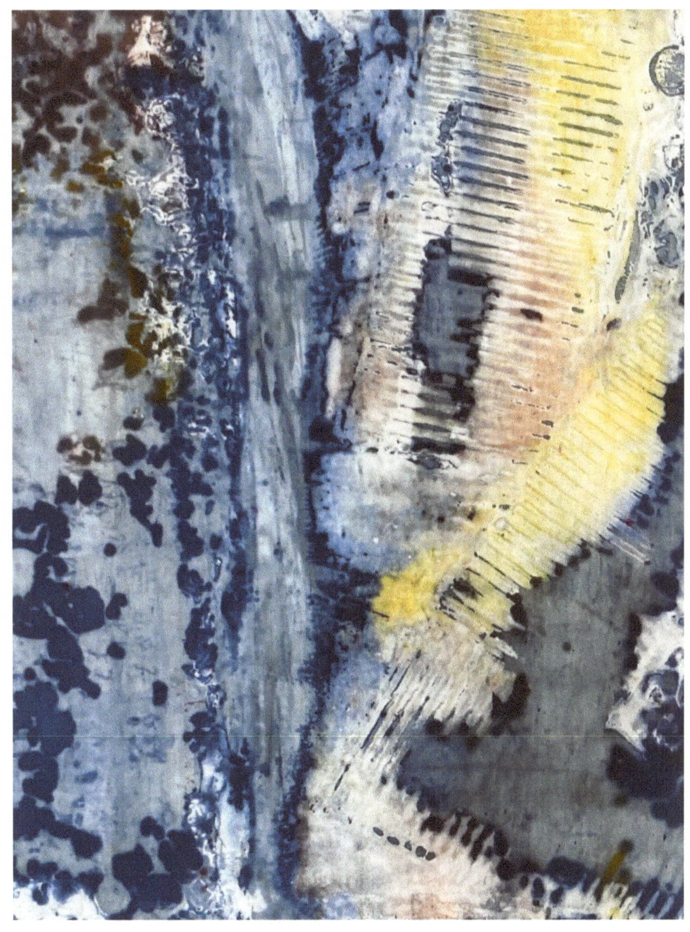

With deconstructed screen printing, colors blend in unexpected and delightful ways. Visual texture can be created with common household items like corrugated cardboard and bubble wrap.

1. Thickened dyes are painted onto the surface of a silk screen to create patterns or designs.

2. The screen is placed in the sun or a warm room until the dye is dry.

3. The screen is placed on a piece of fabric to be printed, then a print is "pulled" using alginate (print paste).

4. Some of the dried dye will remain after the first pull, so the screen can be used to make multiple prints.

5. As the image on the screen "deconstructs," each print will be unique.

In the following chapters, I walk you through the supplies you'll need and provide recipes for mixing the alginate (print paste). Then, I cover using the print paste to thicken dyes for painting your design. You'll learn how to pull prints onto fabric and how to add layers and textures. Along the way, I hope you'll be inspired by the samples and artwork you'll find in each chapter.

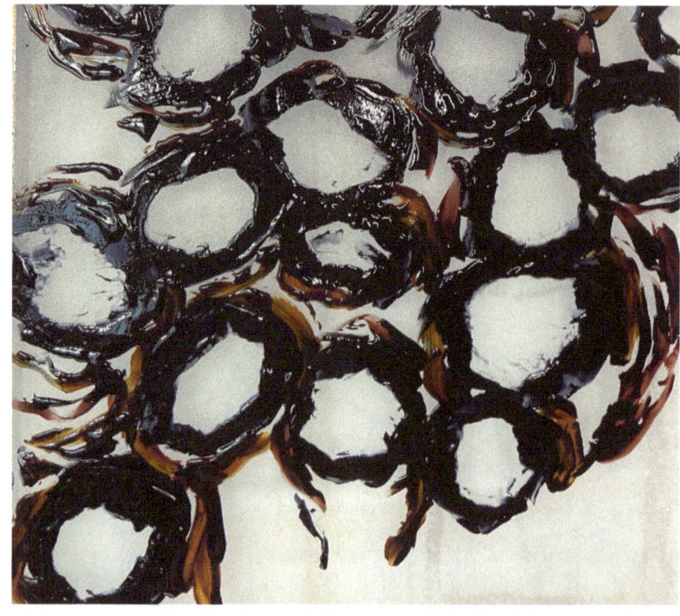

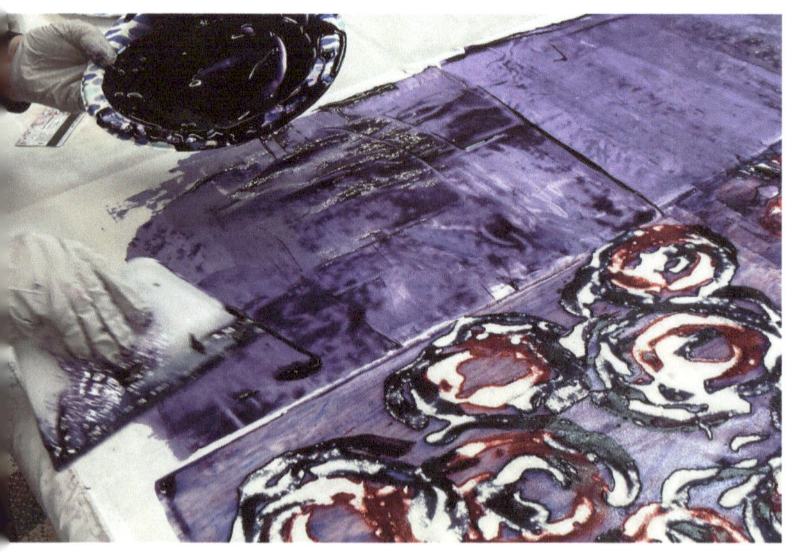

Left: After pulling a print, you can use the alginate mud to "paint" your fabric as well.

NOTE:
The most difficult part of the process is cutting into the fabric after it is printed! Try using your printed fabric to create:
- *Art quilts*
- *Bags or journal covers*
- *Framed wall art*
- *Clothing or scarves*

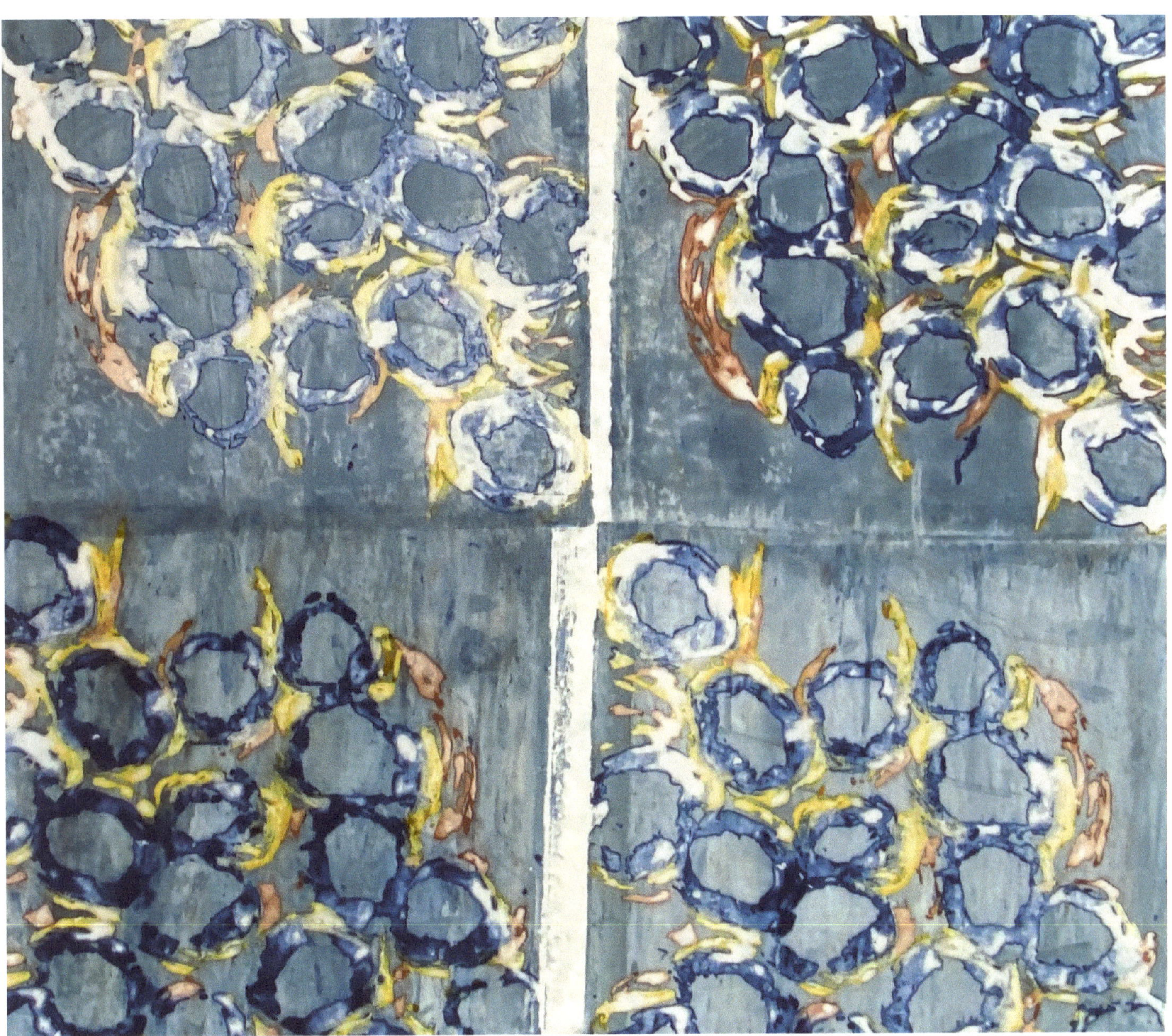

A series of prints was pulled from the painted screen shown opposite. Areas of the screen that aren't painted will fill in with color on the print. Print 1 is on the top left. Print 2 is top right. Print 3 is bottom right, and print 4 is bottom left. Using clear alginate for each pull keeps the background color consistent. The background appears blue because the alginate has picked up color from the Indigo and Gold dyes, which were painted on the screen.

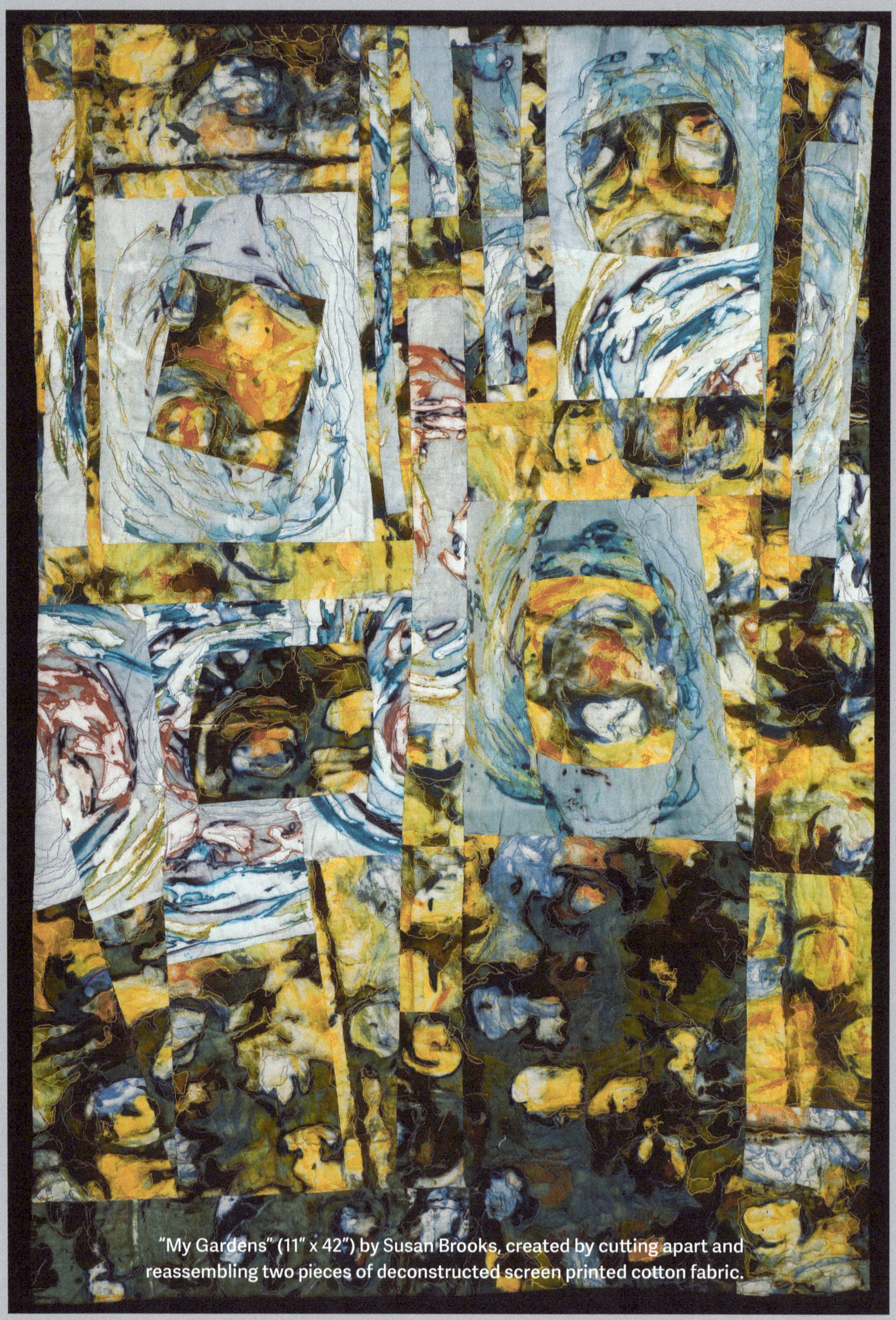

"My Gardens" (11" x 42") by Susan Brooks, created by cutting apart and reassembling two pieces of deconstructed screen printed cotton fabric.

chapter 1

Supplies

All supply companies are listed in Resources on page 107.

- Portable 4-by-6-foot tabletop printing pad (see instructions on page 101) or materials to cover your table surface (several layers of thick batting, then plastic, then a sheet or piece of cotton)
- All natural fabric: cotton, silk, wool, linen, rayon, silk organza, bamboo
- Silk screens: one or two, any size from large to small with 12xx mesh
- High-quality duct tape (for silk screen wells only)
- Procion MX dyes (purchase dyes in a range of colors or mix your own colors by purchasing a few basic colors)
- Sodium alginate
- Urea
- Soda ash
- Ludigol
- Metaphos
- Blender (designated for chemical mixing only)
- N95 particulate mask
- Plastic gloves
- Plastic cups

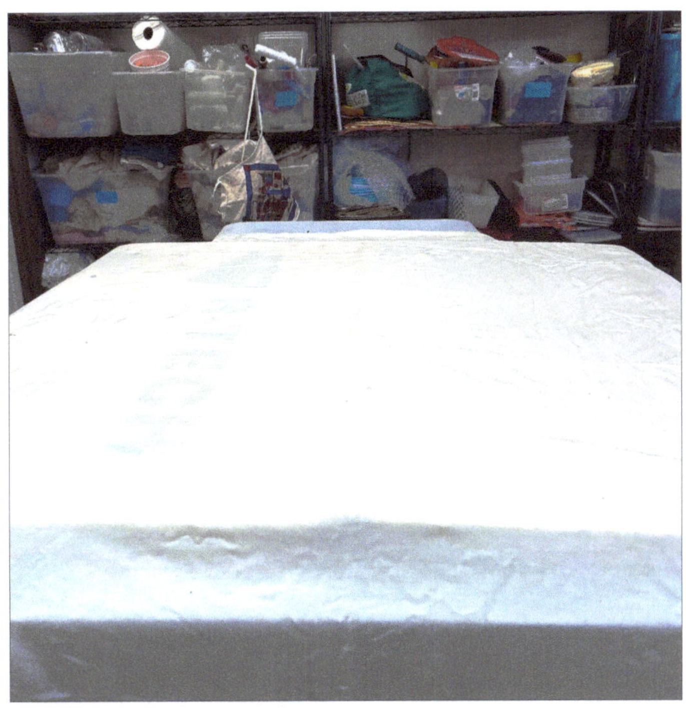

Portable 4-by-6-foot tabletop printing pad

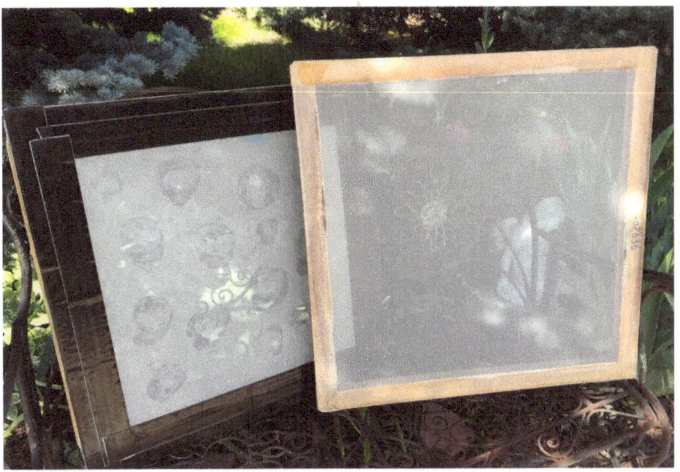

The silk screen on the left has a well made by placing duct tape around its perimeter. The screen on the right has no well.

- Plastic spoons
- Paper or plastic plates
- Blue tape for identifying mixed dyes in cups
- Foam paint brushes
- Squeegees for pulling prints
- Discarded credit cards or gift cards
- T-pins or blue painters tape to keep fabric taut while printing
- Sheets
- Painters .2 mil plastic for tabletop and batching
- Synthrapol for washing out fabrics (use low-suds Synthrapol for low-water washing machines)

OPTIONAL SUPPLIES
- Watercolor paper
- Paint brushes
- Extruders
- Plastic bottles (wide mouth)
- Soy wax
- Electric skillet for melting soy wax
- Stamps and soy wax tools
- Clorox toilet bowl cleaner
- Anti-Chlor powder
- Respirator for vapor protection (for discharge pastes)

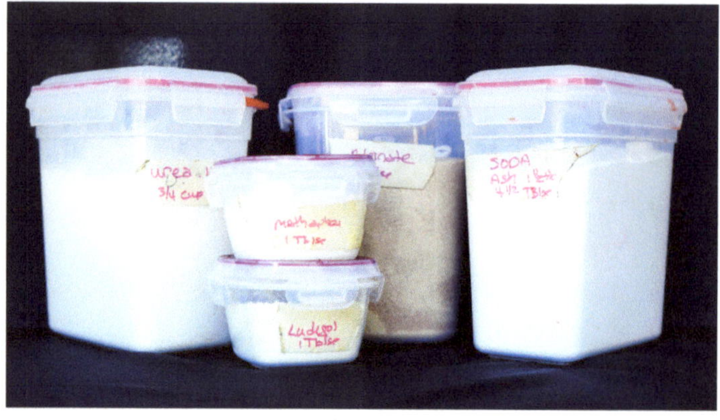

Chemicals used for dyeing

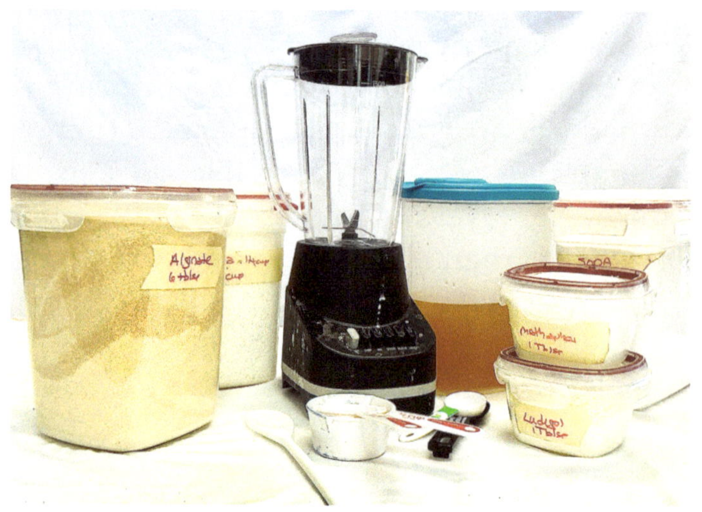

Chemicals and mixing supplies

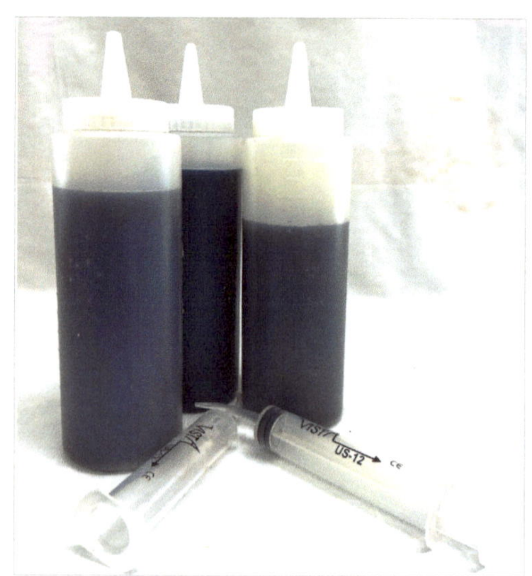

Bottles and extruders for creating fine lines with dye

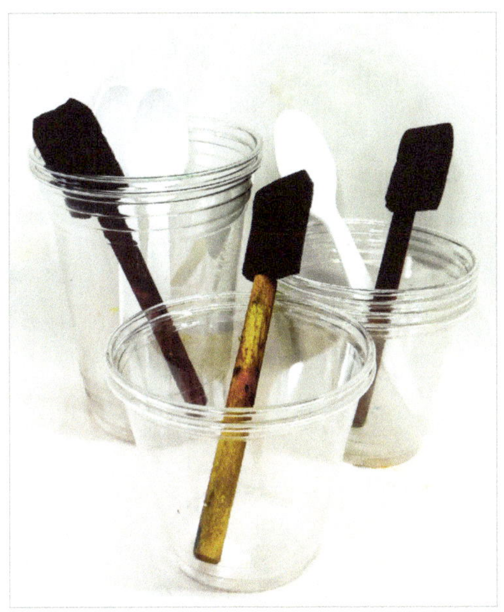

Cups, spoons and foam brushes

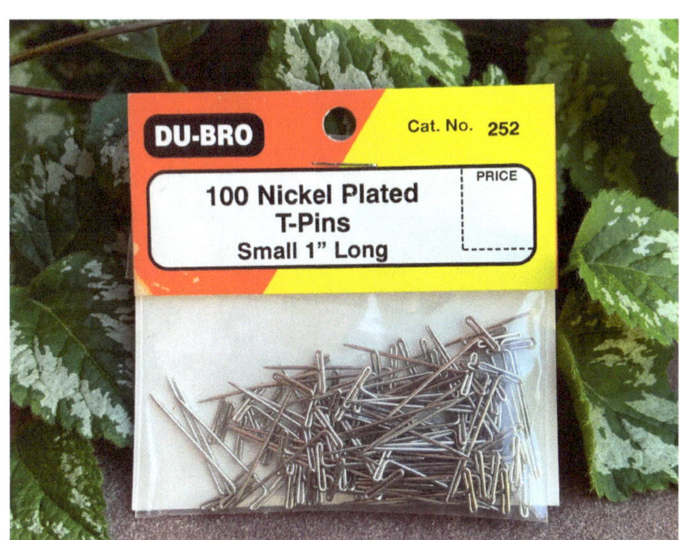

T-pins

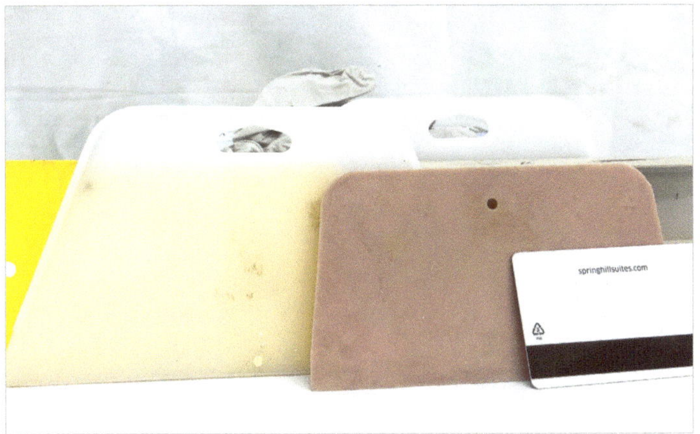

Squeegees for pulling prints

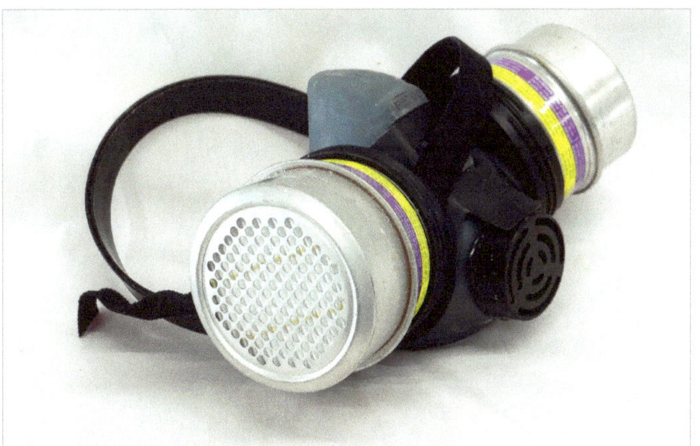

Respirator to avoid breathing fumes

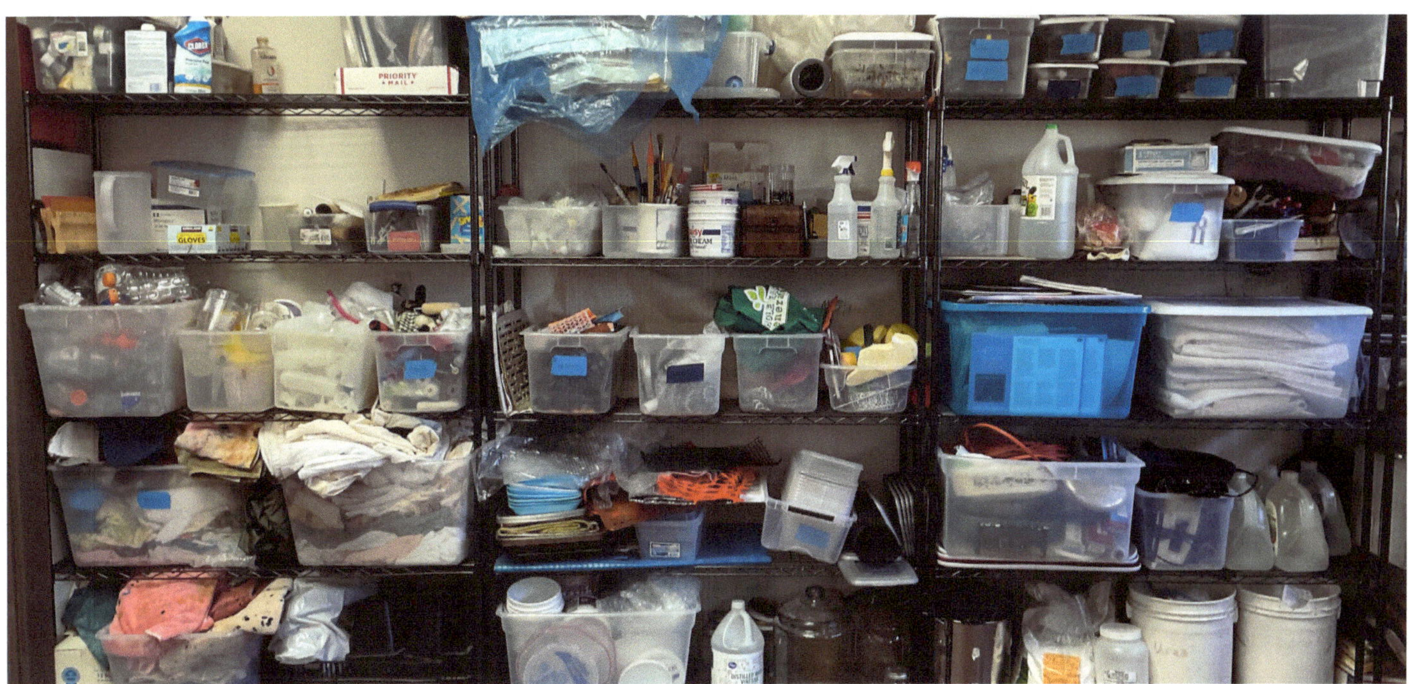

Garage studio supply storage

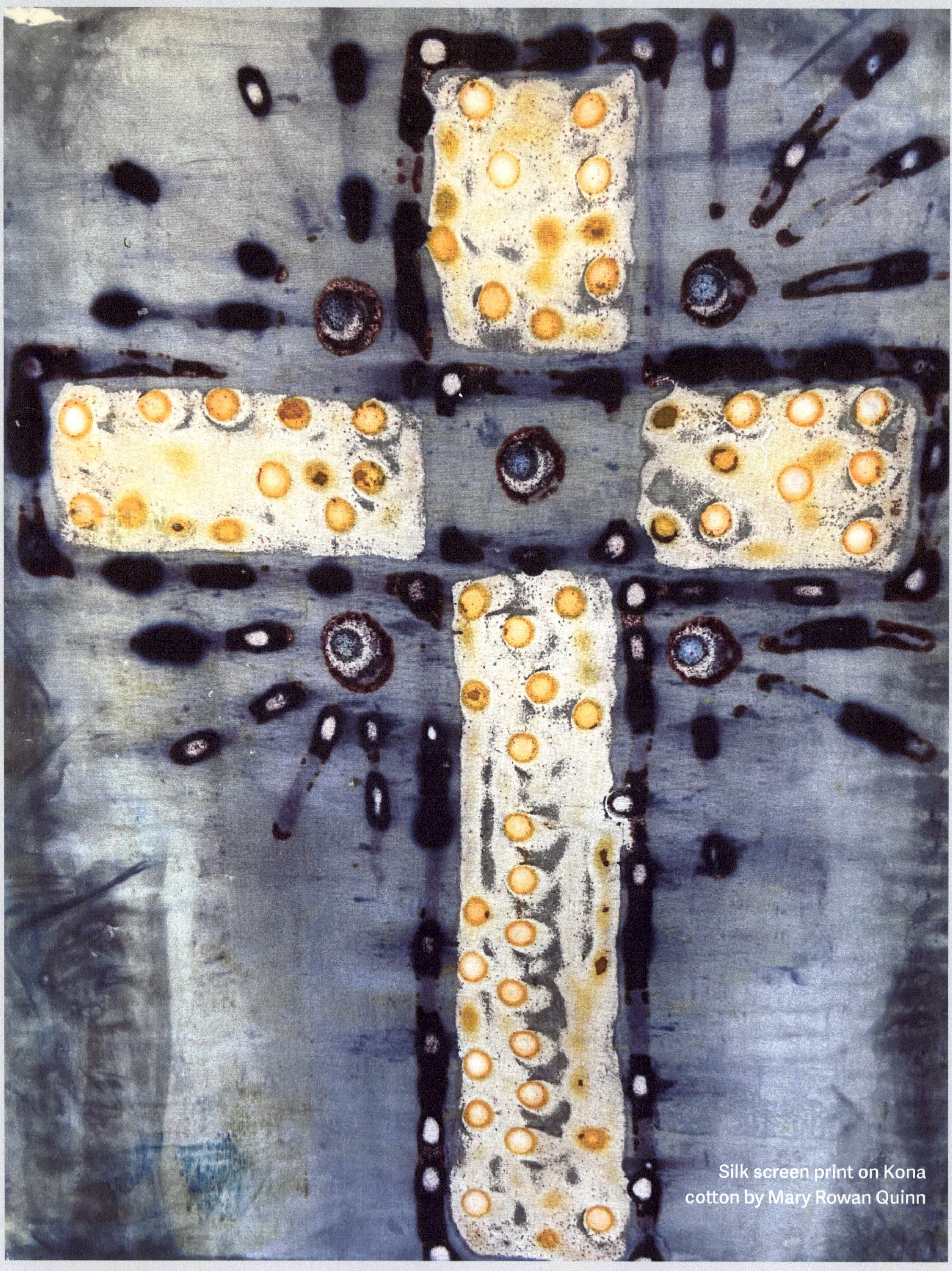

Silk screen print on Kona cotton by Mary Rowan Quinn

chapter 2

Fabrics and Dyes

FABRICS

Choose white or off-white:
- Pimatex PFD (prepared for dye) for the most vibrant colors
- Kona cotton, for a lighter and more subtle effect
- Muslin cotton, for even lighter saturation
- Linen
- Rayon
- Bamboo
- Hemp
- Silk
- Organza

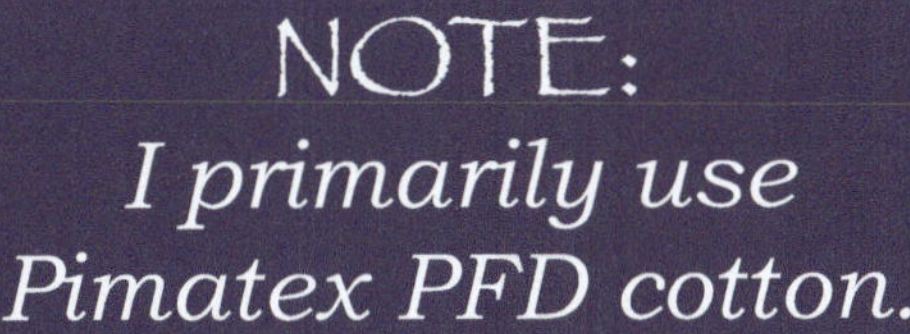

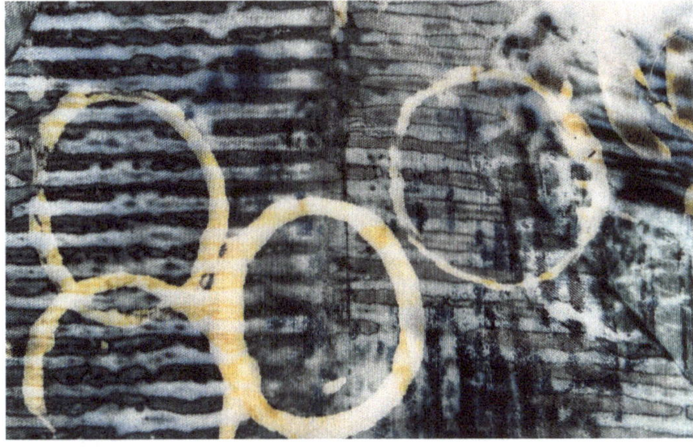

The pattern of lines on this print on rayon fabric was made by pressing corrugated cardboard into the thickened dye. The circles were made by discharging the color with disharge paste.

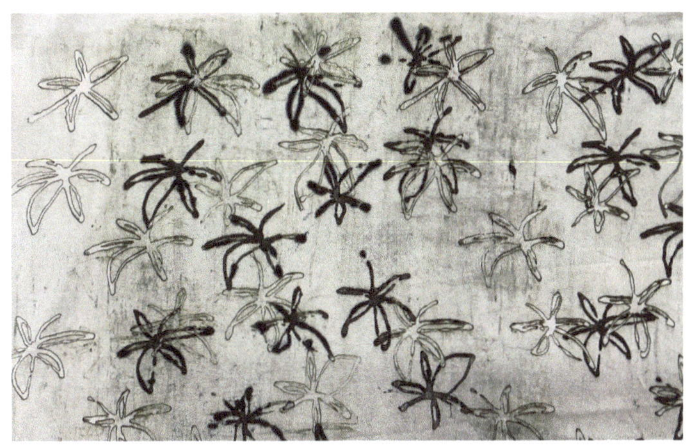

This print on hemp fabric was made by pulling clear alginate across a screen painted with a flower design. The thickened dye was Moss Green.

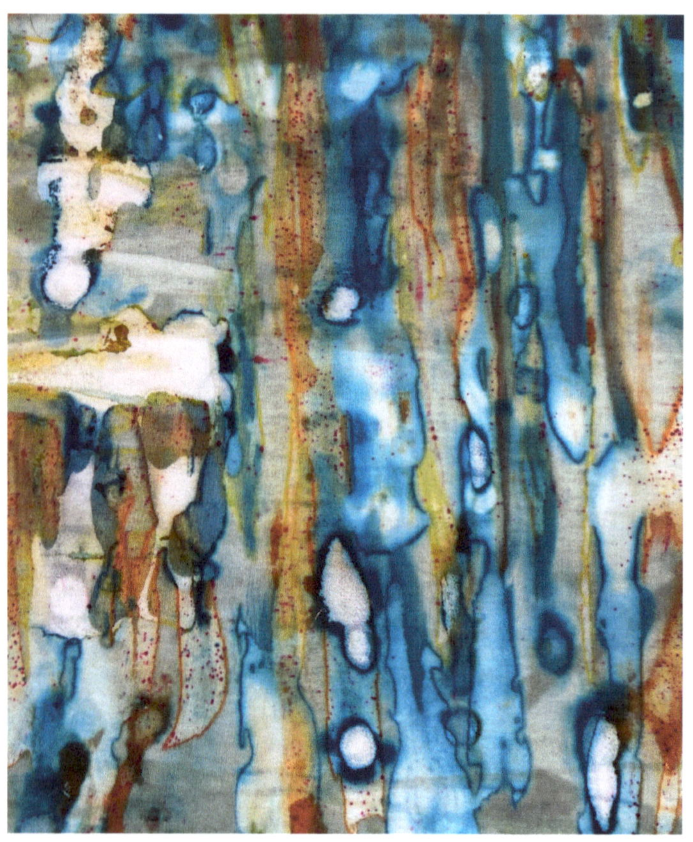

Red dots on prints can be caused by dye that's not completely dissolved.

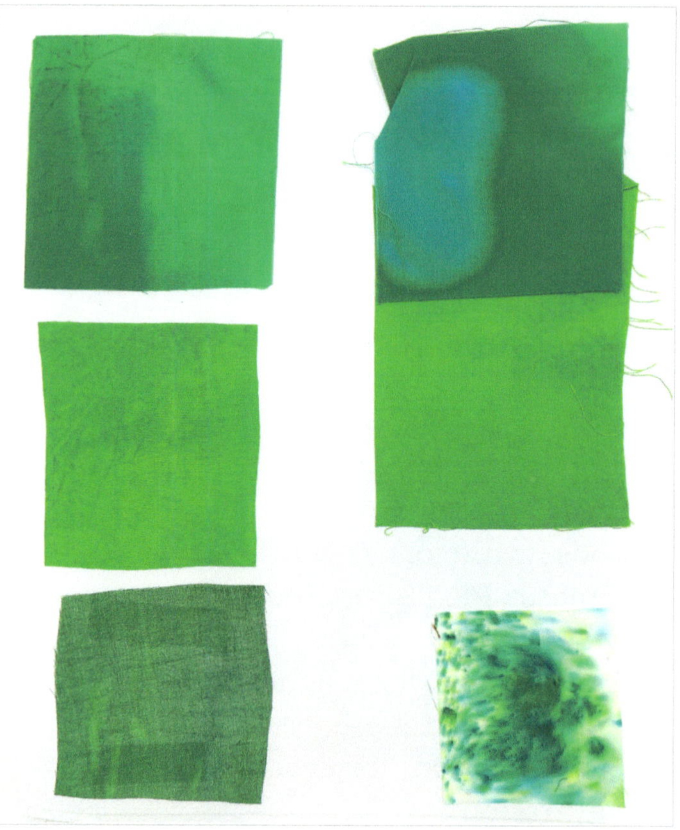

Green dye looks slightly different on different fabrics: cotton (top left), silk (middle left) and organza (bottom left). The top right swatch shows how the color changes when discharged with bleach. The bottom right swatch shows the various color particles within the dye powder.

DETAILS ON PRINTING AND DYEING

Red dye molecules tend to set quickly on cotton fabrics if the alginate (print paste) is used right after it is mixed.

Experiment with dye powders before using them on your finished piece by sprinkling a small amount of dye powder on a piece of silk or cotton and spritzing it with water. You will see how much red is in the dye powder. Wash out the fabric when you are finished to prevent the dye from becoming airborne.

If you place a plastic sheet under the fabric to be printed, the wet dye will blend and morph under the fabric and on top of the plastic, blurring any lines in your print.

I place my fabric to be printed on a cotton bedsheet. As the dye absorbs into the sheet underneath, it makes a more defined line.

Allow your fabric to dry entirely before using an extruder to add additional lines.

If you overdye fabric that is screen printed, the print will be covered up. Here's why: Fibers have "open spaces" that the dye molecule "fills up." The looser the weave (i.e. Kona fabric), the larger the open space and more muted the color

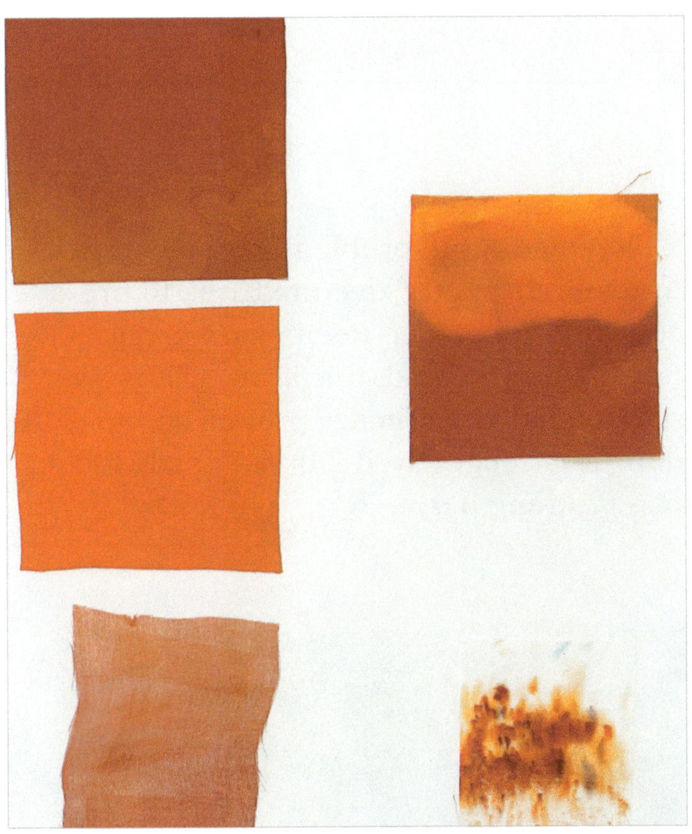

Pumpkin dye on cotton, silk and organza; discharged with bleach and with its various color particles (bottom right).

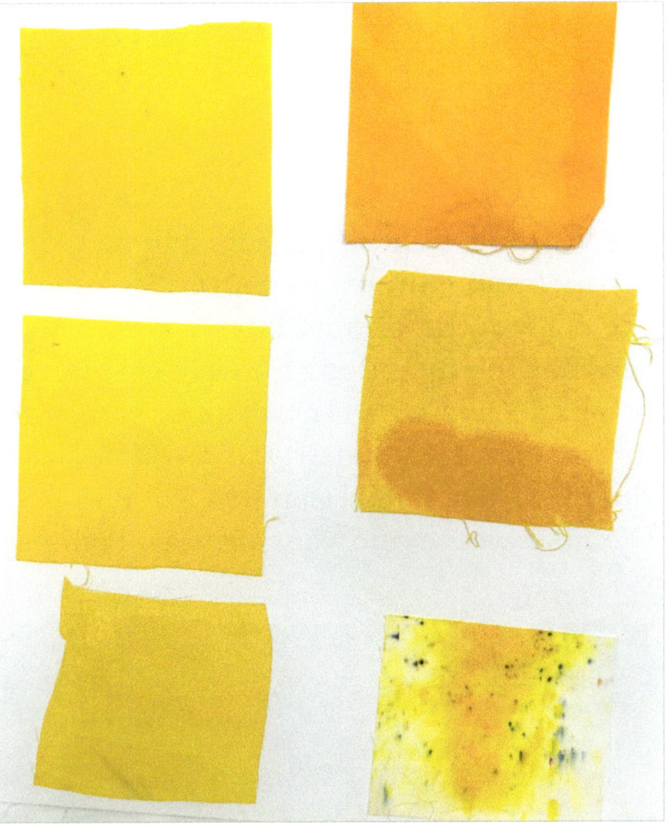

Yellow dye on cotton, silk and organza. The color when discharged and with its various color particles (bottom right).

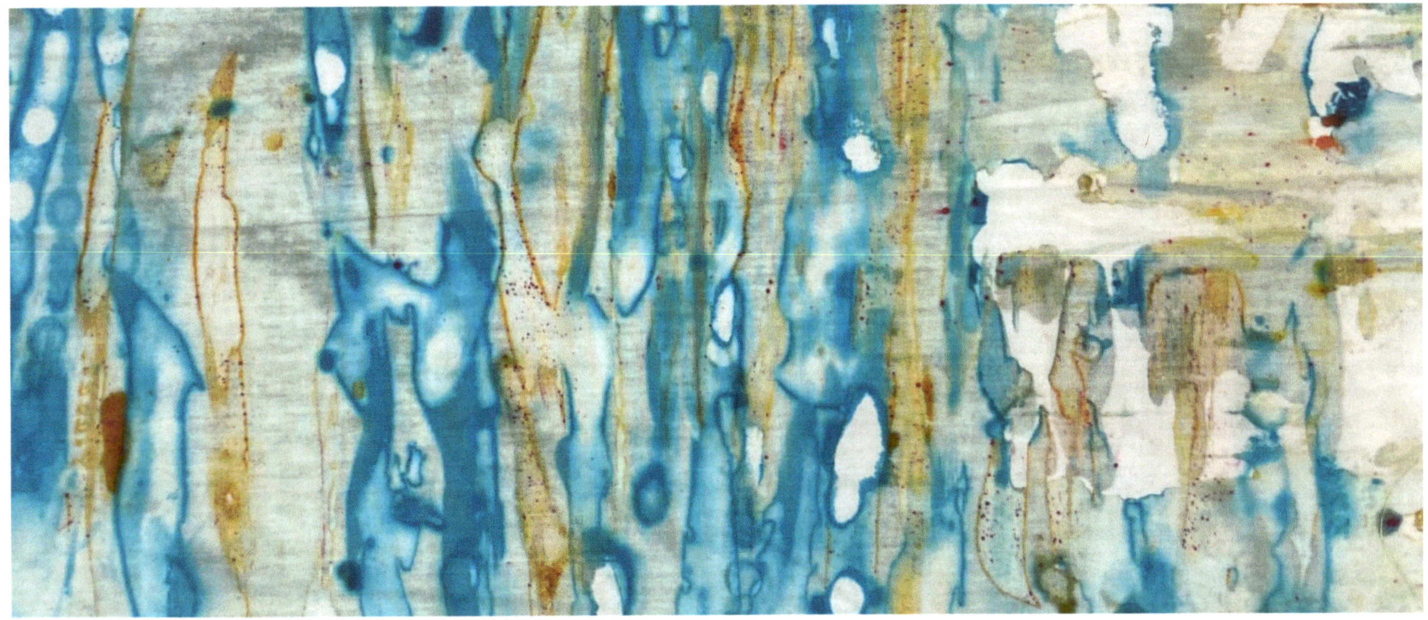

The reverse side of the fabric shows the dye does not completely bleed through to the back.

when using the same amount of dye. If the weave is tight, the colors will be more distinct and vibrant. When you look at the back of the printed fabrics, you will see that the dyes don't entirely permeate, or fill up the fibers. Therefore, if you do an immersion dye after you have made the print, the immersion dye will fill up the fiber weave and your print will almost entirely disappear.

To remedy this problem, you can use "quarter strength" dye mixtures to pre-dye cotton fabrics. (See Recipes on page 25.)

Using this method, the fabric will receive the deconstructed image printed on top of the quarter-strength dyed fabric. For silk fabric, use ⅛ strength dye.

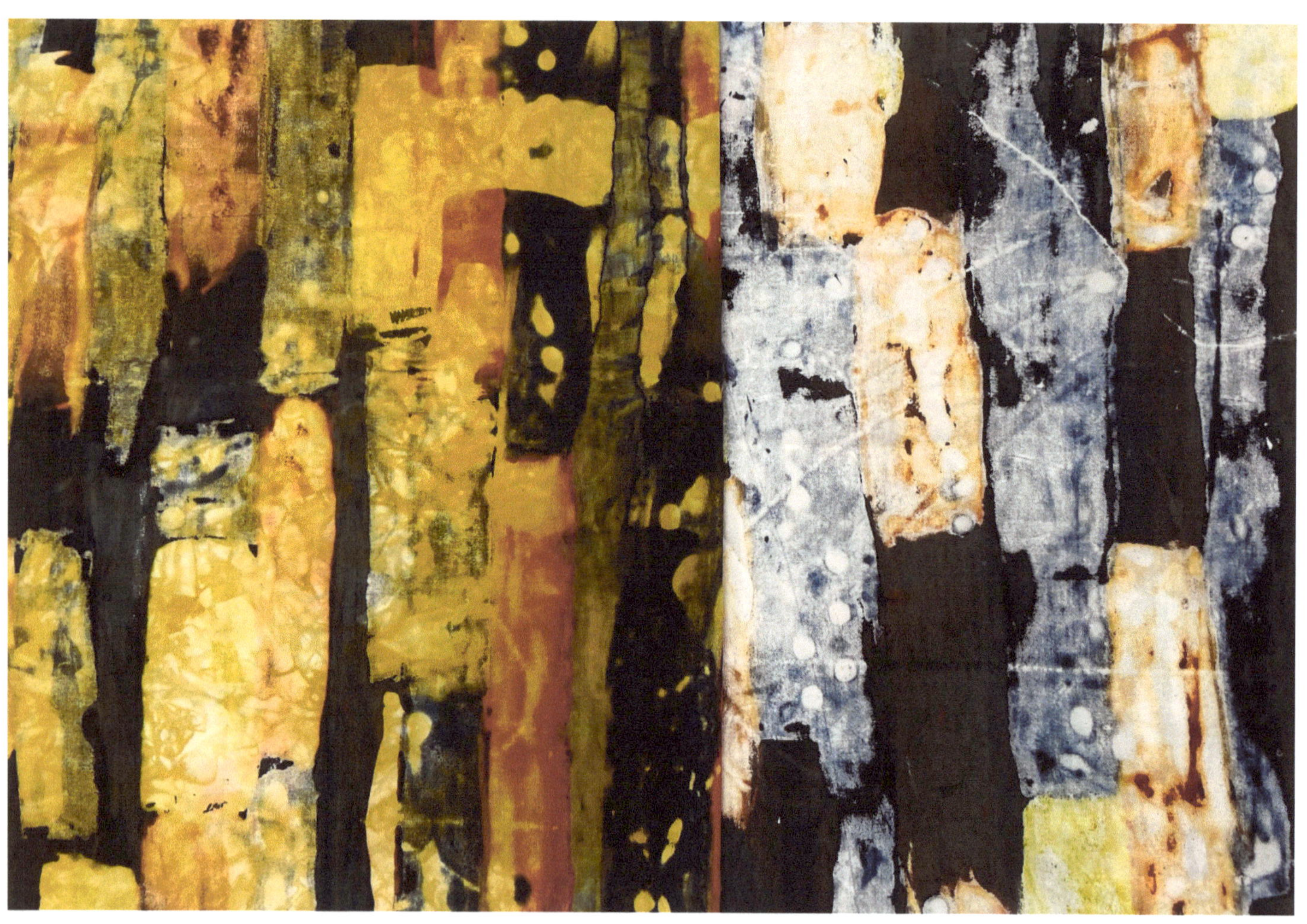

Pre-dyeing fabric changes the look of the print. On the left, the fabric was pre-dyed with ¼ strength dye. On the right is a print on white (undyed) fabric.

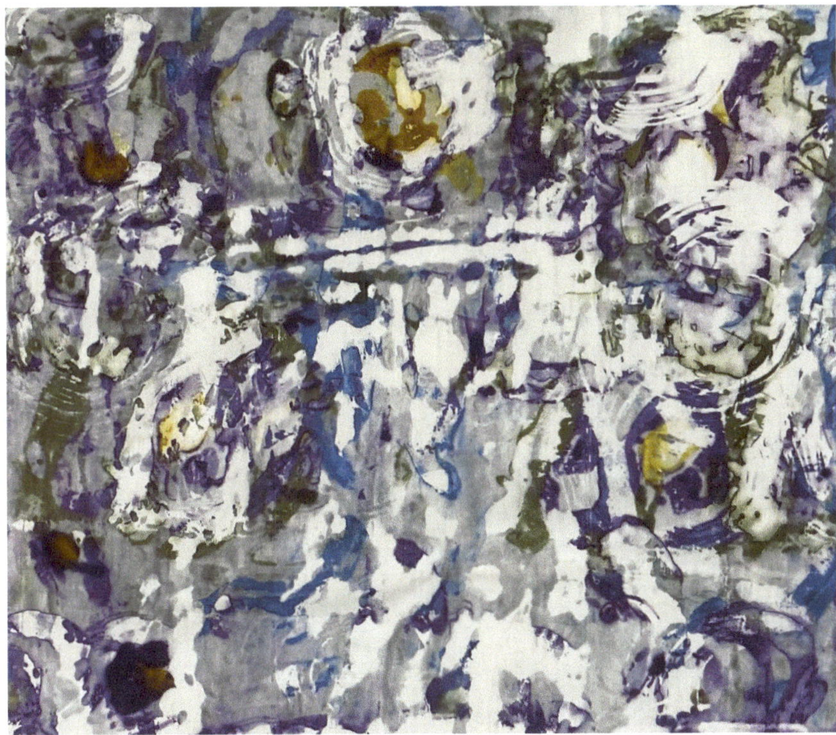

The edges of the silk screen create prints with clear, sharp edges.

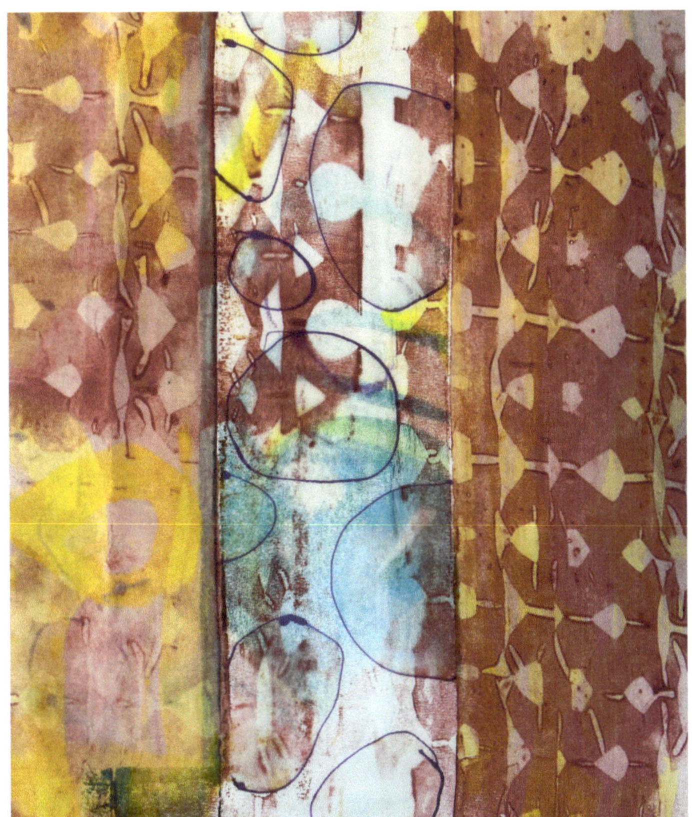

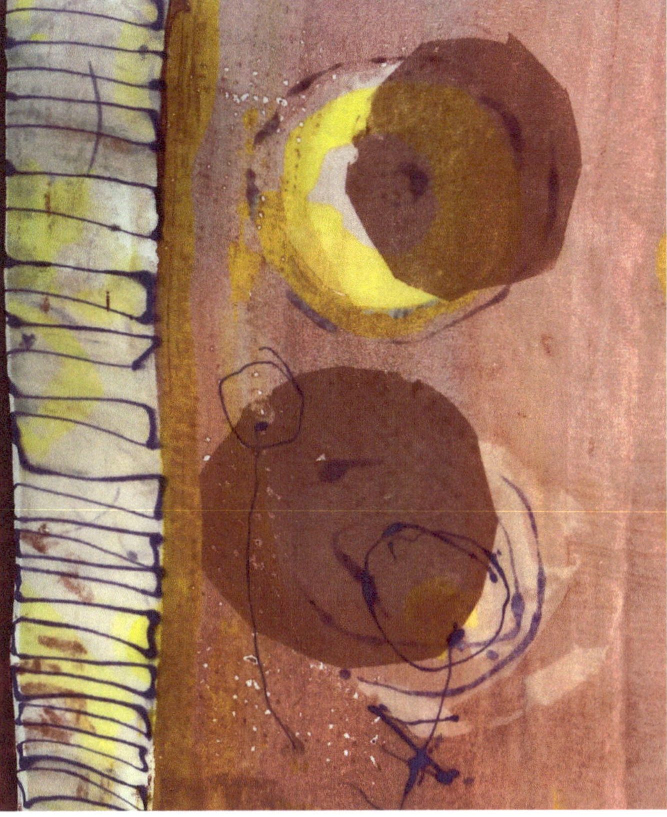

Artist Kerr Grabowski puts plastic under her fabric to be printed. Then when the print is pulled, moisture trapped on top of the plastic causes the colors to blur and morph. Right: Another sample of Kerr's work shows how she lets the pulled print dry, then adds line work by drawing with an extruder filled with dye.

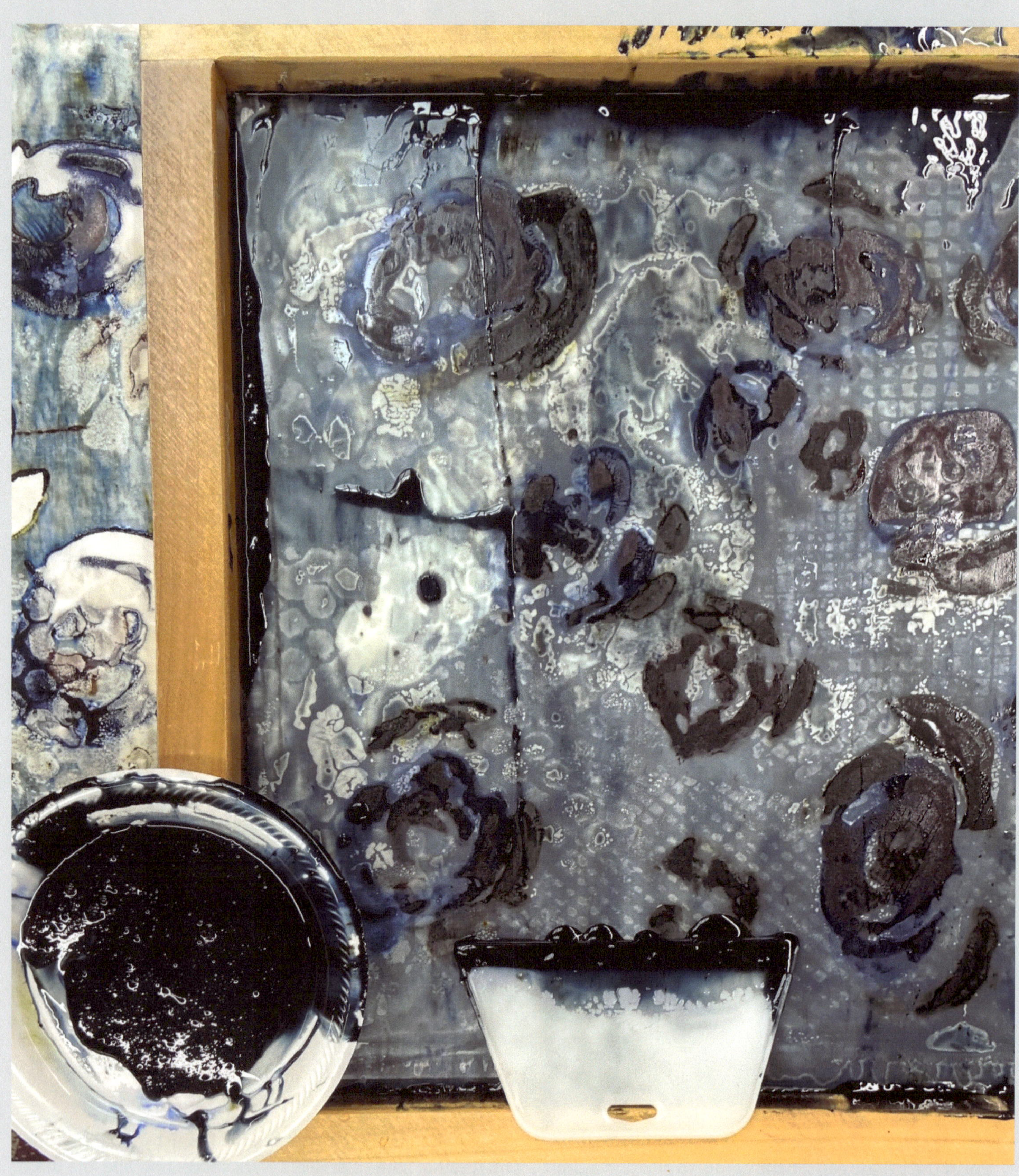

When pulling this print, a squeegee was used to remove the mud and scoop it out onto the plate as there is no well on the screen.

Silk Screens:
Wells vs No Wells

When you purchase screens from a craft store or online retailer, the wooden frame is not water-resistant. You will either need to varnish or tape the wood with a good duct tape to prevent warping.

Using duct tape, you can create a "well," which is just a taped-off perimeter where you can store your "mud" (the print paste that has picked up color) while pulling your prints.

Advantage of having the well: You don't have to use your squeegees and a paper plate to remove the mud between pulls.

Disadvantages of a well: It reduces the size of the printable area of your screen, and therefore the size of your print. Also, over time, the duct tape comes loose on the edges and eventually will need to be replaced.

Disadvantage of no well: You must be careful to not put a hole in the screen with the edge of the squeegee. If the screen is damaged, it cannot be replaced.

Screens will be laid in the sun on a sheet for drying before pulling a print. The sheet will collect the dripping dyes.

This deconstructed printing method works best in the spring/summer/fall

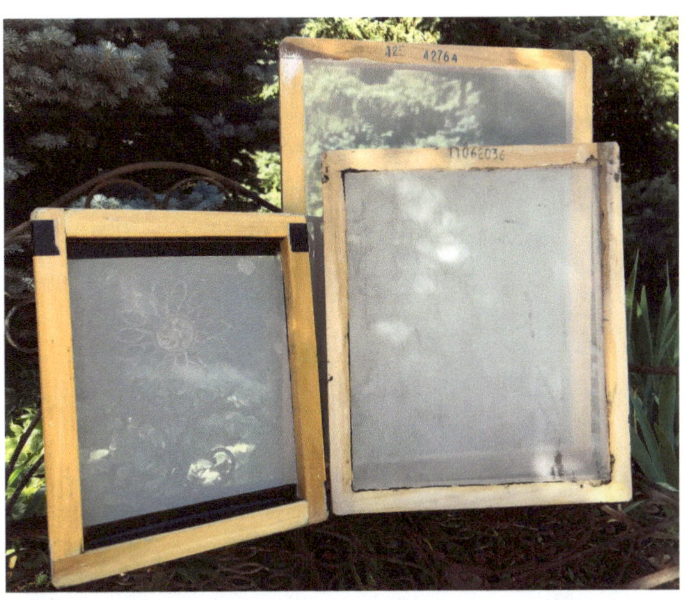

You can use a screen as is with no well, like the ones on the right, or add a well with duct tape, like the silk screen on the left.

NOTE:
American Frame Company varnishes their wooden frames, so you don't need to varnish the frame or "seal" it with duct tape.

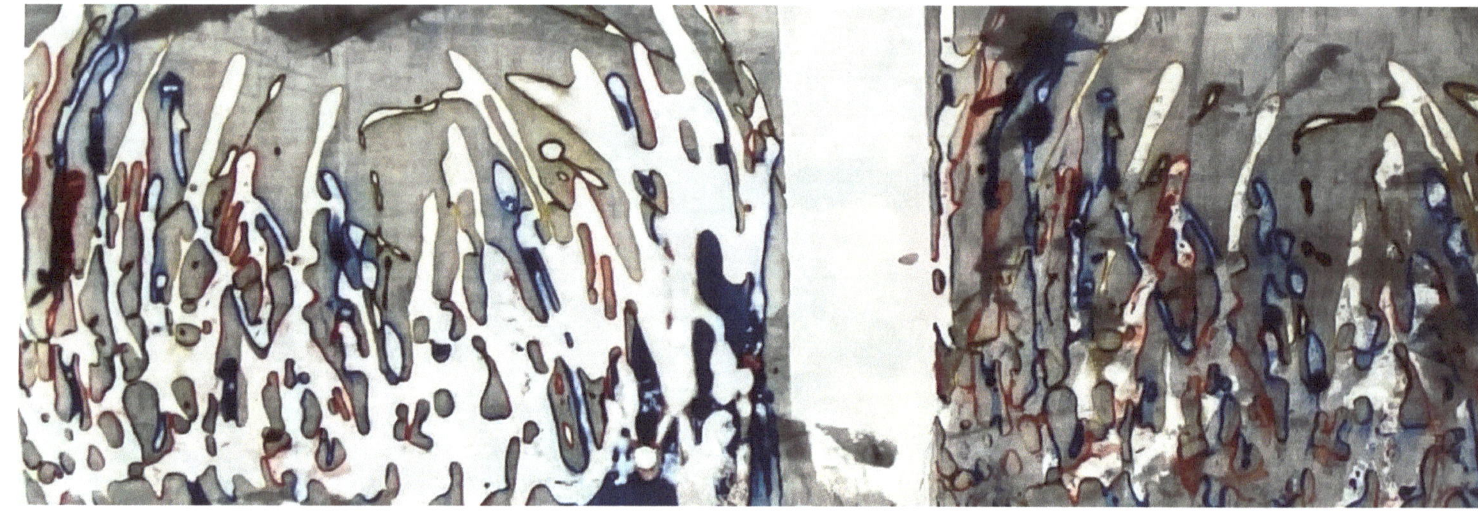

I pulled this series of three prints by using clear (uncolored) alginate for each print. The paste picks up colors from the thickened dye that was originally painted. Note how the design changes between prints as the thickened dye starts to break down on the screen.

months because of the heat of the sun. Screens can be dried inside your house, garage or studio during the winter. They usually take several days to dry, and the images are not quite as crisp.

NOTE:
I prefer to not use a well and have the full size of the screen, as I almost always remove the "mud" between the pulls. Removing the "mud" and replacing with new, clear alginate makes a lighter print. Reusing the "mud" makes the prints much darker with each pull.

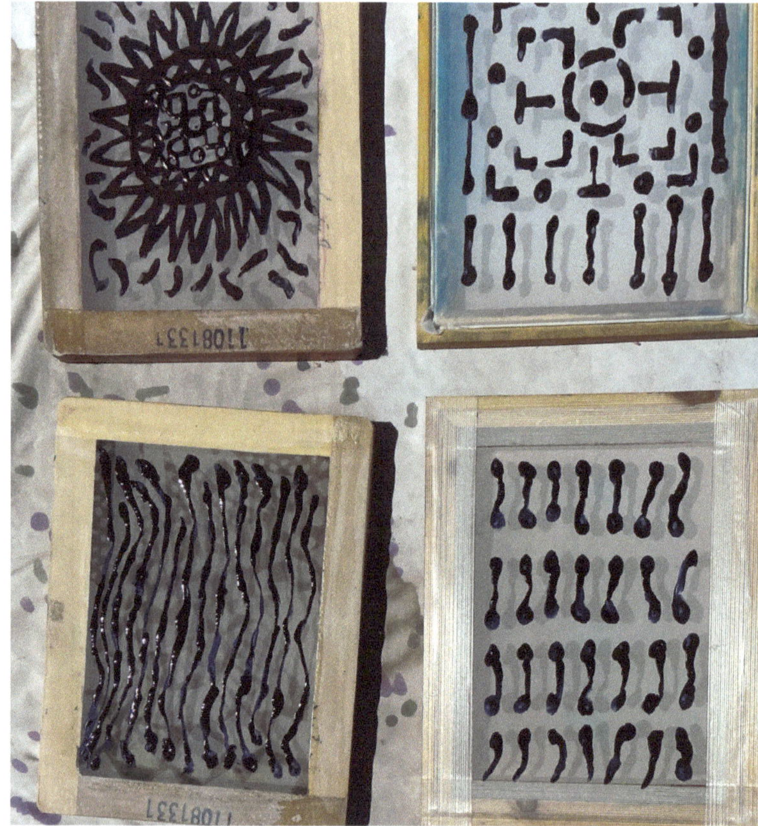

Four screens with linework designs by Jeanne Gray are set on a sheet in the sun to dry.

  Deconstructed Screen Printing: The Beauty of the Organic Line

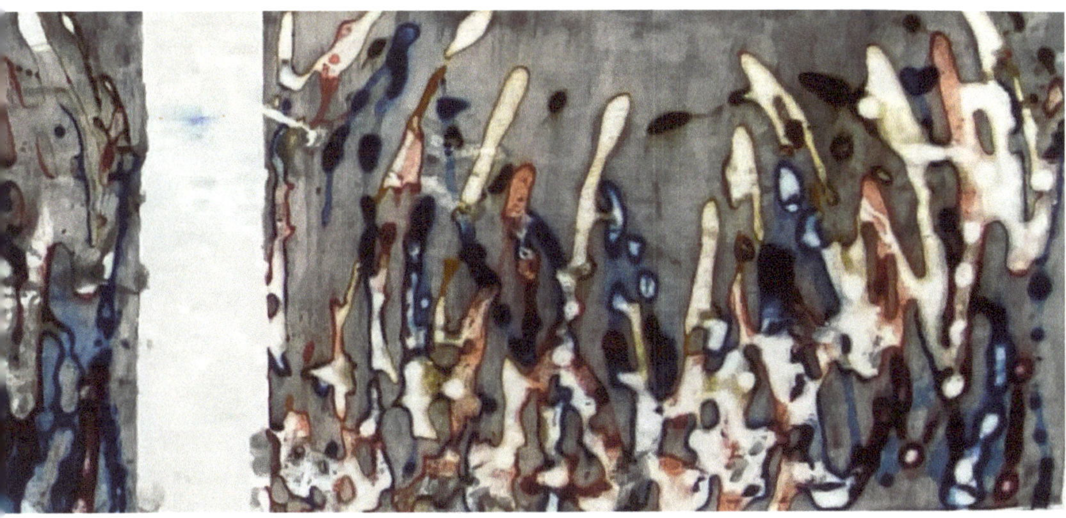

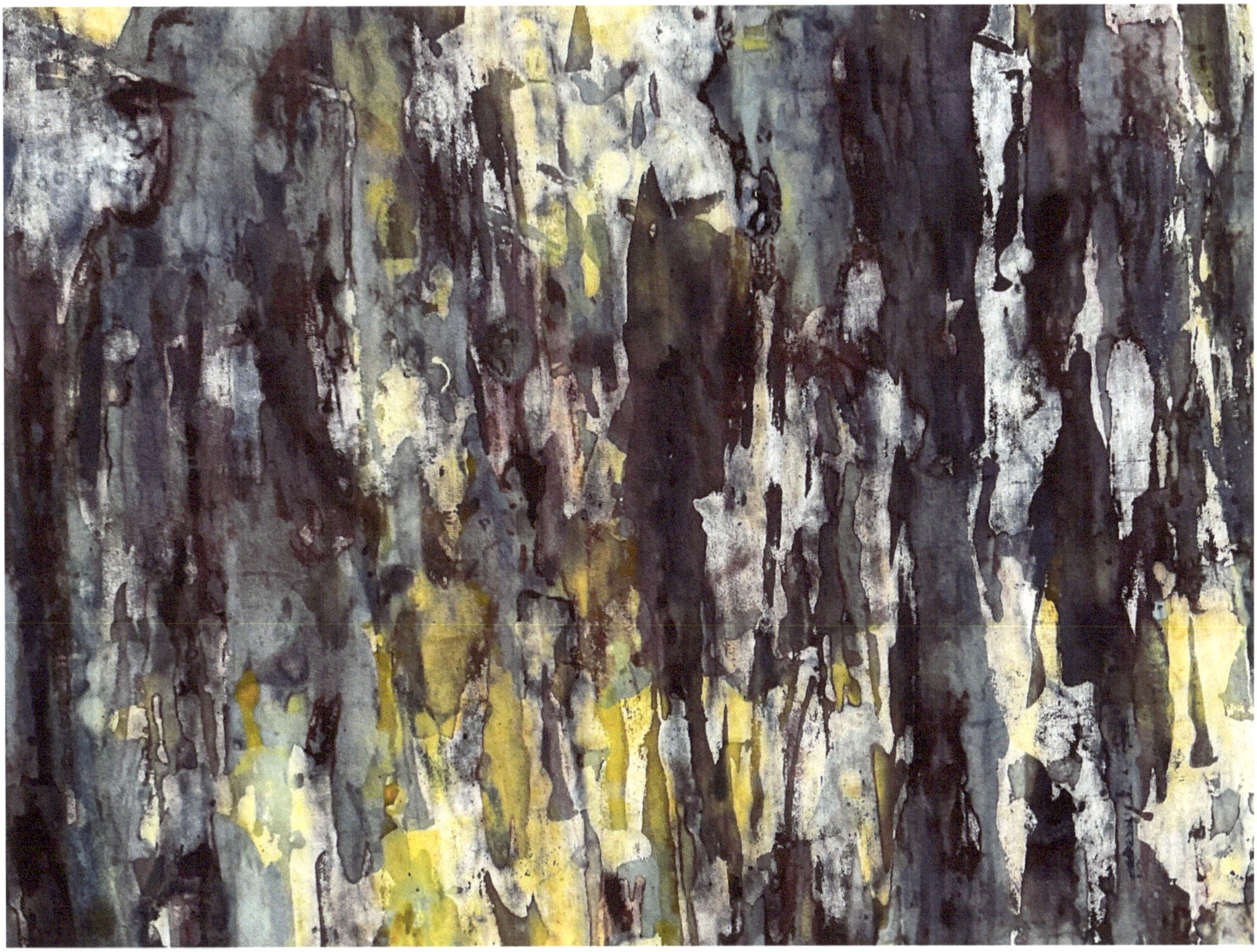

As with yeast, temperature affects the reaction of dyes. This print was taken from a design painted on a screen in winter. The result is a more blurred, watercolor effect. Two colors of dye were used to paint the screen: Black and Marigold. The colors blend as the clear alginate is pulled across the screen to make the print.

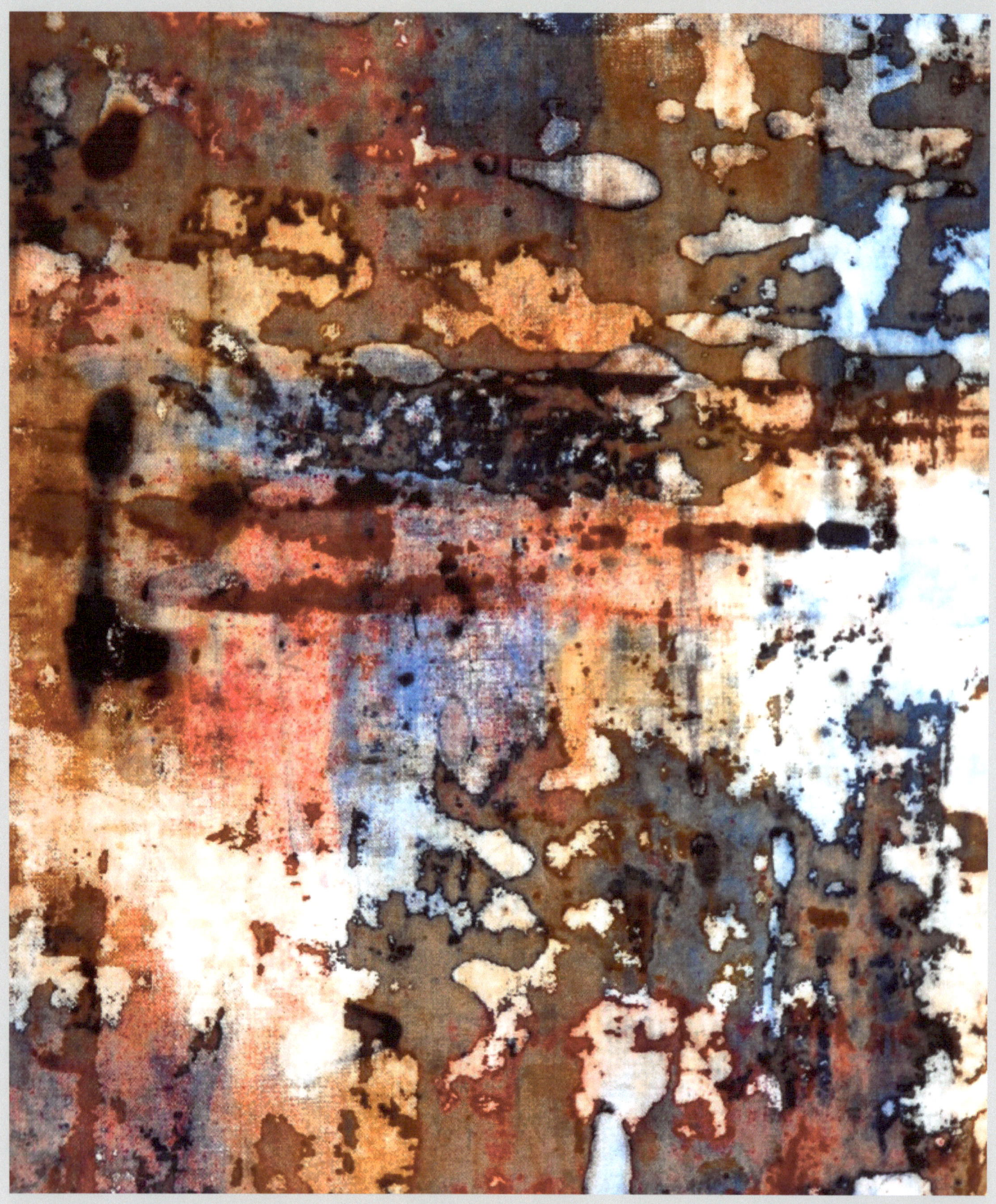

On this print, the light-colored places show where built-up areas of thickened dye acted as a resist. The clear alginate used to pull the print picks up color from the design painted in Indigo, Marigold and Brick. With each subsequent pull, the thicker areas of dye will break down, allowing more color to seep through, and there will be fewer white areas.

chapter 4

Recipes
For Print Paste and Dyes

ALGINATE (PRINT PASTE) to use for thickening dyes and pulling prints

In a blender, mix:
- 4 cups warm water
- ¼ cup urea
- 1 teaspoon Metaphos
- 1 teaspoon Ludigol
- 2 tablespoons sodium alginate

Mix for about 30 seconds until you hear the blender motor become slightly labored.

When pouring the alginate mixture into your container, it will be thin and runny. Keep stirring until it thickens. It will become the consistency of honey.

Mix the alginate paste at least two hours before use. Alginate can be mixed and used several days later. Store any unused alginate in the refrigerator. If it has an ammonia smell, discard.

SCOURING FABRIC

Before printing, you will need to scour fabrics that contain sizing. There's no need to scour PFD (prepared for dye) fabrics. The following recipe makes up enough solution for scouring up to 10 yards of fabric with sizing.

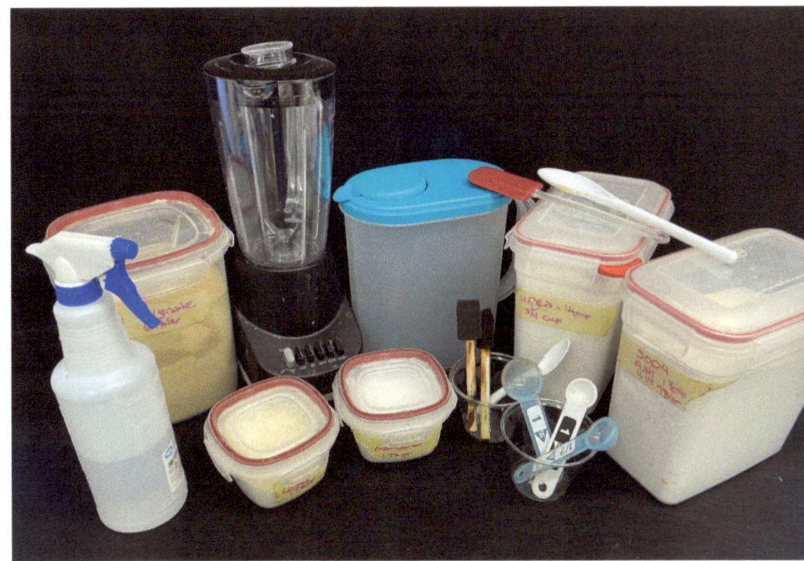

Supplies for mixing alginate (print paste)

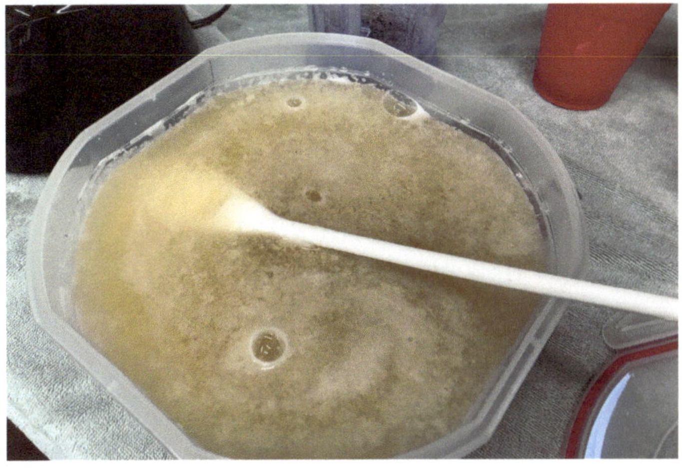

Alginate (print paste) should have the consistency of honey.

In washing machine add:

- ½ teaspoon Synthrapol
- ½ teaspoon soda ash

Wash fabric through a regular wash cycle with no detergent.

PRE-SOAK FOR IMMERSION DYEING (OPTIONAL)

If you'd like to dye your fabric, this water/soda ash solution primes the fabric to accept the dye.

Mix:

- ½ cup soda ash to 1 gallon hot water (16 cups)

Soak fabric until fully immersed and saturated in soda ash water solution; about 5 minutes. Wring out excess water/soda ash solution. You can immersion dye while the fabric is still wet.

You can also store dry soda ash soaked fabrics for future use. Cotton can be kept indefinitely. Silks can only be kept six months before the soda ash starts to deteriorate the fabric.

Keep the soda ash mixture in a gallon-size jug until ready to use. Pour excess soda ash water back into the jug after soaking the fabric. Discard after several uses.

DYES FOR IMMERSION DYEING AT FULL STRENGTH, ¼ STRENGTH AND ⅛ STRENGTH (Optional)

If you'd like to dye your fabric prior to printing, you can use dyes at full strength, ¼ strength or ⅛ strength, depending on the depth of color you want.

To create urea water, mix in a 16-ounce plastic bottle:

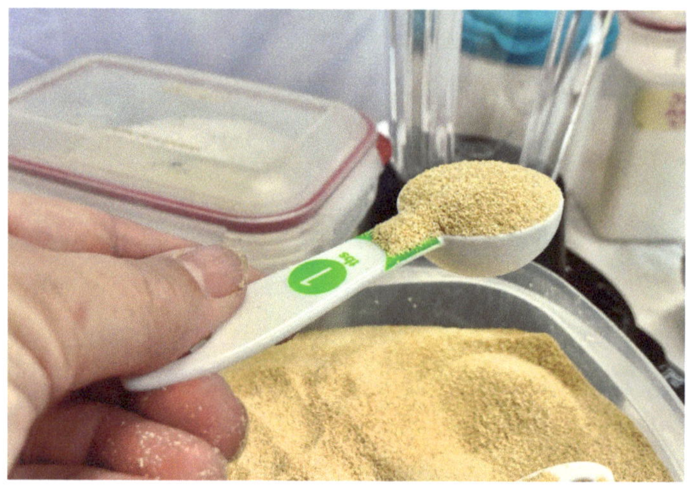

Sodium alginate in a rounded teaspoon.

- 2 cups warm water
- ¼ cup urea
- 1 teaspoon Metaphos
- 1 teaspoon Ludigol

This mixture will dye up to 2 yards of fabric.

- Add dye powder (enough for your preferred color and strength) to the urea water mixture.

Very dark color: 2 teaspoons of dye powder

Medium color: 1 teaspoon dye powder

Light color: Add 1 teaspoon dye powder and an additional 1 cup of water to mixture

Quarter strength: ¼ teaspoon dye powder to the two cups of urea water

Eighth strength (for silk): ⅛ teaspoon dye powder to the two cups of urea water

IMMERSION DYEING INSTRUCTIONS

In a large plastic container (i.e., a cottage cheese carton or plastic shoebox), place the fabric you pre-soaked in soda ash solution and pour the liquid dye mixture over the top, flipping the fabric several times to make sure it is fully saturated in the liquid dye.

Let the fabric sit in the container, with a lid, overnight in a warm environment. Use an electric blanket and wrap around the containers or bundles if it's cold overnight.

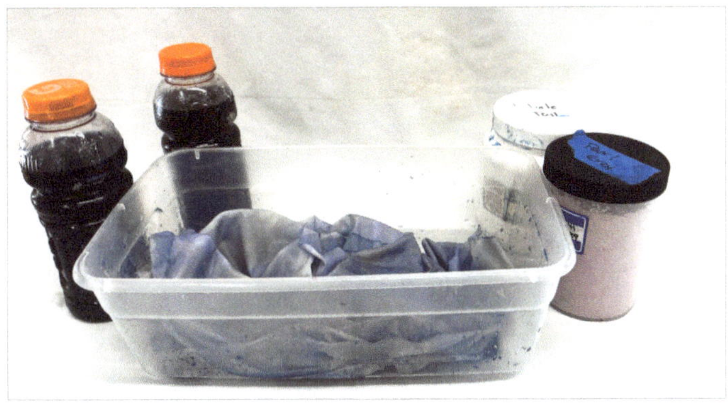

Immersion dyeing fabric in a plastic shoebox.

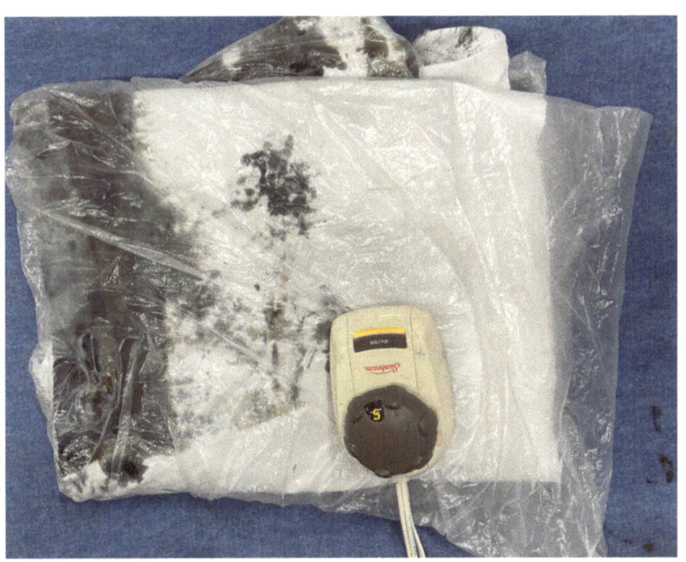

Bundle of fabrics wrapped in an electric blanket overnight to help set the dye.

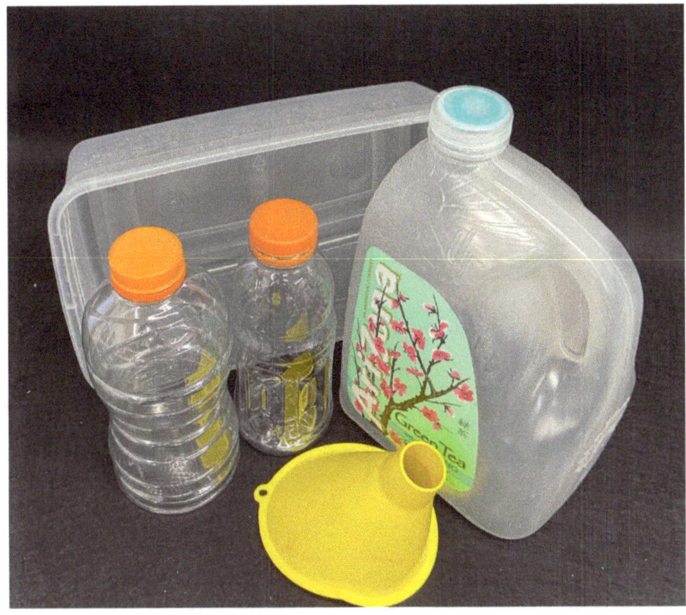

Immersion dyeing supplies include small bottles, a plastic shoebox, a funnel and a gallon jug for soda ash solution.

NOTE:
Dye is like yeast: If it's too cold, it won't activate. Temperatures that are too hot will kill the dye.

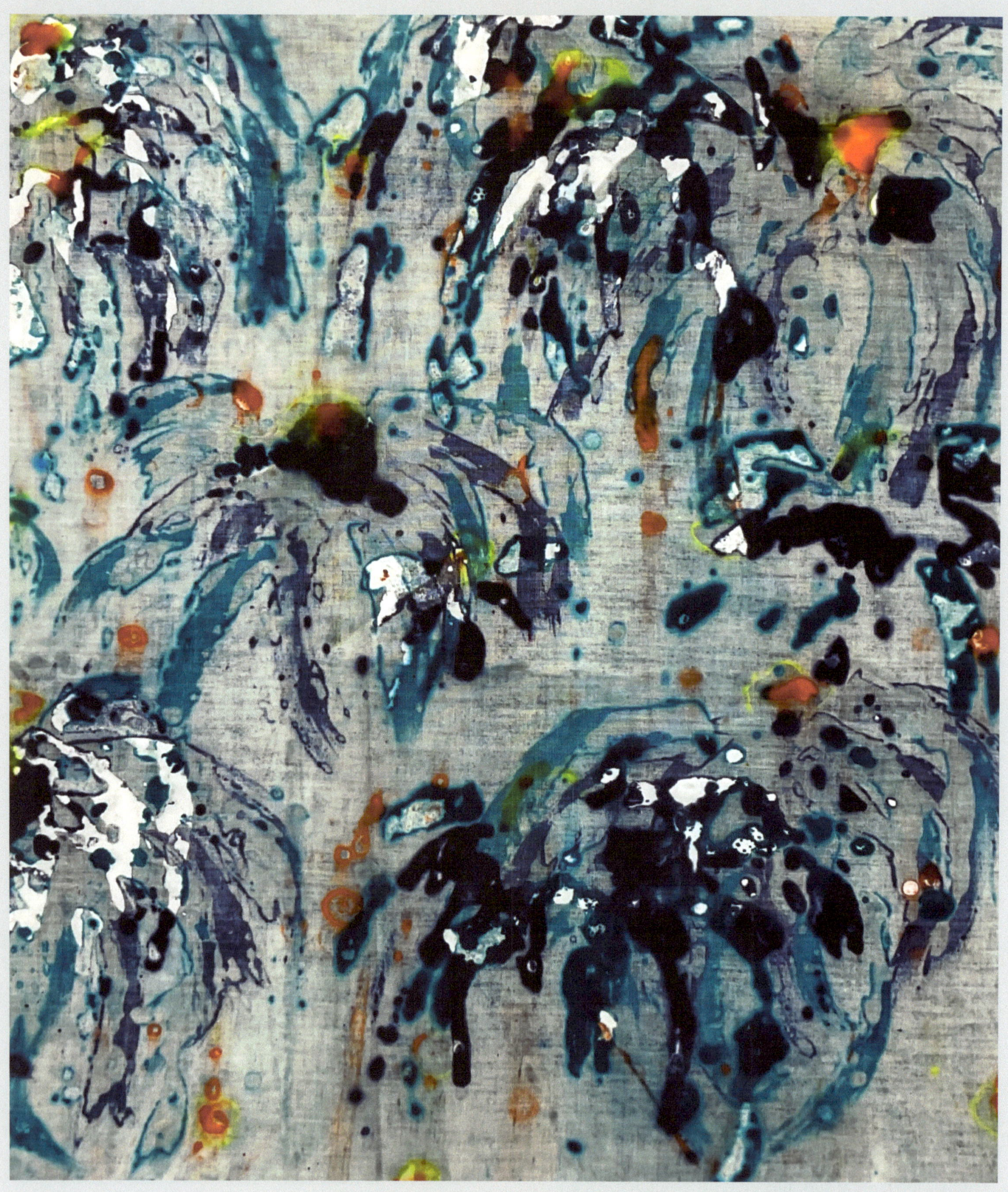

A floral pattern appears in a print pulled from a screen painted with Indigo Blue and Golden Yellow in a flower design.

chapter 5

Painting Designs
With Thickened Dyes

THICKENED DYE FOR PAINTING DESIGNS

Mix in individual cups:
- 1 cup alginate
- Procion dye powder
    - *½ teaspoon for light color*
    - *1 teaspoon for medium color*
    - *2 teaspoons for dark color*

To lighten colors, use less dye powder or add more print paste (alginate) to your cup of dye. You can also use Winter White dye powder (PRO Chemical #010). This method is much like adding white paint to lighten a darker paint. Use half dye color and half Winter White in a 50/50 mixture.

Mix our alginate the night before and your dyes about 10 minutes before using. This allows the dye chemicals to fully dissolve, resulting in fewer red dots and more true colors.

Use a gallon-size plastic container to store your alginate.

Pour the alginate into the individual cups and, using blue painter's tape, LABEL the color of dye power used on the cups.

You can use a small corner of a paper towel to check the color.

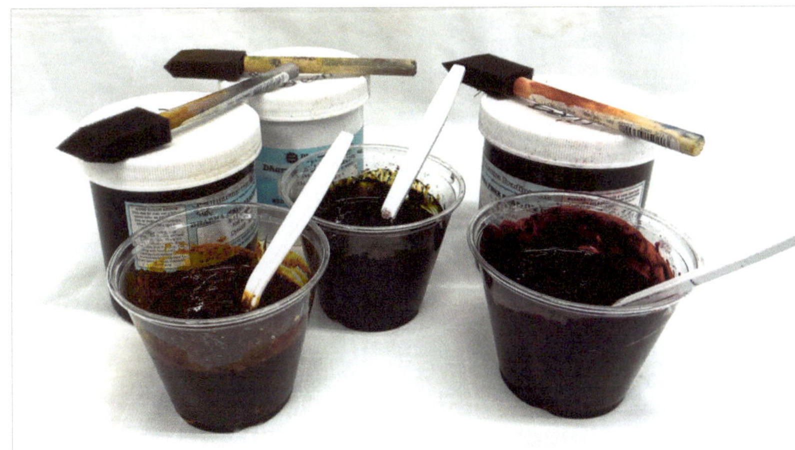

Alginate (print paste) is mixed with three different dye colors in individual cups and ready to be painted on a screen.

NOTE:
When working with dye powder, wear your mask and gloves. You can remove the mask once the powder is mixed with the alginate or other liquid.

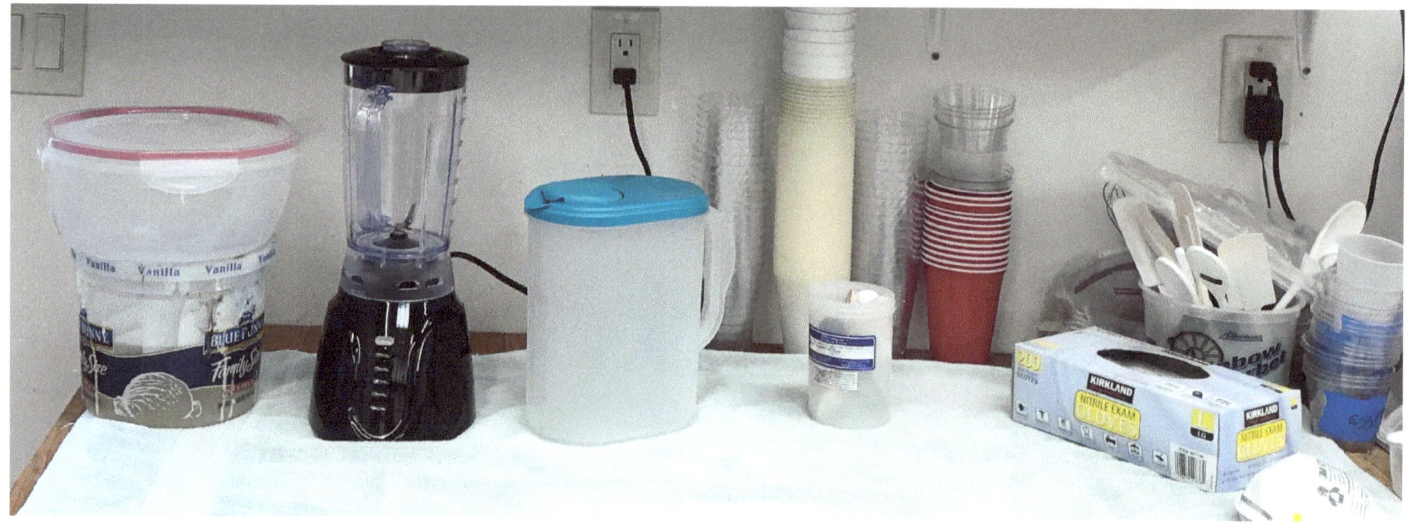

Gallon size storage for alginate

FOR BOTTLES AND EXTRUDERS

When mixing dyes for a line image or writing, pour your alginate into a wide-mouth bottle.

Use measuring spoons to measure and add the dye powder.

Mix with a long-handled plastic mixing spoon.

When using an extruder for a thin line image, mix dye and alginate in an individual cup.

Insert extruder into the cup of dye and pull the plunger to create a vacuum and pull the dye up into the extruder.

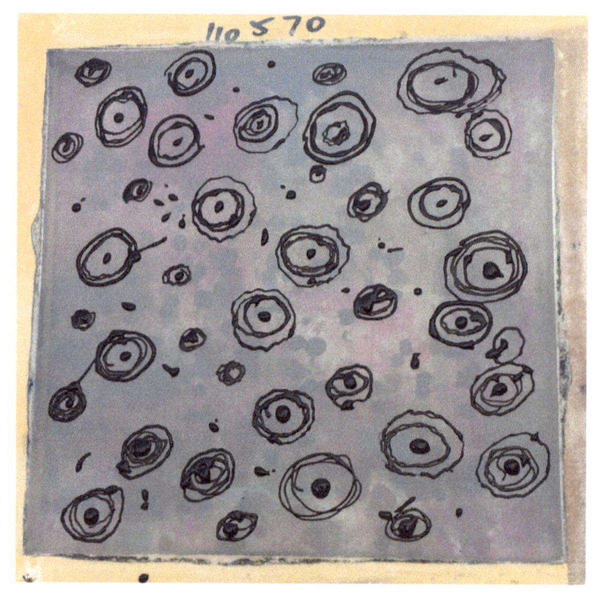

Bottles and extruders are used to create fine lines.

> ## NOTE:
> *I use dental extruders rather than a straight syringe as they don't drip as much onto the screens.*

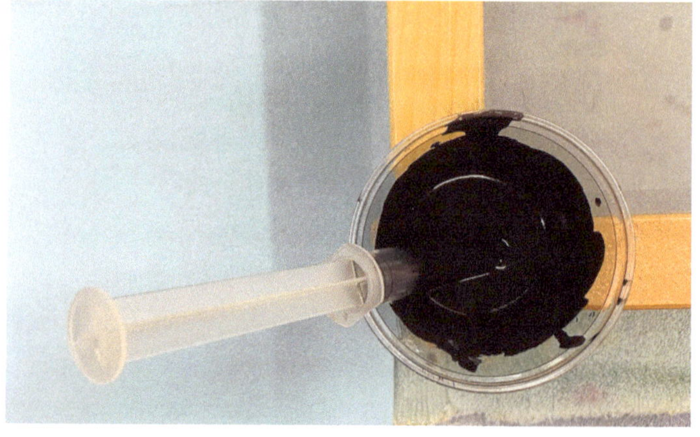

Extruder in cup of print paste

PAINTING YOUR DESIGN

To create the image, you will apply thickened dye (or print paste) to the front, or flat, side of the silk screen. You can use a brush, foam brush or any painting tool to create the design on your silk screen with the thickened dye.

When you have finished painting your design, set the screen in the sun to dry.

One of the easiest designs to make on the screens is to paint shapes with the thickened dye using a foam brush, paintbrush, bottle or extruder. Choose one or two colors. Think about how the colors will blend. If using a single color, the background color will be a very light version of that color (i.e. a black image will produce a gray background).

You can choose to apply a designed image, leaving open space on the screen. When you pull the print, you will get the blended colors as your background color (i.e. if you use red and blue, you will get a purplish background color).

You can also choose to cover the entire surface of the screen with the thickened dye. By doing this you have more control of the background color. Note in the strawberry print on page 35 that the foam brush also creates a texture pattern.

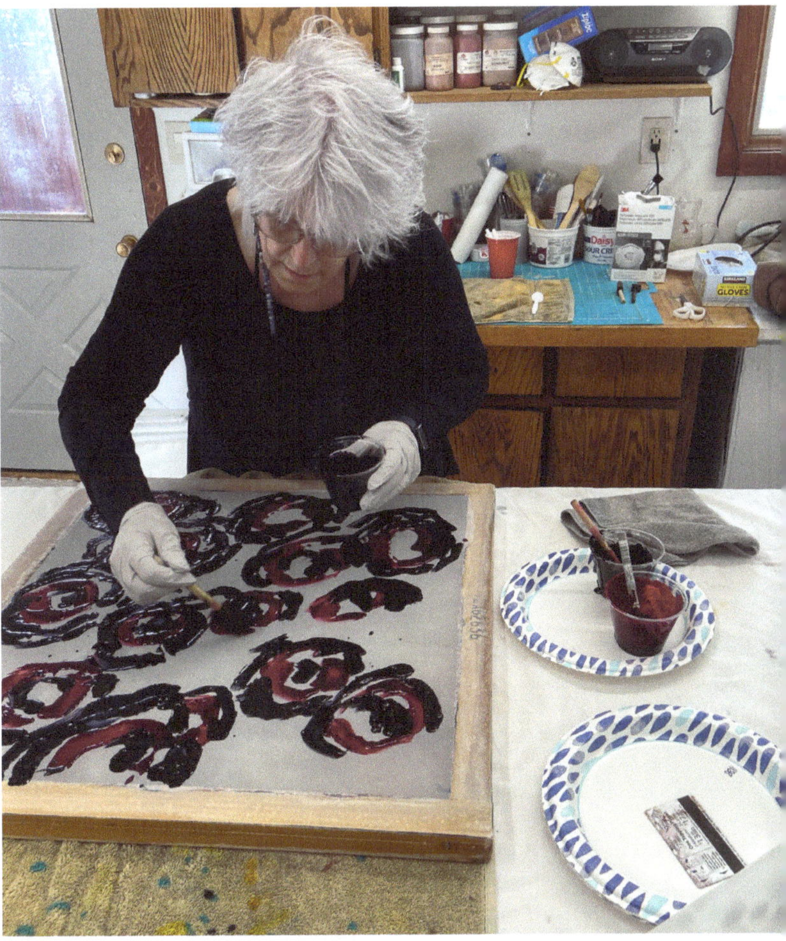

Using a foam brush and three colors of dye, I painted a loose rosebud design on a large silk screen.

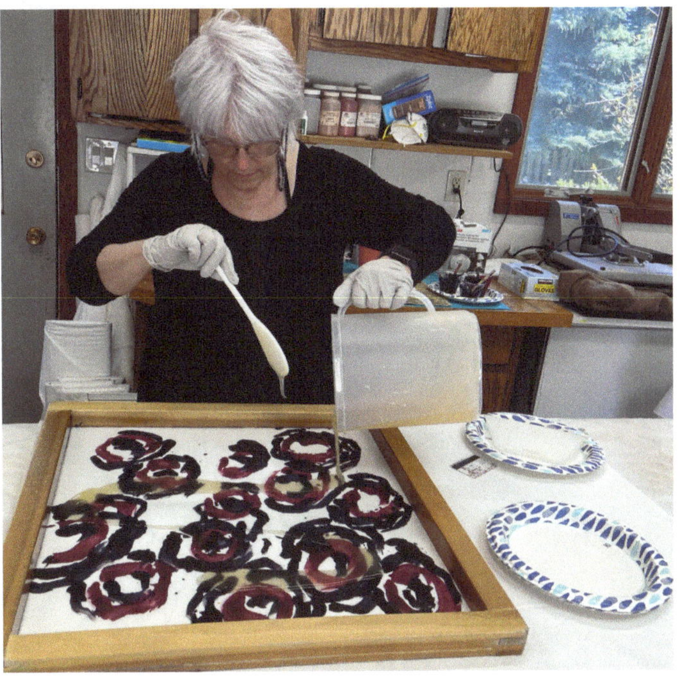

Once the paint was dry, I prepared to pull the first print by pouring clear alginate onto the inside of the screen.

You can use fabric that has been pre-dyed with ¼ strength dye for background color. You can pull the image using another color of thickened dye (print paste) for the background color.

To see how thickly you've applied the thickened dye (print paste), hold the screen up to the light. If the dye application seems thin, you will only get one pull from the screen. If it's too thick, you will get a resist from the dyes with the first pulls. As your screen dries, thickened dye may drip off in small drops. These dots will act as a resist and take several pulls to release. When pulling the print, you can leave the dots as the background color (usually white) or you can use your mud to dye the dots. (See "Red Painting" on page 44 as an example of the drips left as a white resist.)

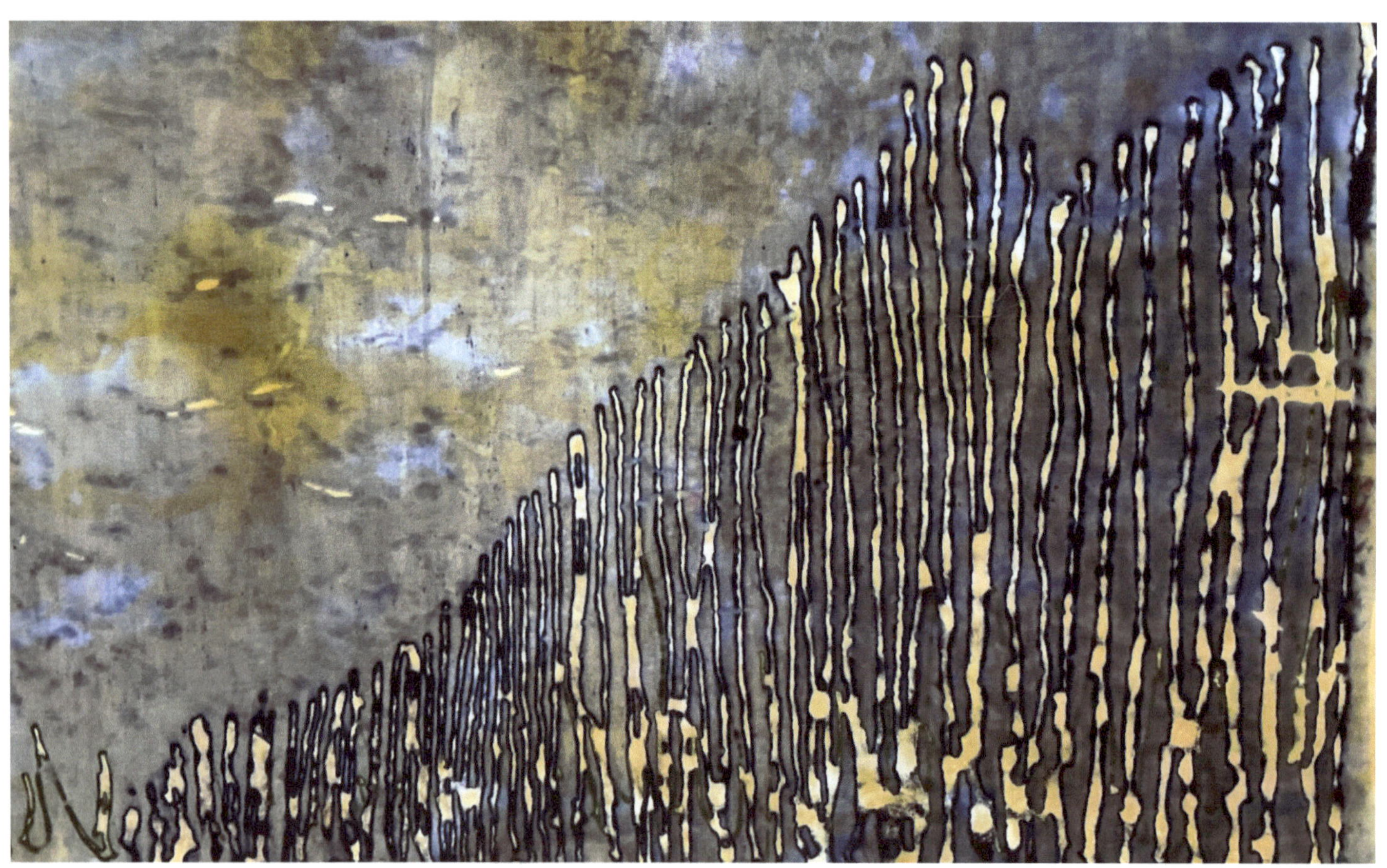

Fabric pre-dyed with 1/4 strength dye is the background for this print. The lined design was painted on the screen in black. This is the first pull from the painted screen.

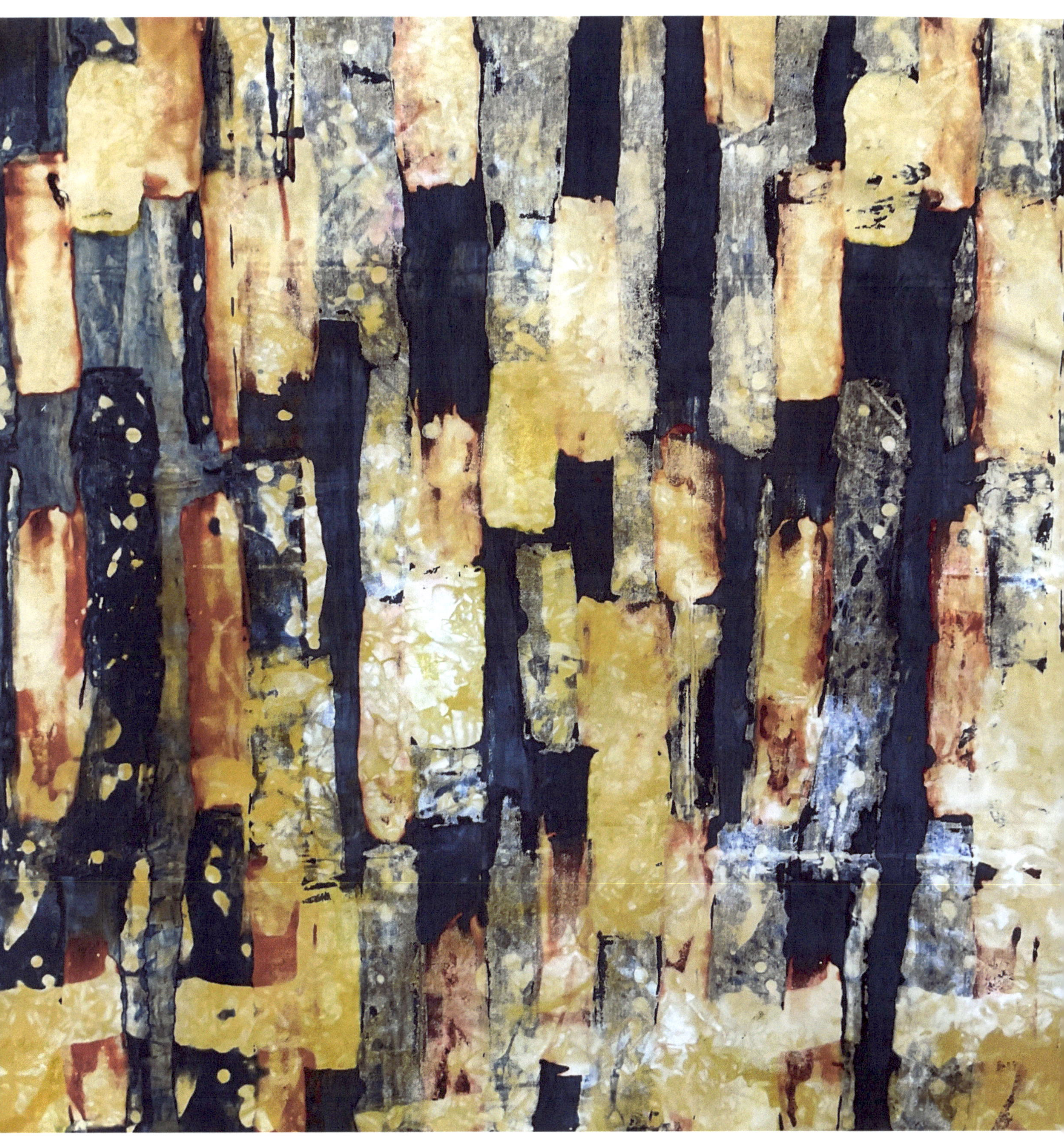

Fabric pre-dyed with ¼ strength yellow dye is the background for this print. The design was made by painting "brick" shapes with thickened dyes in a range of colors left over from a class session.

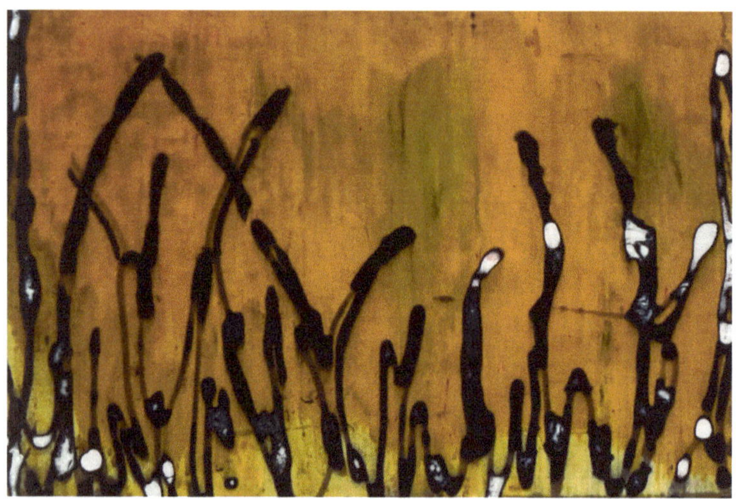

To create this print, I used alginate (print paste) colored with a yellow dye.

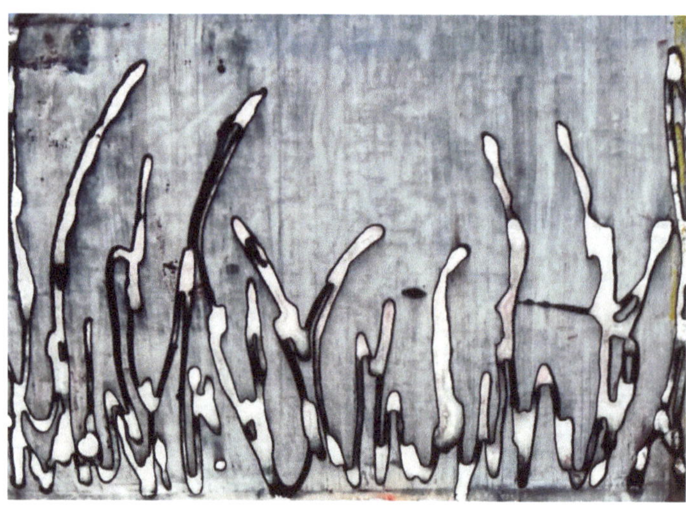

For this print, I used clear alginate (print paste). The light gray background color appears as the image, painted with black thickened dye, starts to break down.

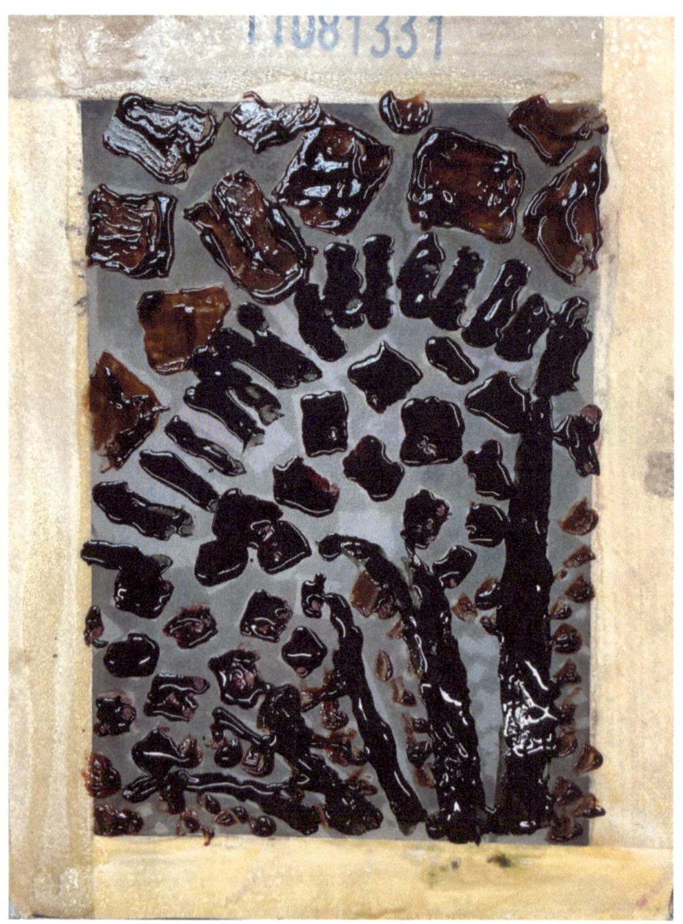

Thickened dye on screen with open background.

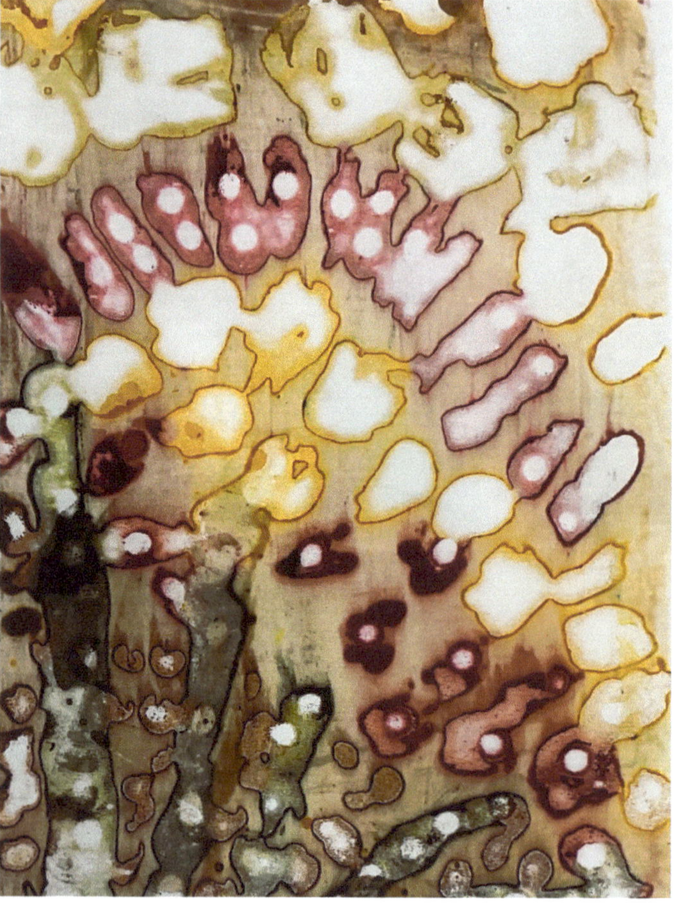

Print pulled from the painted screen at left.

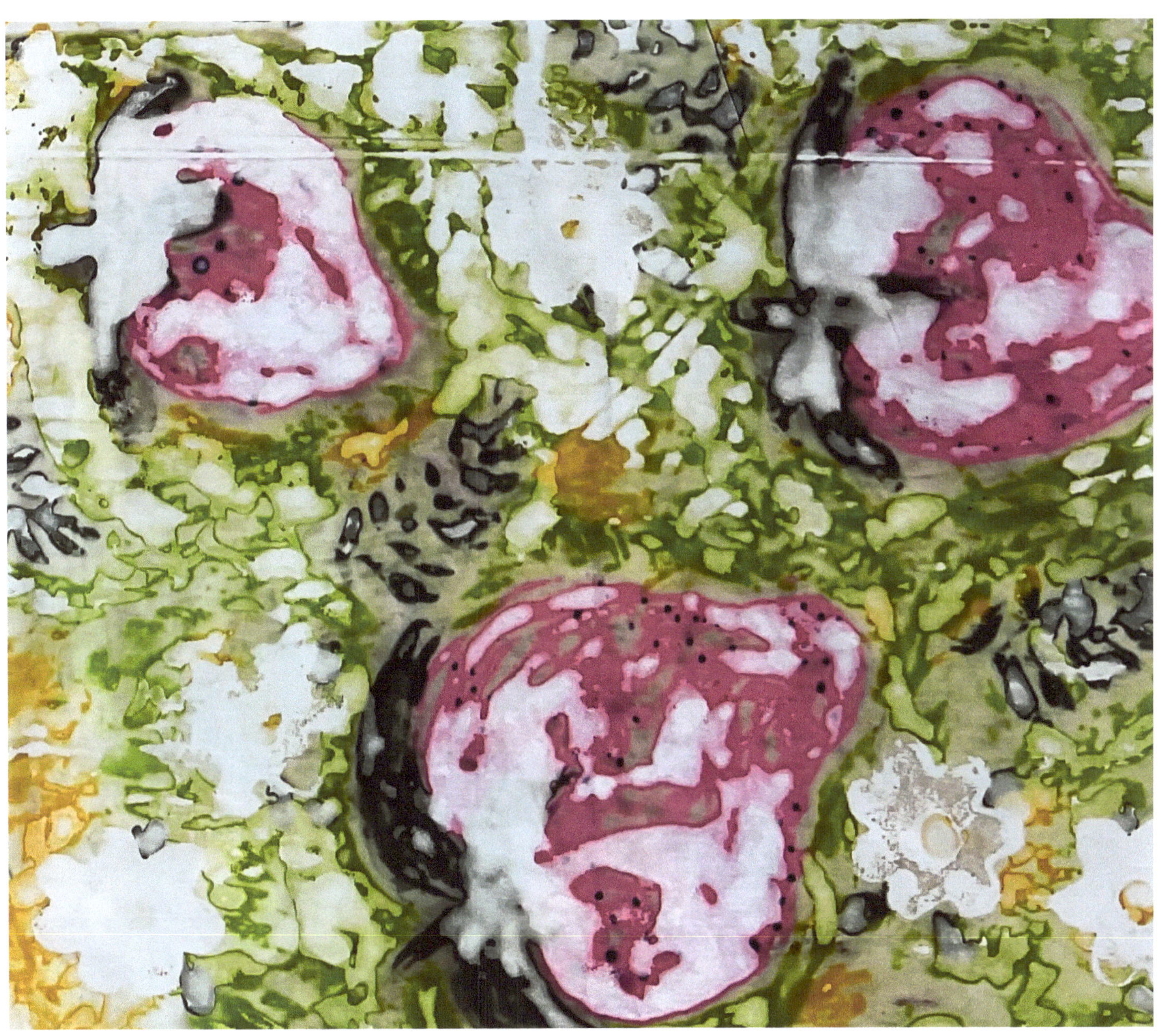

My student Chara DeWolf created this print by first painting around the strawberries with dye using a foam brush, which creates a lot of visual texture. She also used stamps of flowers and leaves in the background of her strawberry design.

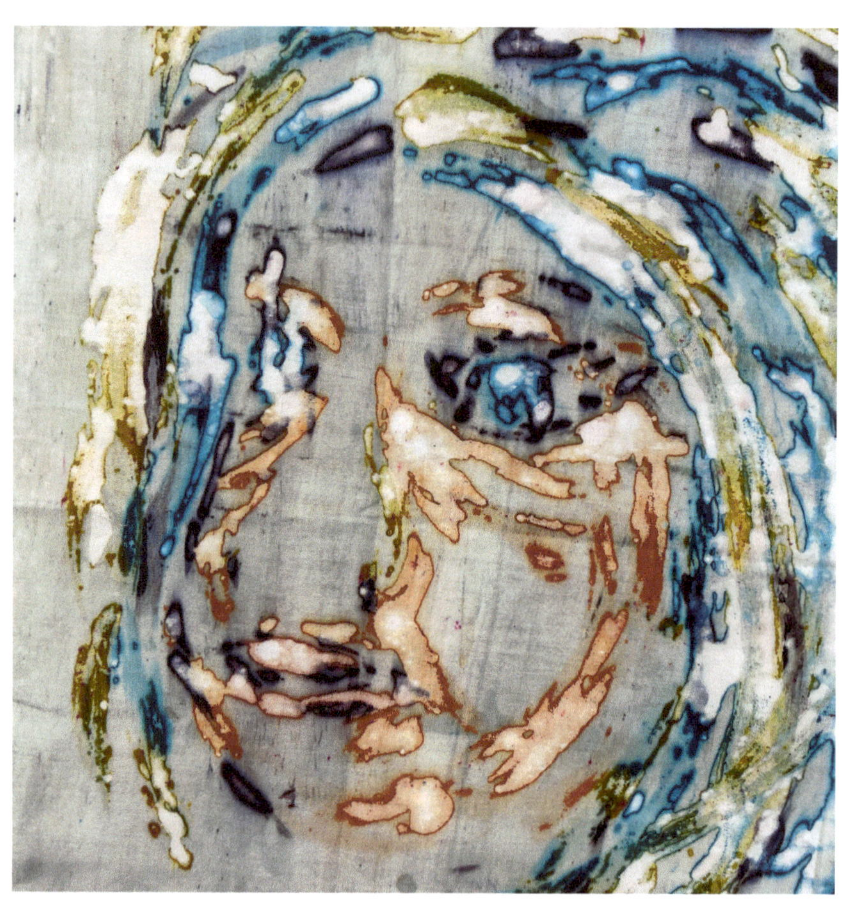

A face image was created freehand by painting with a brush on the screen using three dye colors: New Aqua, Palomino Gold and a touch of Jet Black.

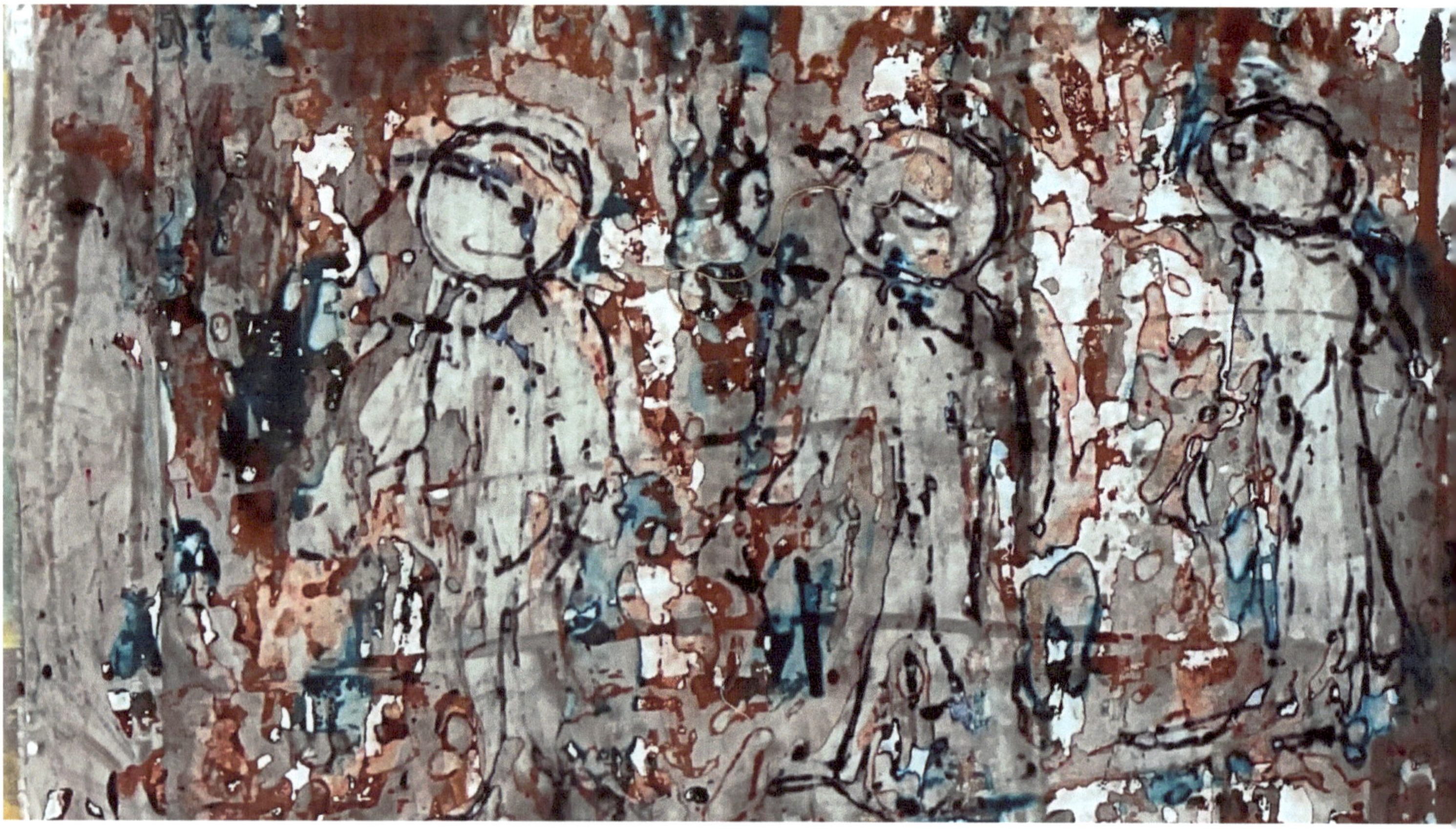

To make these prints, which are part of a series on human trafficking, the entire screen was painted using a foam brush. The figures were drawn using an extruder.

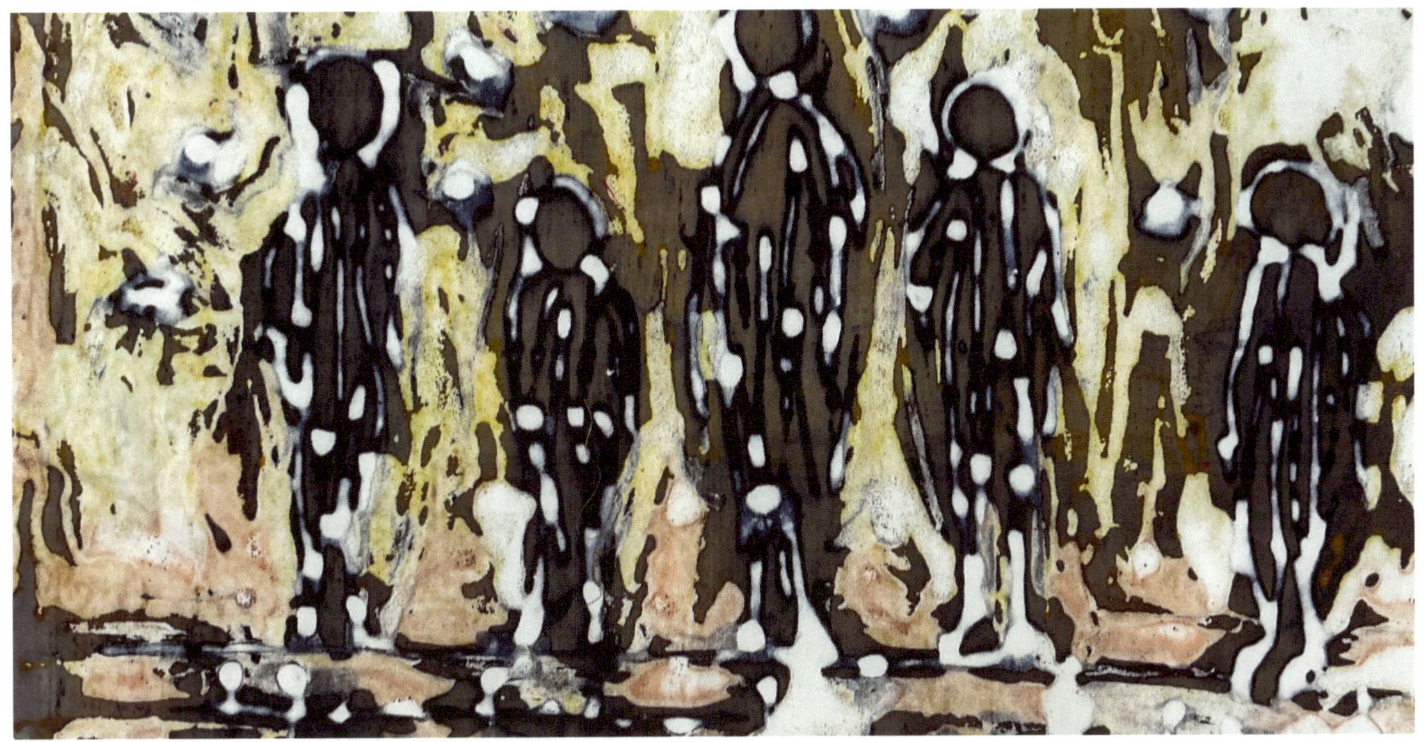

By painting the entire background of this design with thickened dye, the alginate only filled in the open spaces around and inside the figures with color. The gray color occurs when pigment is picked up from the black outlines of the figures.

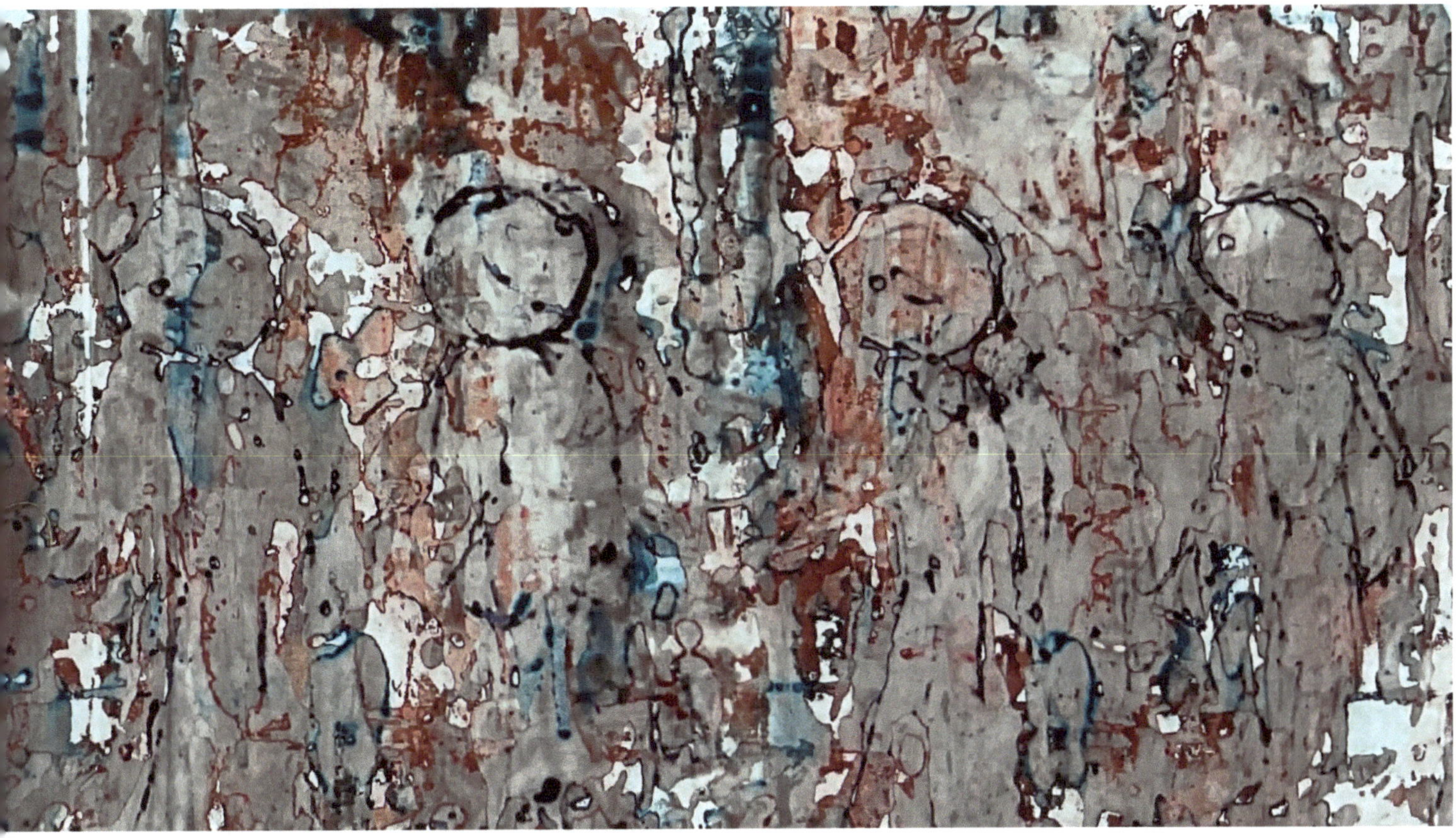

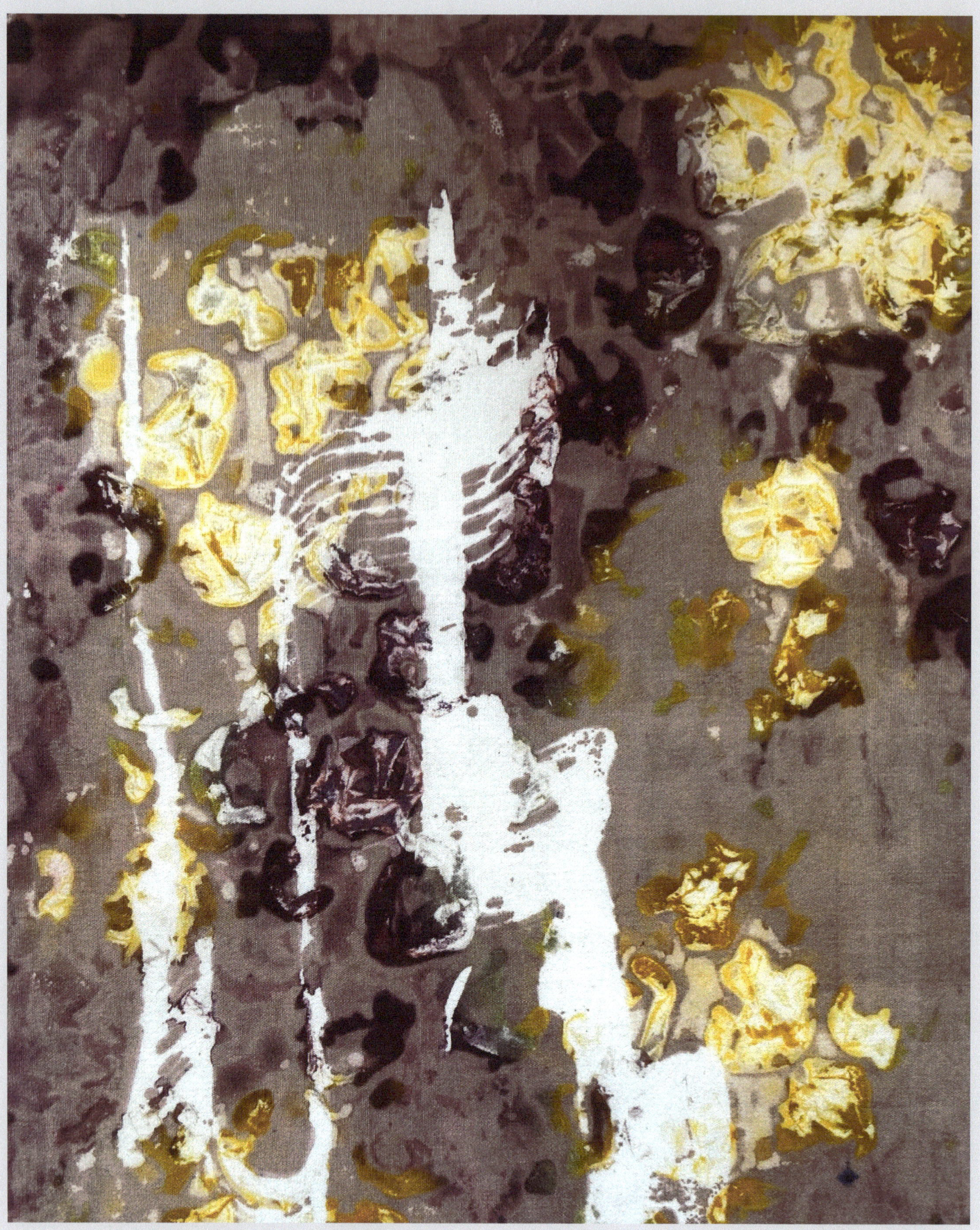

Background dyed with the mud. Soy wax was used as a resist on the screen, creating the white marks.

chapter 6

Pulling a Print

Once the dye on the silk screen is completely dry it is ready to use for printing.

To create a flat, even surface for printing, I use a 6-foot table with a tabletop printing pad. (See instructions on how to build your own tabletop pad on page 101.)

To raise the table to a more comfortable height, I use a set of table (or bed) risers. (Risers can be purchased at bath and linen stores or online).

Cover the tabletop printing pad with an inexpensive bed sheet.

Cut the fabric to be printed to a size that will fit at least four screen prints.

Pin the fabric down securely to your tabletop printing pad or the table coverings with 1-inch T-pins. If you are printing on silk or wool, keep in mind that these fabrics expand when wet, so they need to be pinned down very securely, or you will need to move pins after several pulls to prevent wrinkles.

To create the print, you will remoisturize the dried image using alginate (print paste). This paste can be uncolored or colored with dye, depending on how you want the final print to look.

Lay the silk screen face down on the fabric to be printed.

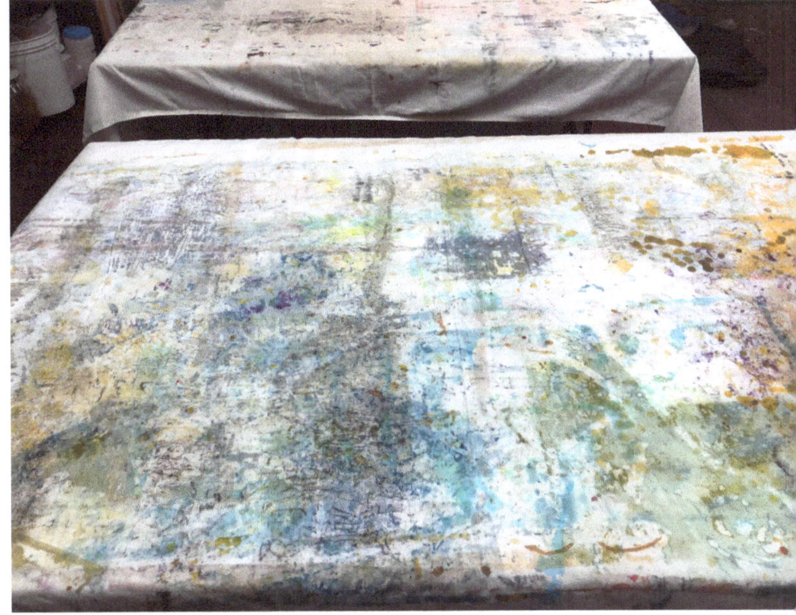

The sheet you use to cover your tabletop may become a colorful piece of art too!

> NOTE:
> *Instead of a tabletop pad, you can cover your table with several layers of batting, covered with plastic and then an inexpensive bed sheet.*

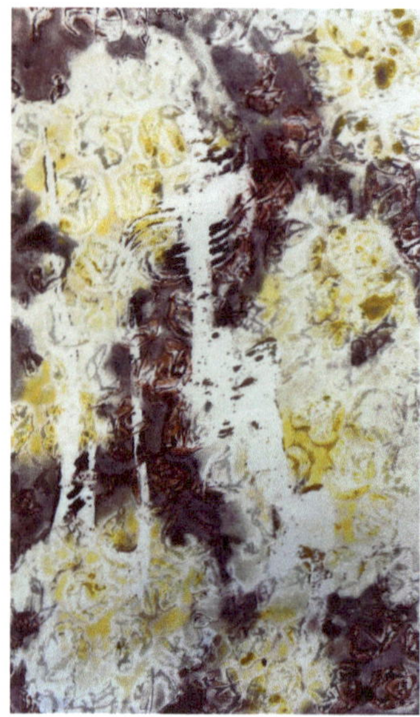
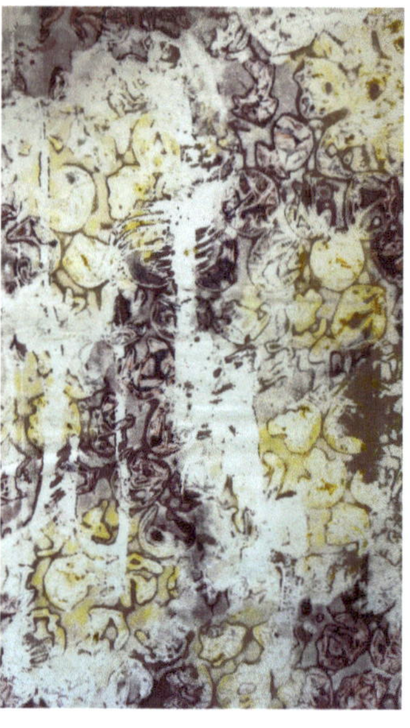
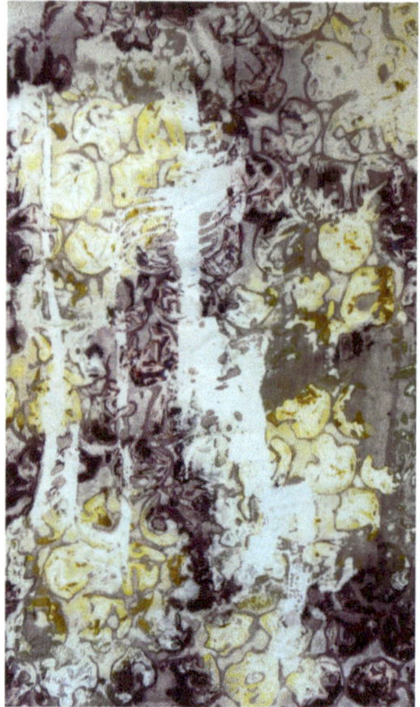
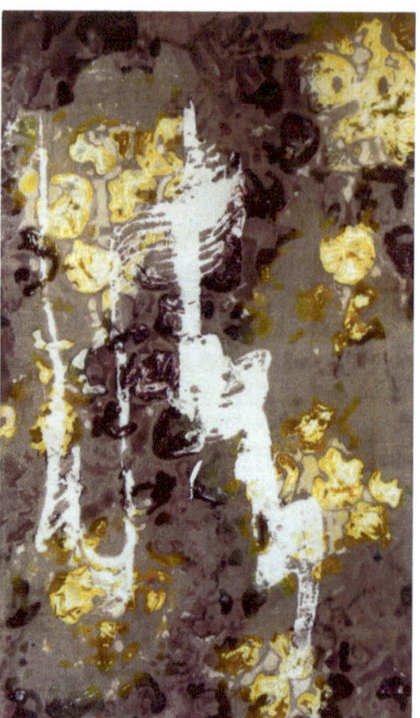

In this series of four prints and final print below, you can see the soy wax resist creates white marks that stay the same as the rest of the painted dye design breaks down.

Pour alginate/print paste on the inside of the screen; enough that you can spread it to cover the entire inside surface.

Allow the alginate to set for several minutes as the dried dye is like hard glue. For this reason, usually the first pull is the weakest print in terms of color saturation.

Pull the first print using a good bit of pressure on your squeegee. (You'll use less pressure with each subsequent print as the dried dye dissolves.)

> ### NOTE:
> *If your first pull is very faint, you can realign your screen and pull a second print on top of the first.*

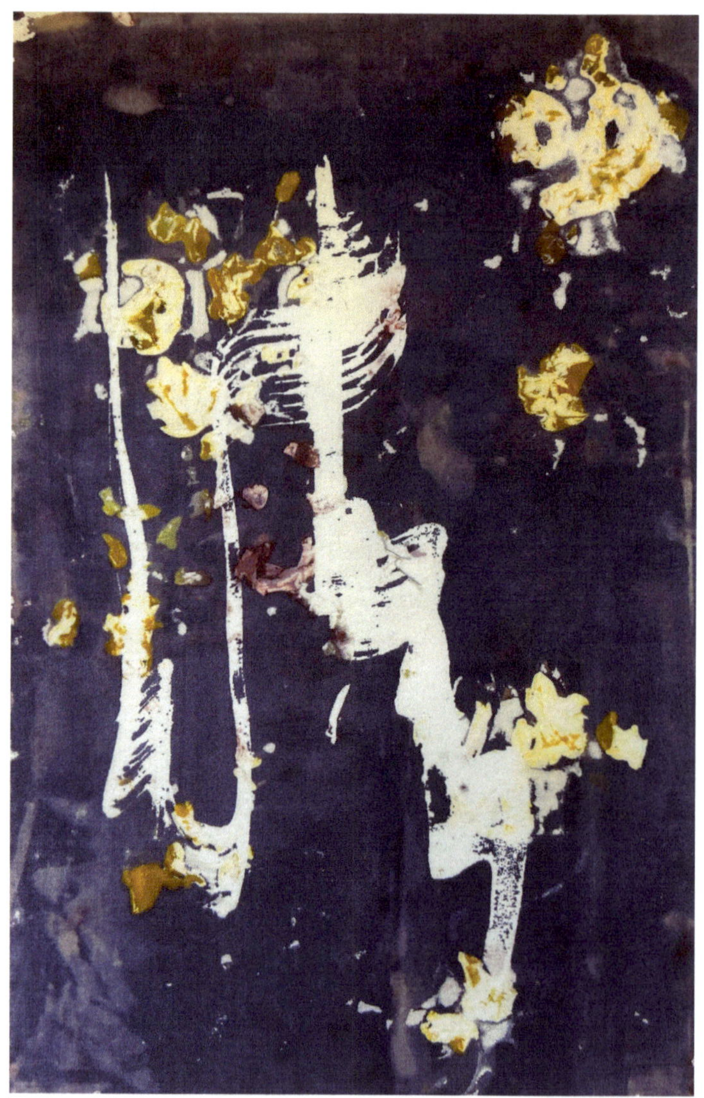

MAKING "MUD"

When you pull the alginate through the screen, it blends all the colors of the dyes you used in your design. After every pull, more dye is released, and the alginate "mud" becomes darker. Decide if you want to use the darker mud for the next pull or remove the mud from the screen and apply a clean, clear coat of alginate.

If you want to remove the mud, scoop it off the screen and onto a paper plate using a squeegee.

Pull prints until the image on the screen is almost gone – or has deconstructed.

Take the leftover mud on your paper plate and, using the squeegee, paint the edges of the fabric. Doing this will create color-coordinated fabrics to use with your deconstructed prints.

Wash the screen outside with a high-pressure hose nozzle or in a utility sink.

NOTE:

When washing the screens outside, the lawn and gardens love the mud as it is a fertilizer, water softener and contains chemicals that help to hold moisture in.

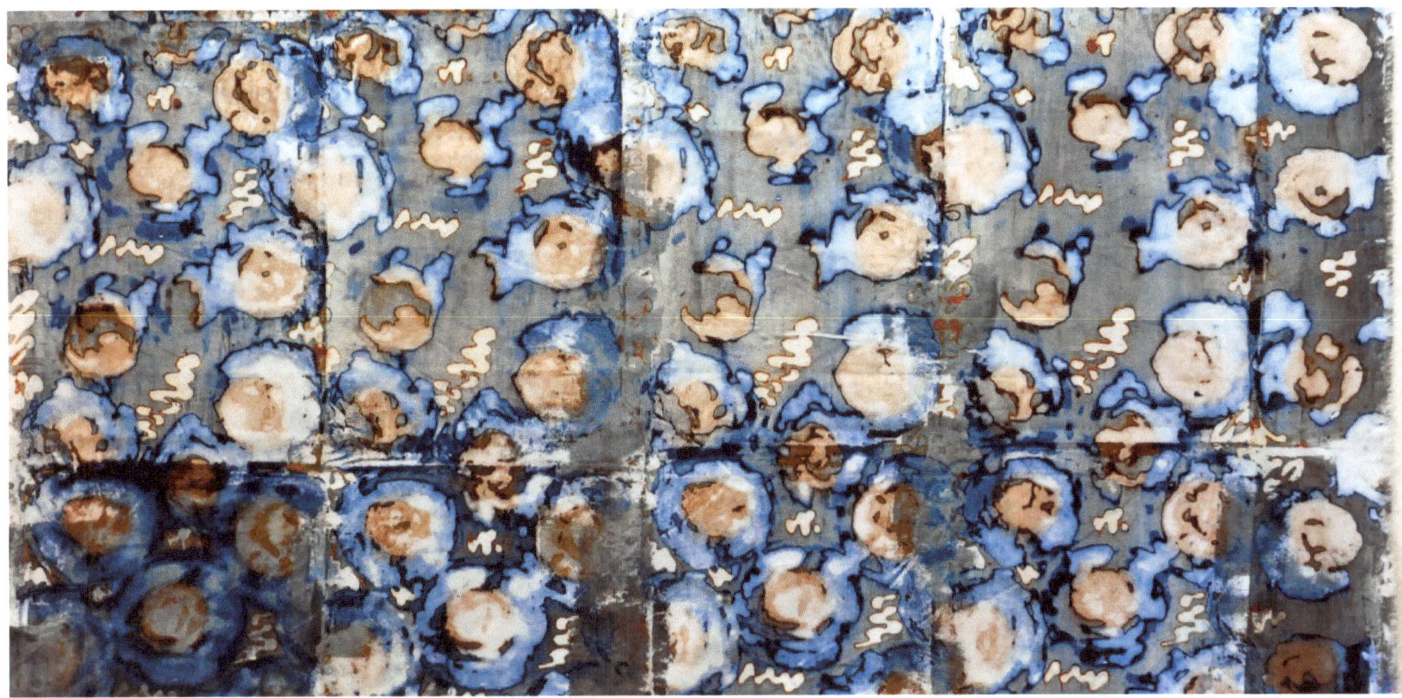

A rose-inspired design was painted on the screen, then clear alginate was used to pull each of these prints. Using clear alginate instead of mud keeps the background color more uniform across all the prints and creates the effect of printed fabric yardage.

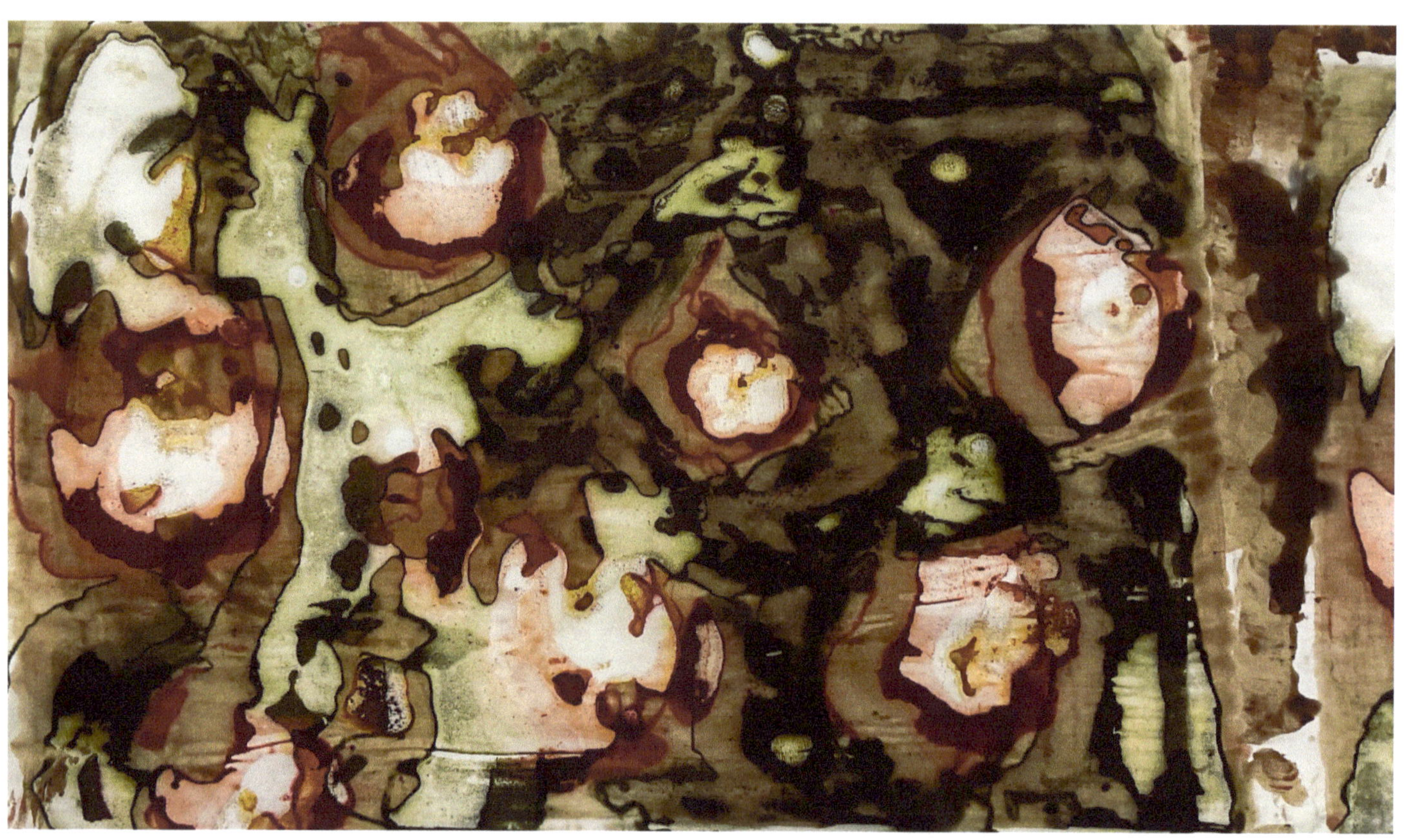

Using mud to pull this print gives it a dramatic, darker background color.

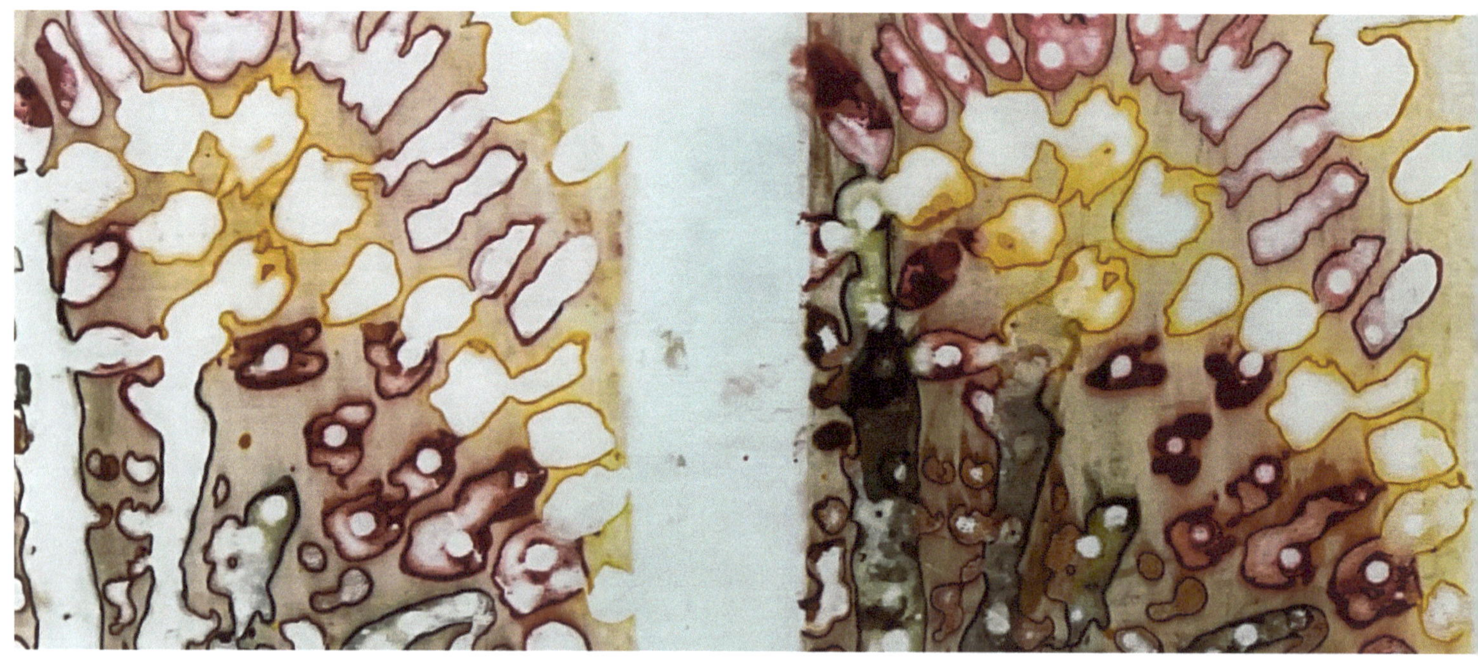

This series of four prints shows how the dried thickened dye acts as a resist, which leaves many white areas in print 1 (far left).

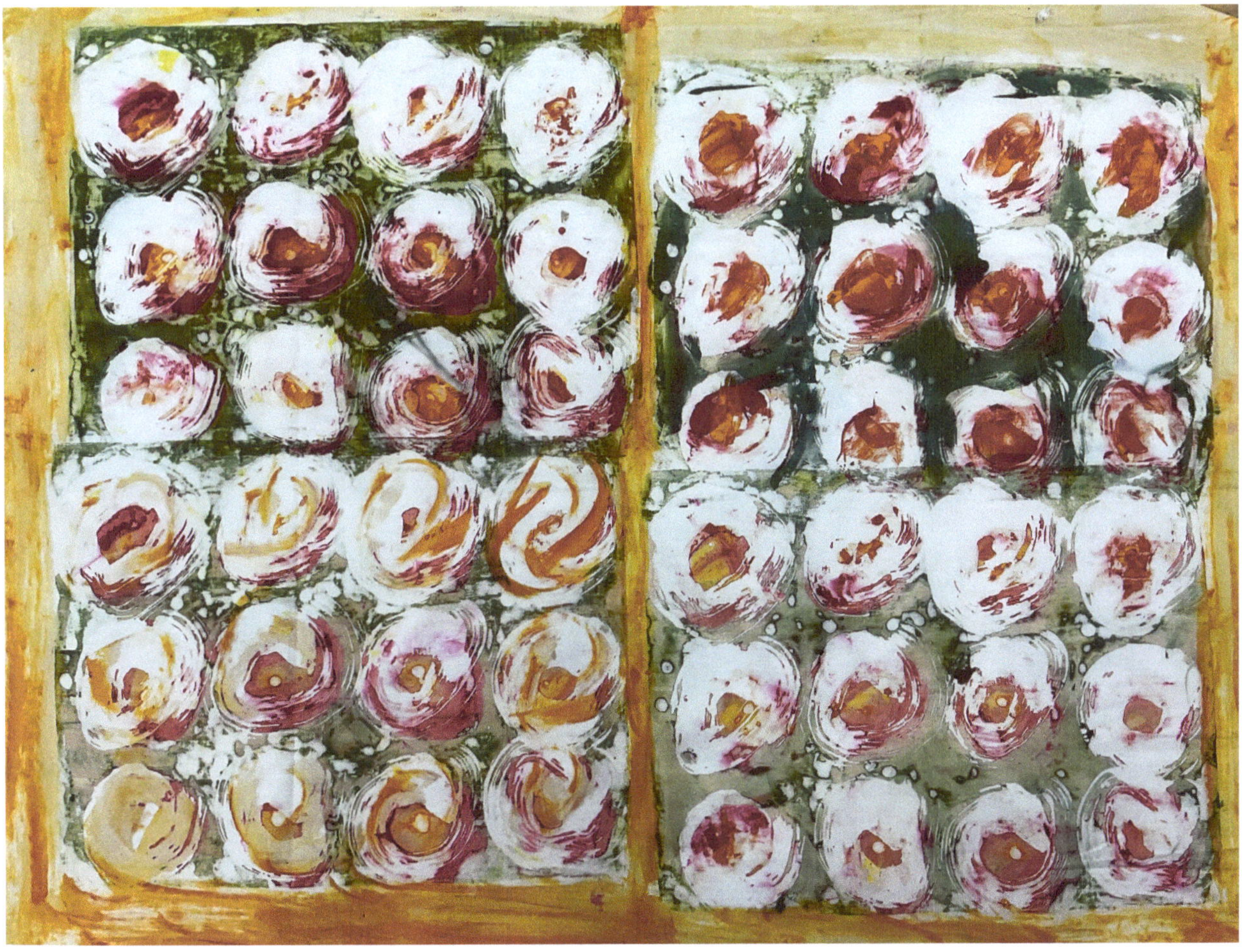

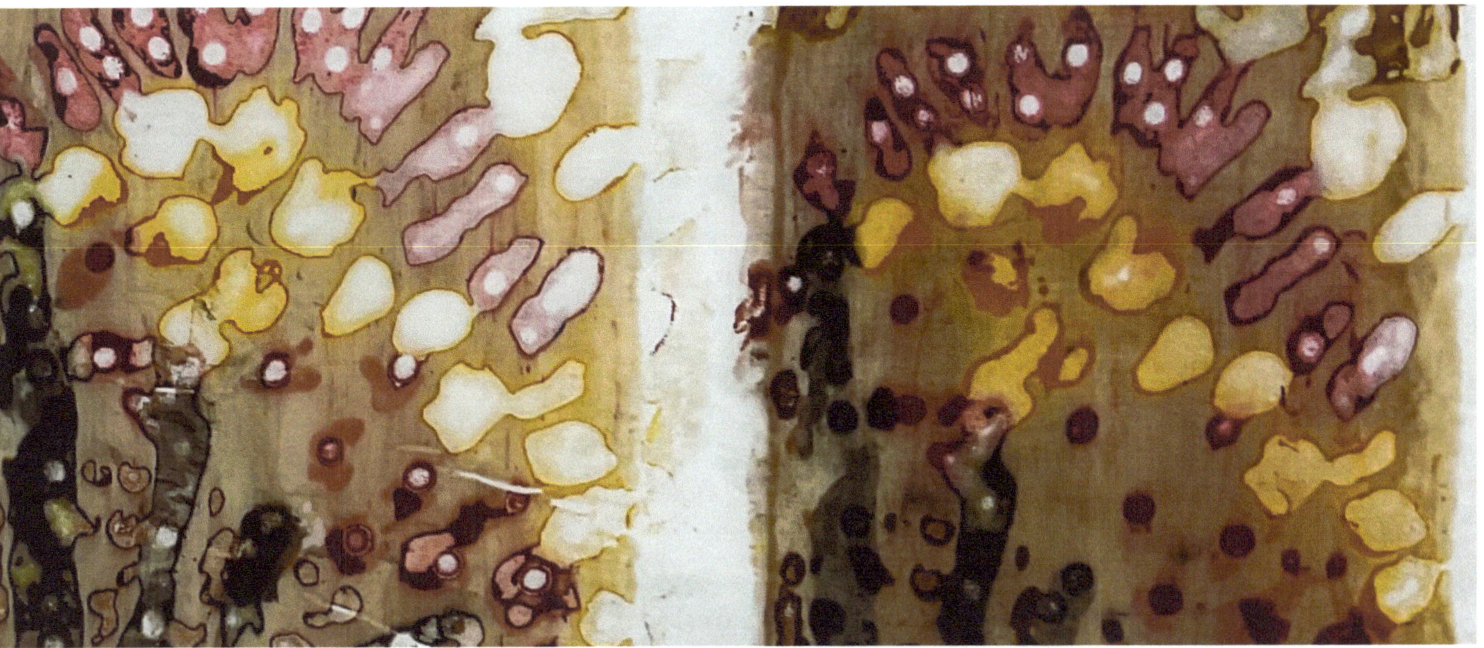

Painting a rosebud pattern in soy wax on the screen creates a resist that leaves bright white areas on each print in this series of four pulls from the same screen. The alginate used to pull the prints picks up an ochre color from the blending of Moss Green and Rust Orange dyes. The ochre "mud" was used to paint the spaces between the prints.

As the dried dye deconstructs, the colors blend, and areas that had thick dried dye before begin to show up as colored in prints 2, 3 and 4. Some parts of the design disappear altogether by print 4.

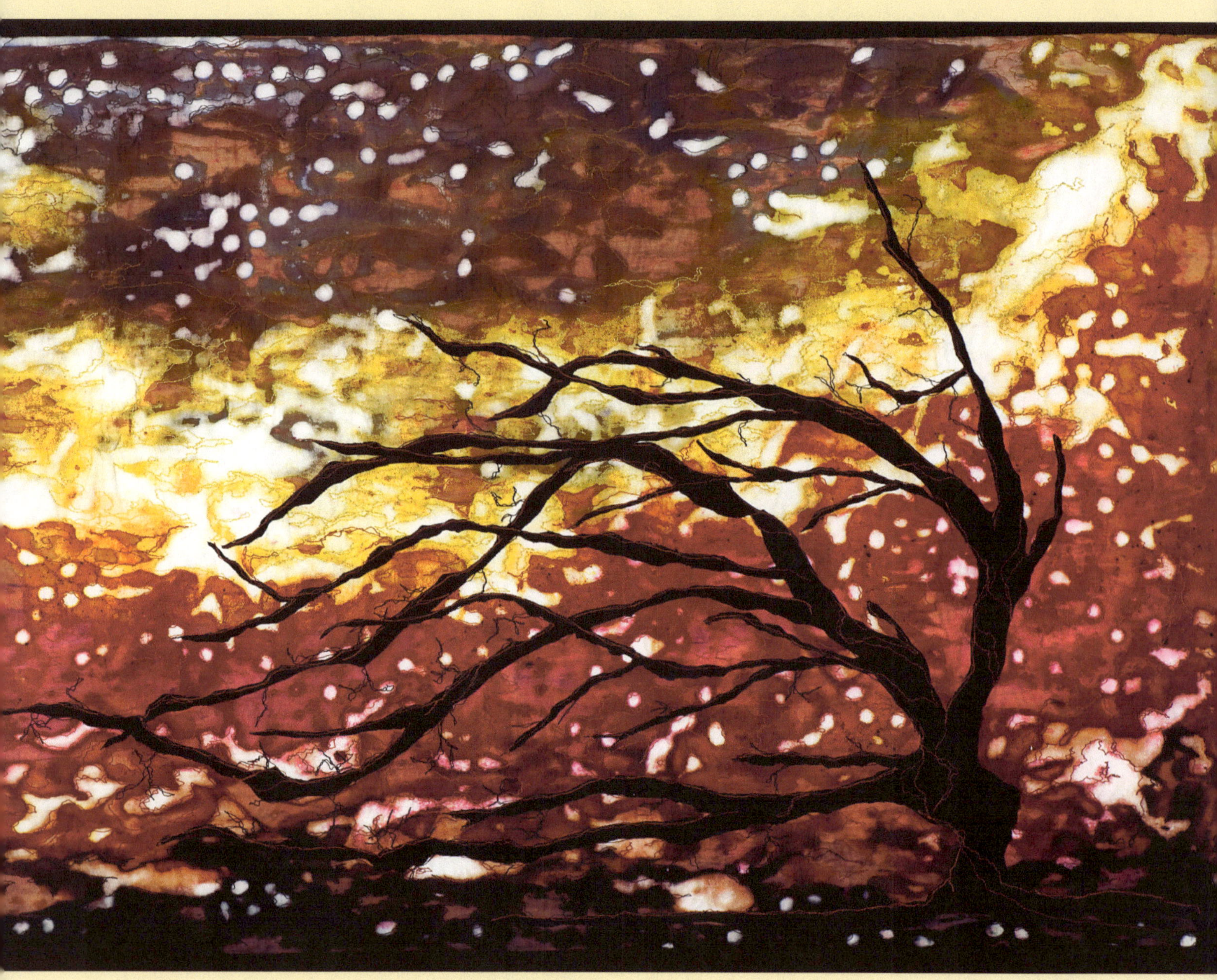

In "Red Painting" (19" x 34") by Susan Brooks, black fabric stitched to a print creates a dramatic tree silhouette. White spots appear on the print in places where the thickened dye formed thick drips as the screen was drying.

chapter 7

Overlapping
and Overprinting

As I am pulling a print, if I see that the piece has very little textural interest, I will start to reposition the screen by a half width between the pulls and overlap the design images. Or the screen can be randomly repositioned to fill in dull or less interesting areas. Using clear alginate to pull overlapping prints keeps the background from getting dark and muddy. If you want to aim for a darker finished piece, you can keep using the mud to pull prints over and over.

Sometimes, after washing out the printed fabric, I might realize that the prints didn't achieve what I had in mind and I am not happy with the results. I will take the piece back into my studio to add a second layer on top, using different colors and images.

By overlapping prints, you can bring layers of depth to your printed design.

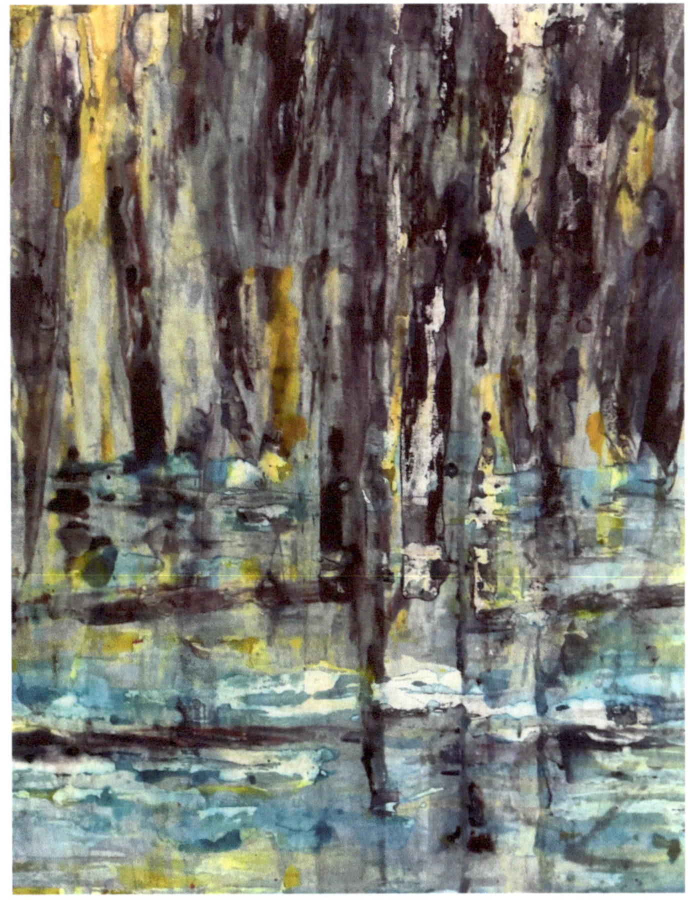

Overlapping prints can add visual interest. When alginate is pulled across the screen, it will pick up colors from the original thickened dye design, blending them in a painterly way.

Meanwhile, overprinting allows you to add new colors to a design, or you can layer a new design altogether onto an existing print.

Your fabric isn't finished until you are pleased with the outcome and can use it in your own unique art.

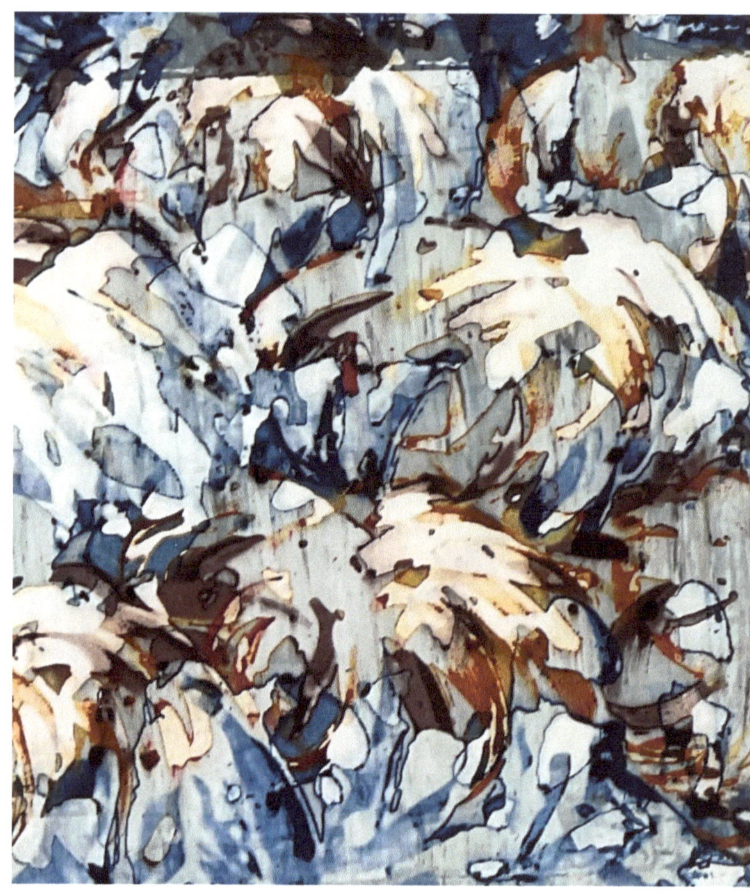

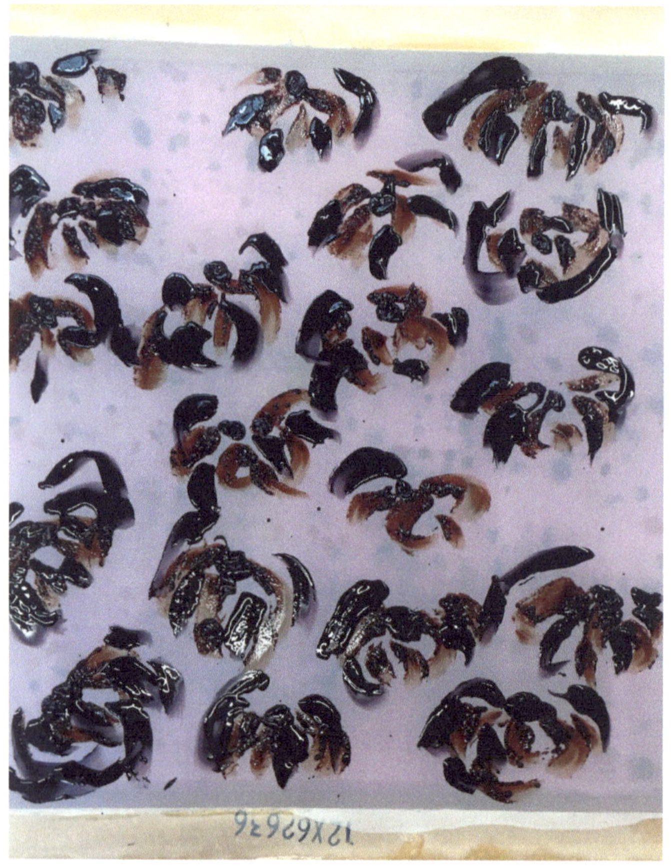

A screen painted with a loose flower design is dry and ready to be used to create the overlapping prints shown at right and above.

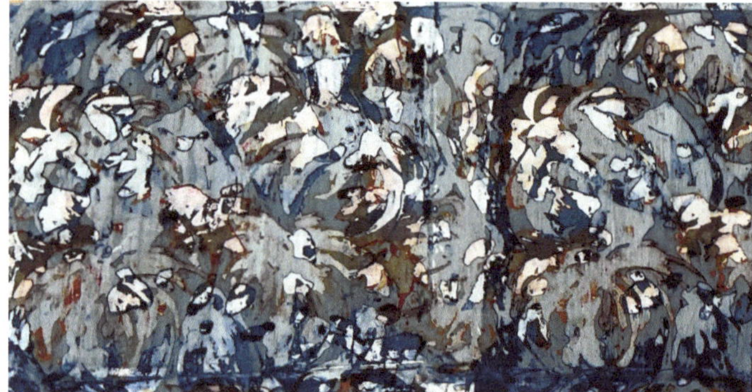

Detail of the overlapping prints.

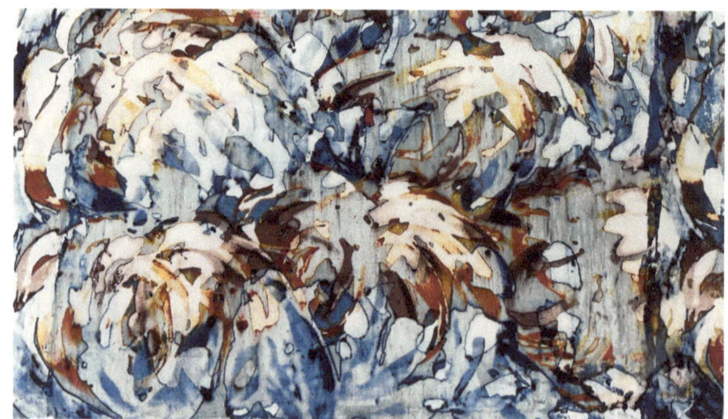

Using clear alginate to pull these overlapping prints keeps the background lighter.

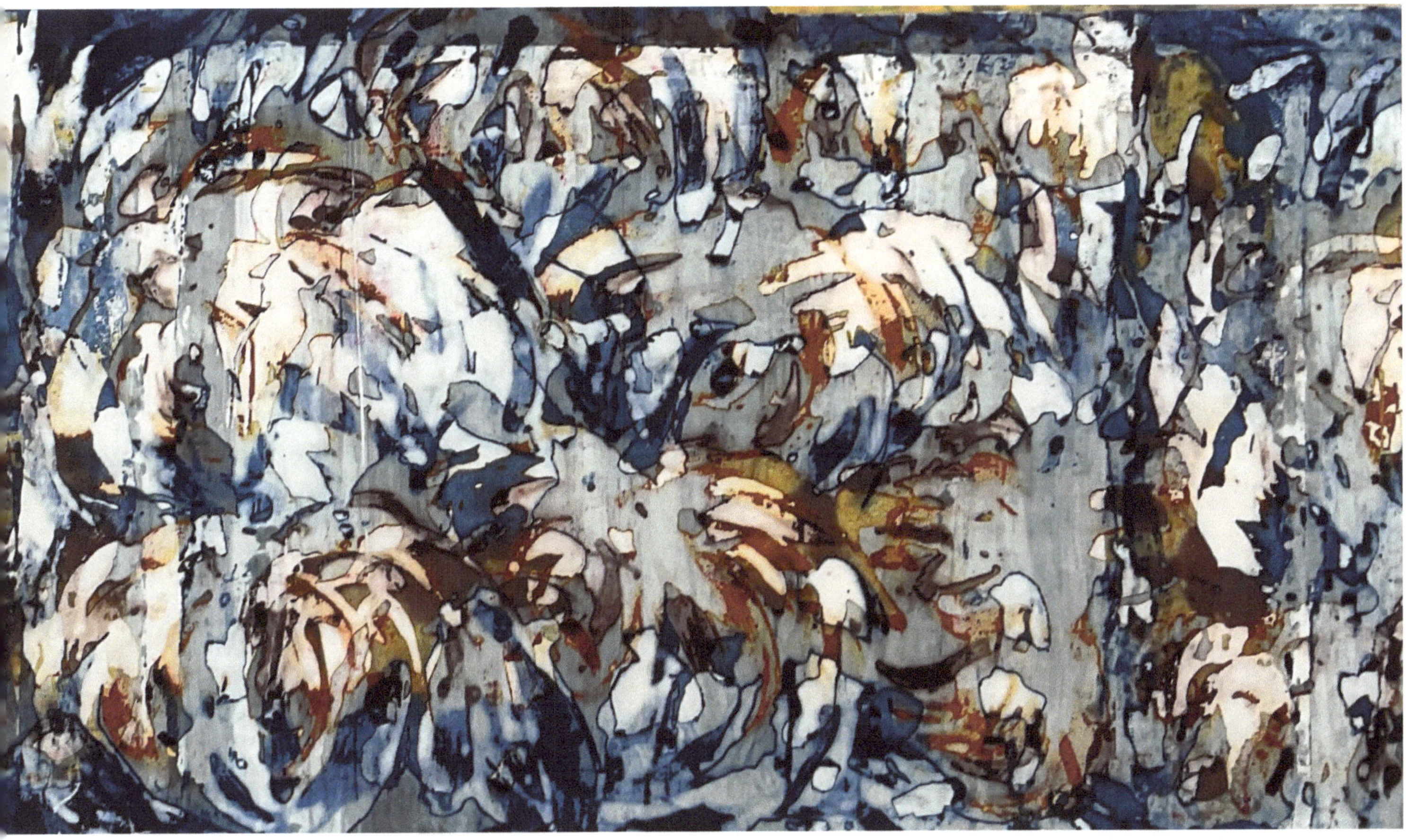

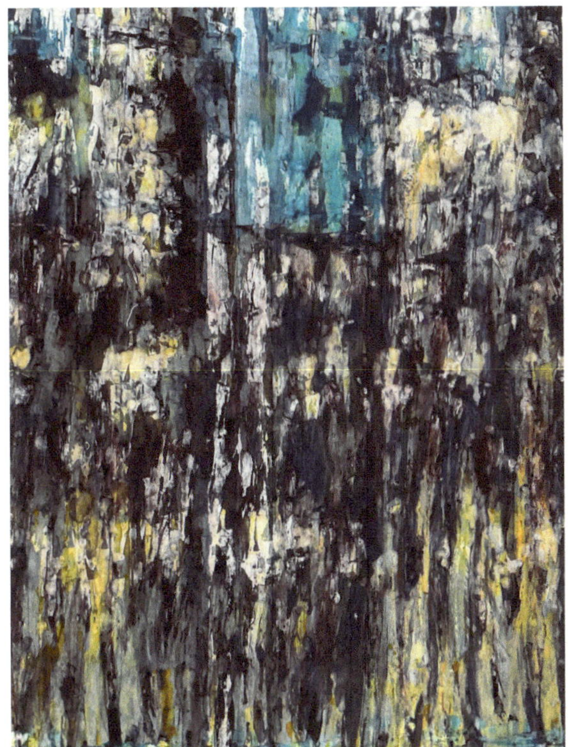

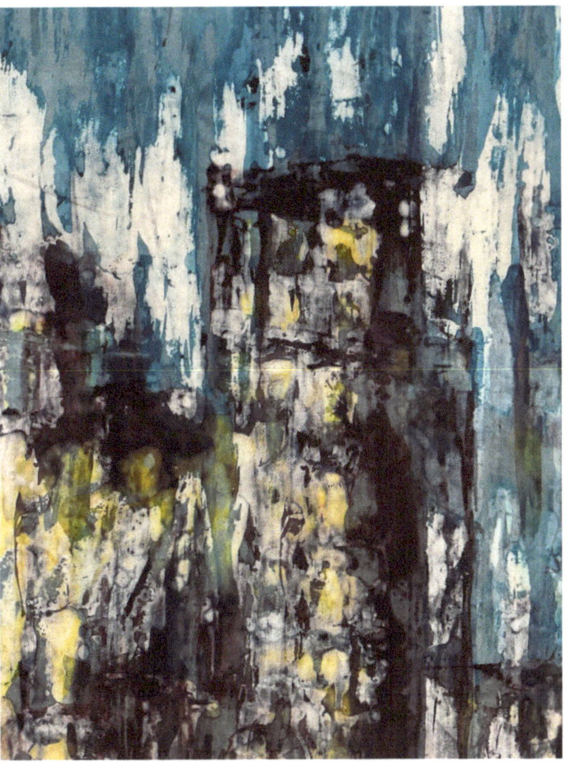

Placing the screen so that it overlaps half of the previous print produces a lively mix of patterns on the fabric.

Two details of the "Remembrances" series show the effects of overlapping prints. The original design was painted on the screen with just two colors of dye: Black and Marigold.

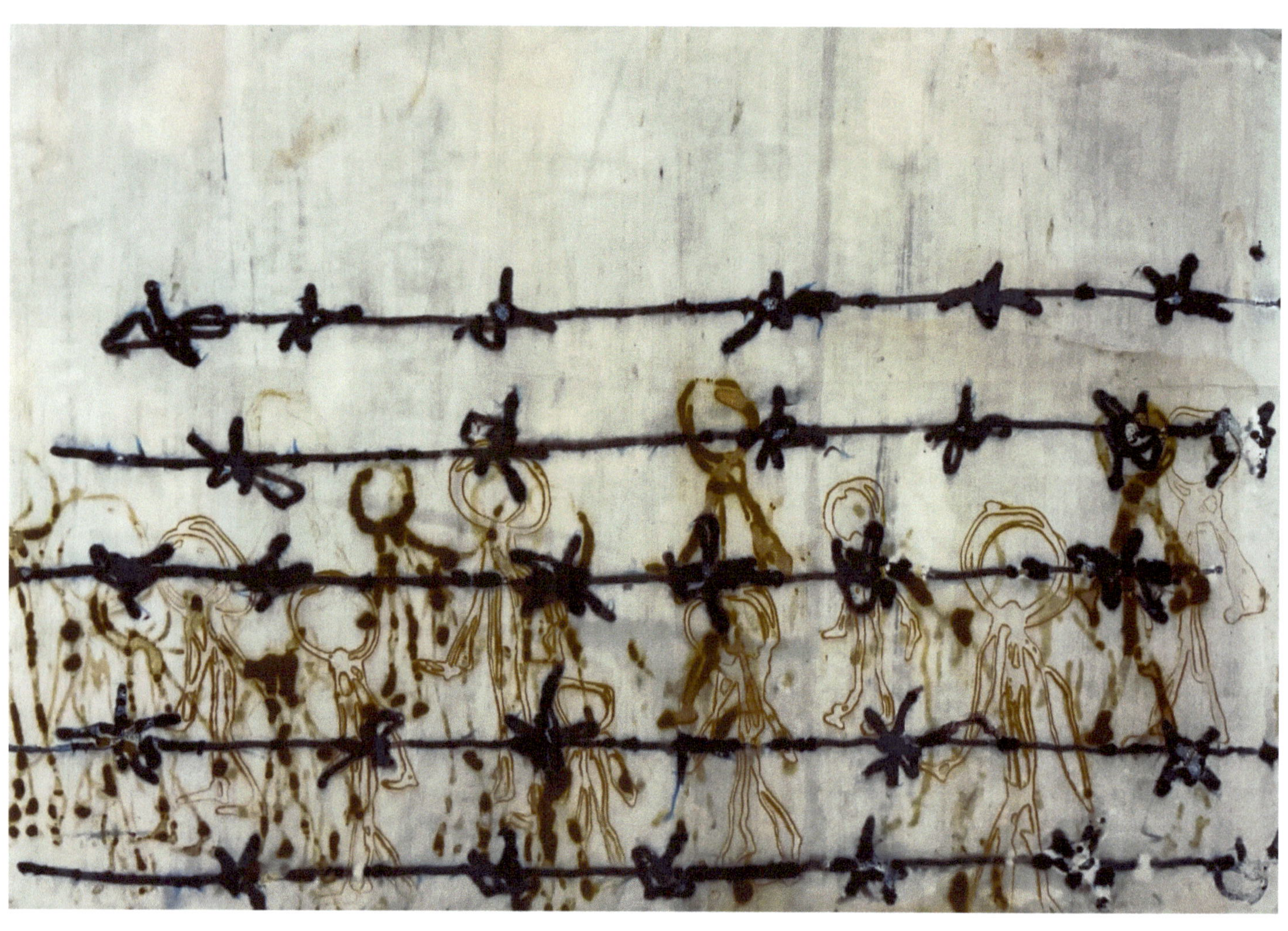

Overprinting is another technique that can be used to alter a print. Here, a print of a barbed wire design was pulled on top of a monotone print of figures. The resulting print makes a statement about immigration.

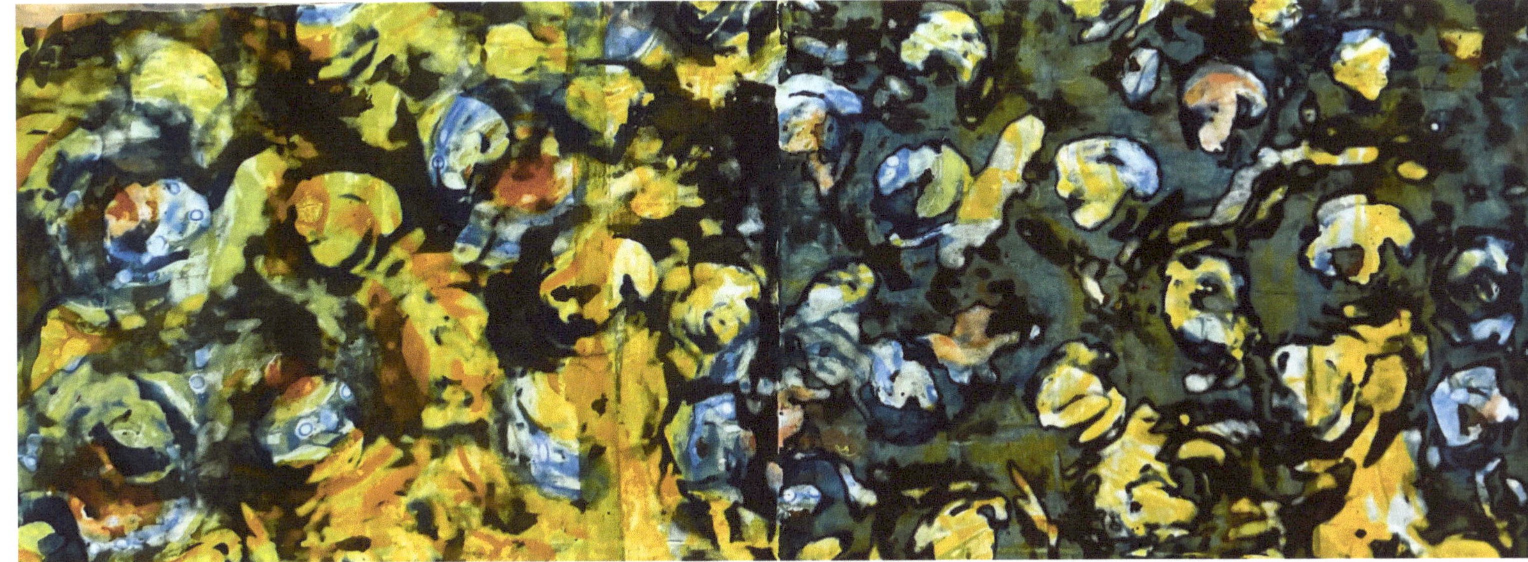

When this large print of a rose pattern design felt flat, I overprinted it with a screen painted in similar colors.

OVERPRINTING

After washing out your printed fabric, if the prints aren't as interesting as you had hoped, you can add similar images in other colors on top or a completely different image. Remember, there are no rules!

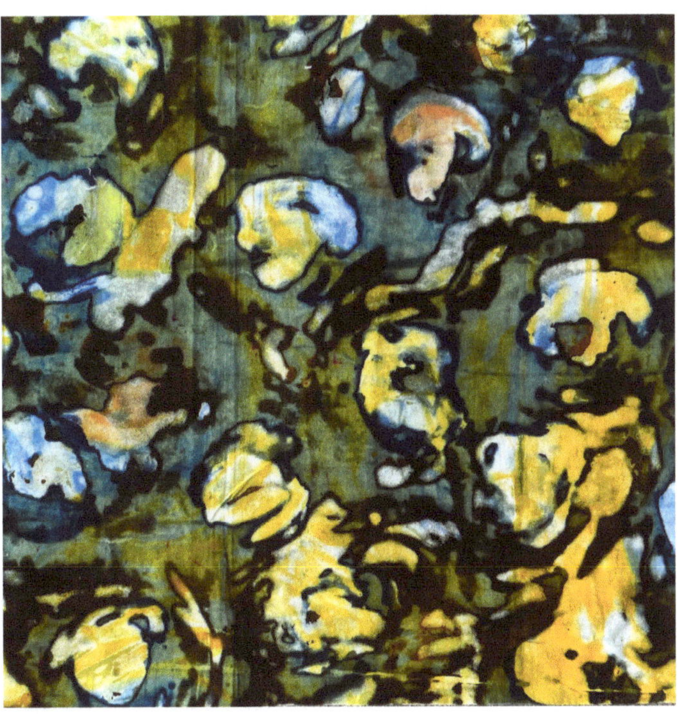

A detail of the overprinting shows the beautiful blend of colors and designs.

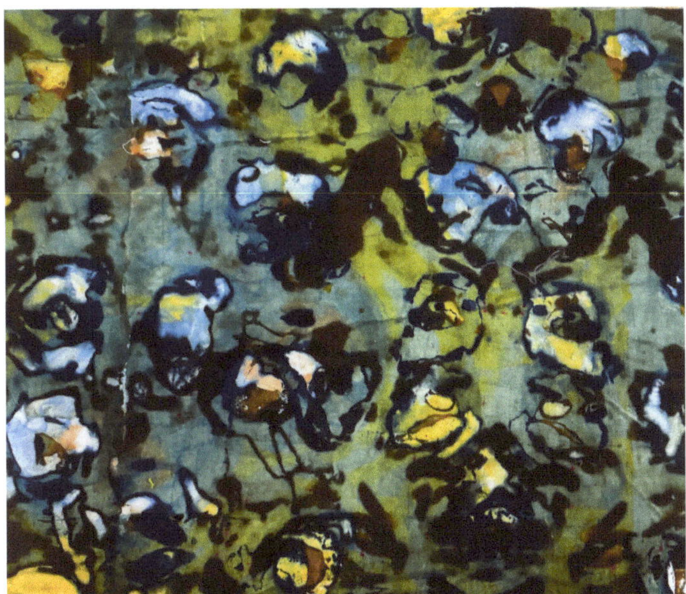

Another detail of the overprinted piece. Clear alginate was used to pull the print.

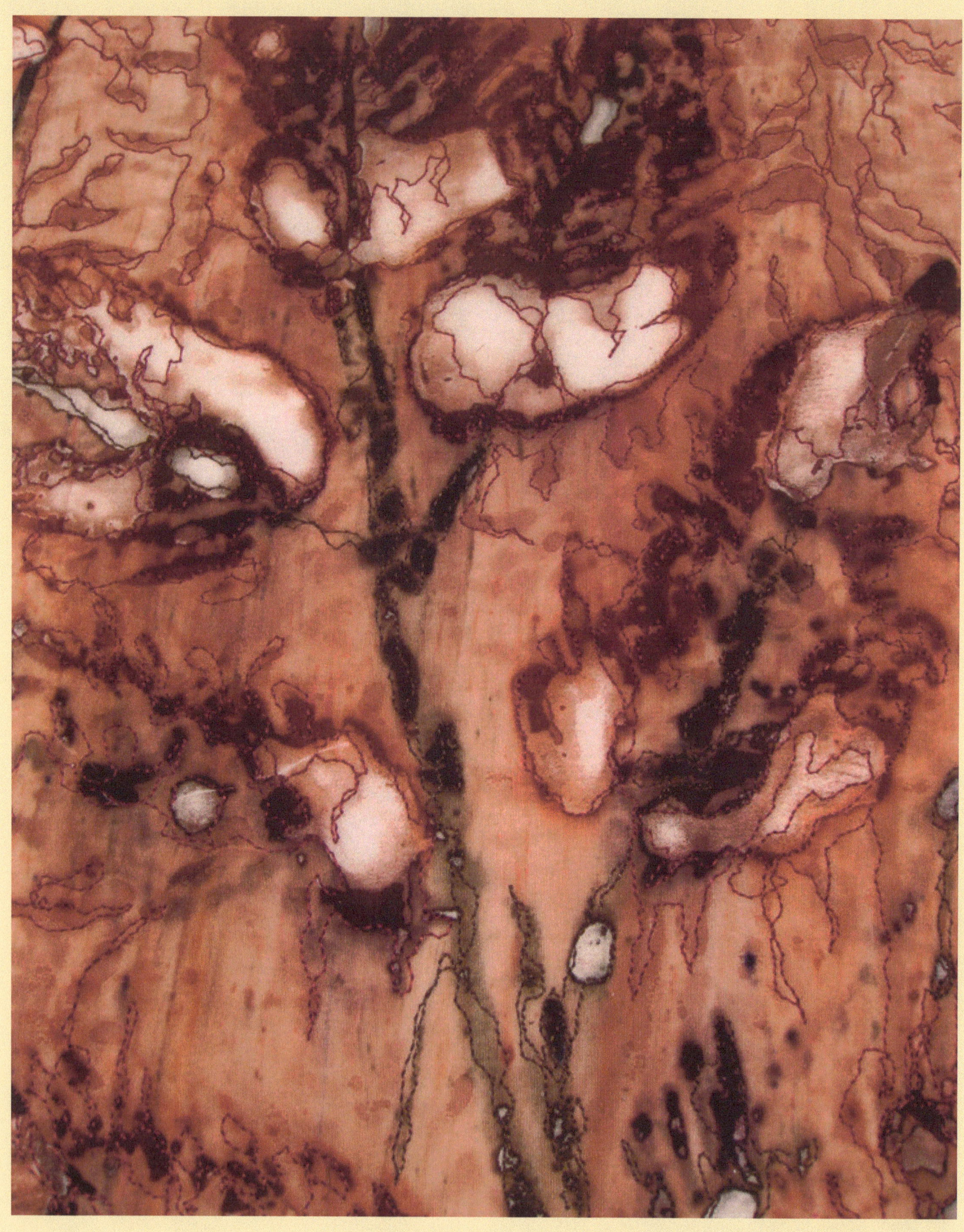

Stitching highlights the floral design of this art piece. The original design was painted with Brick Red and Moss Green dye.

chapter 8

Using Textures, Stamps and Grasses

There are many objects that can be used to create texture on your screens. For best results, the objects should lay flat and have some thickness. If you use leaves, choose those that are thick enough to see the veins.

Some of my favorite objects to use in creating texture:

- Bubble wrap
- Cardboard pieces (Try spritzing the cardboard with water to remove the paper layer and reveal the corrugated ribbing.)
- Thick leaves
- Rubber stamps
- Flat pieces of wood

CREATING TEXTURE

On your tabletop, lay down an old towel and a piece of plastic a bit larger than your screen.

Arrange your objects, making an interesting pattern.

Lay your screen surface (or front) side down on top of your objects.

Paint thickened dye, or dyes, onto the inside of your screen.

Then, using a squeegee or credit card, press the dyes into the textures below.

Very important: Lift the bundle of plastic, textures and screen and carry them together out into the sun. Turn the bundle over so the plastic is on top.

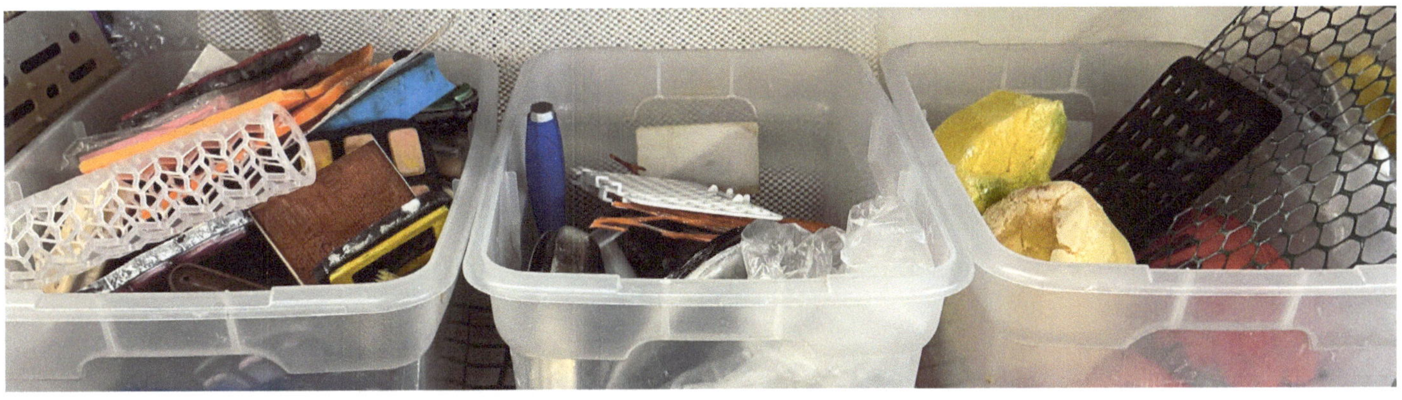

Supplies for making stamps and textures in the thickened dye.

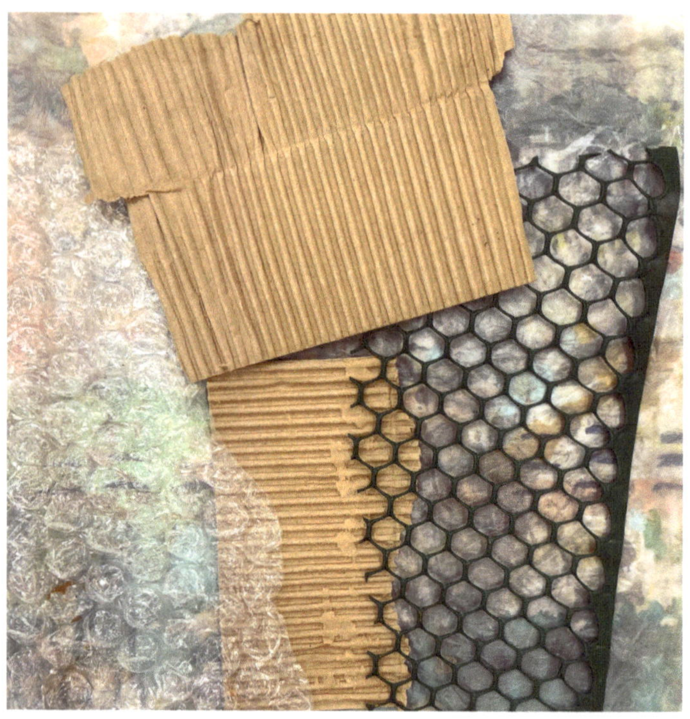

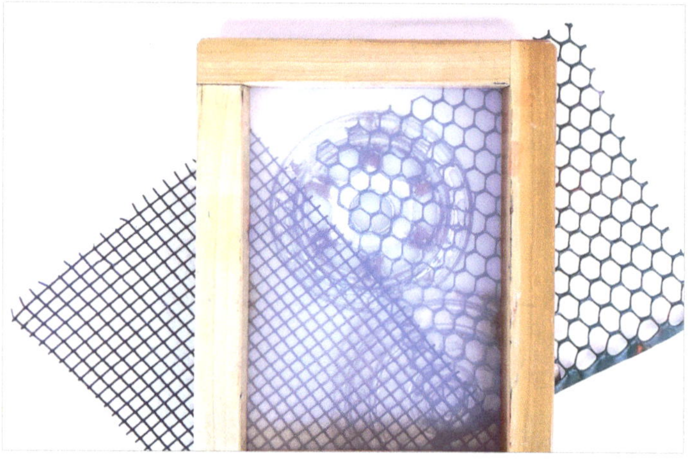

Corrugated cardboard, bubble wrapand plastic fencing are all good materials for creating texture.

Textured materials are placed under the screen.

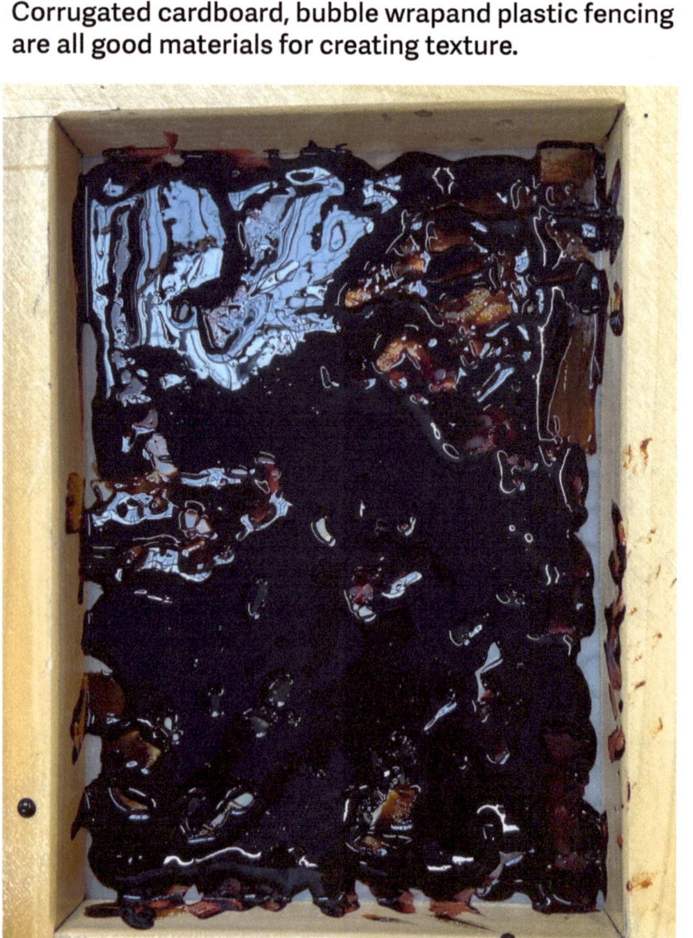

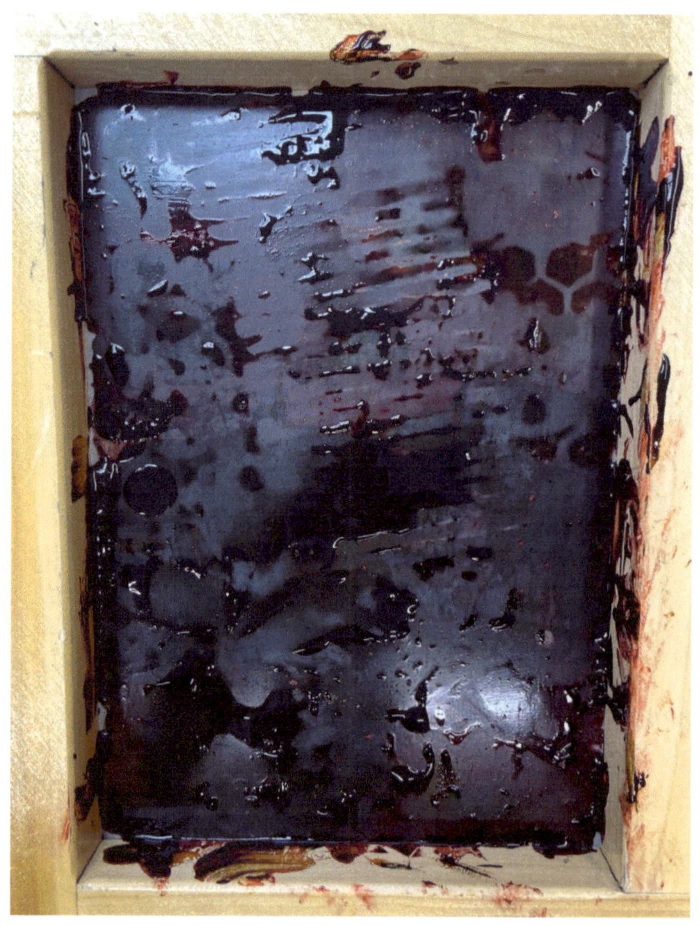

A layer of thickened dye is painted on the screen.

The thickened dye is "squished" down into the textured materials underneath.

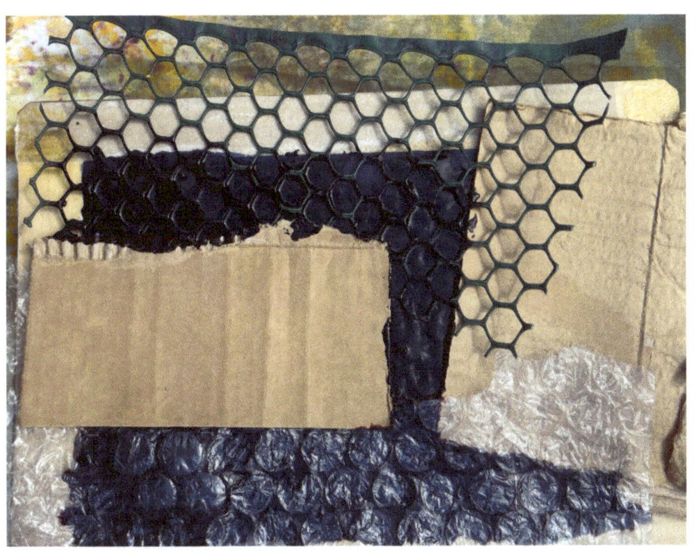

The screen is flipped over so the textured materials are on top while the screen dries in the sun.

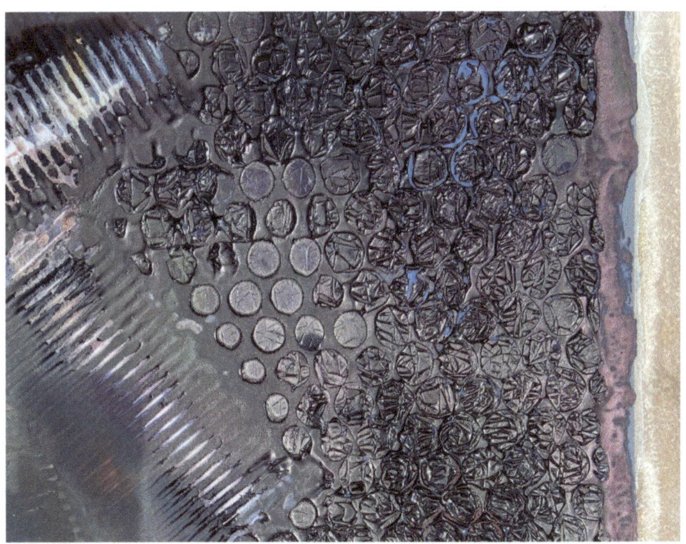

When the materials are removed, the texture stays behind in the dried thickened dye. See prints from this screen on page 54 and 55.

Remove the plastic BUT LEAVE THE TEXTURE MATERIAL on the surface of your screen.

Allow the screen to start drying in the sun, about 30 minutes, depending on how hot it is.

Keep checking until you see the thickened dye is drying and holding the shape of the texture, but is still slightly wet.

If you start to pull off the texture materials and the dyes underneath are runny, then the screen needs to dry longer.

As you pull off the textures, you can print another piece of fabric by using the texture pieces as stamps to monoprint on the fabric.

Allow the screen to thoroughly dry and then pull your prints as usual.

Try other textures underneath, such as a welcome mat. (See page 54.)

Follow the same process by laying down the mat and setting the screen on top of it. Then spread thickened dye (print paste) across the inside of the screen. Pull the paste across the screen, squishing it down into the crevices of the mat. Flip the mat and screen over so that the mat is on top. Allow the screen to dry in the sun for about 30-45 minutes. Slowly remove the mat, making sure the print paste has started to dry and you can see the pattern of the mat. Once the mat is removed, allow the screen to fully dry before pulling the print.

You can also use stamps or stencils to make marks on the screen. Leave the stamps in the print paste while the screen dries in the sun.

When using plants or flowers, make sure they are thick enough to see the veins. Thin plants will not print.

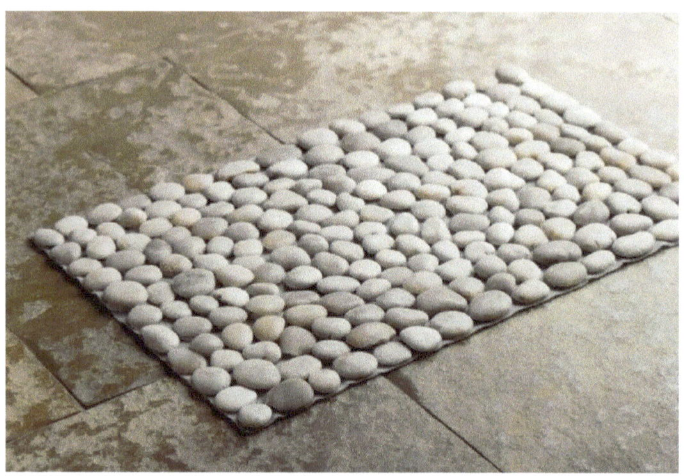

A pebbled mat makes interesting textures.

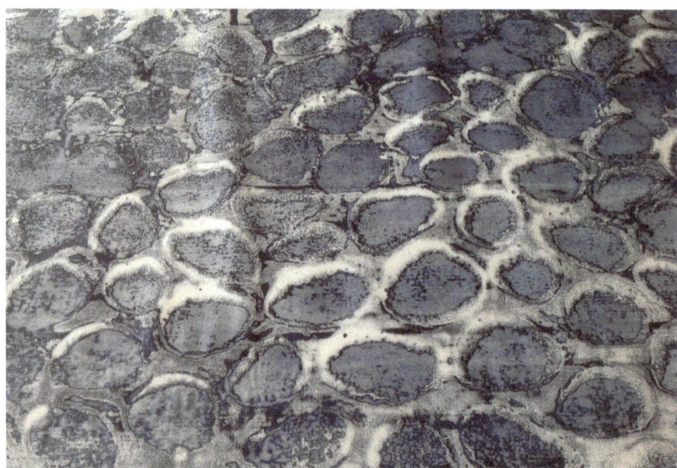

A print created with pebble mat texture.

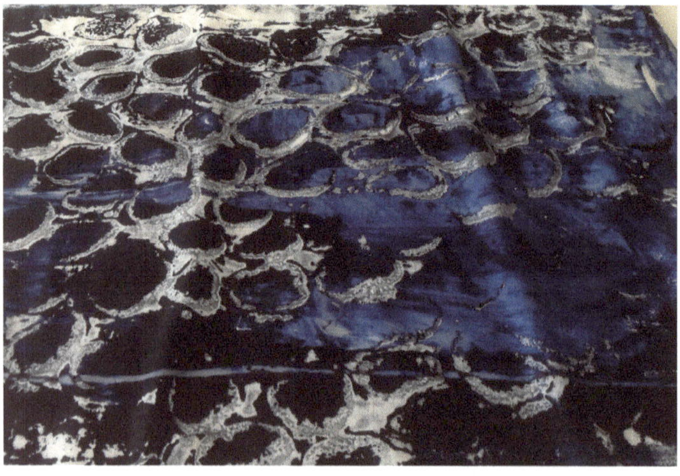

The second print is darker as the design deconstructs.

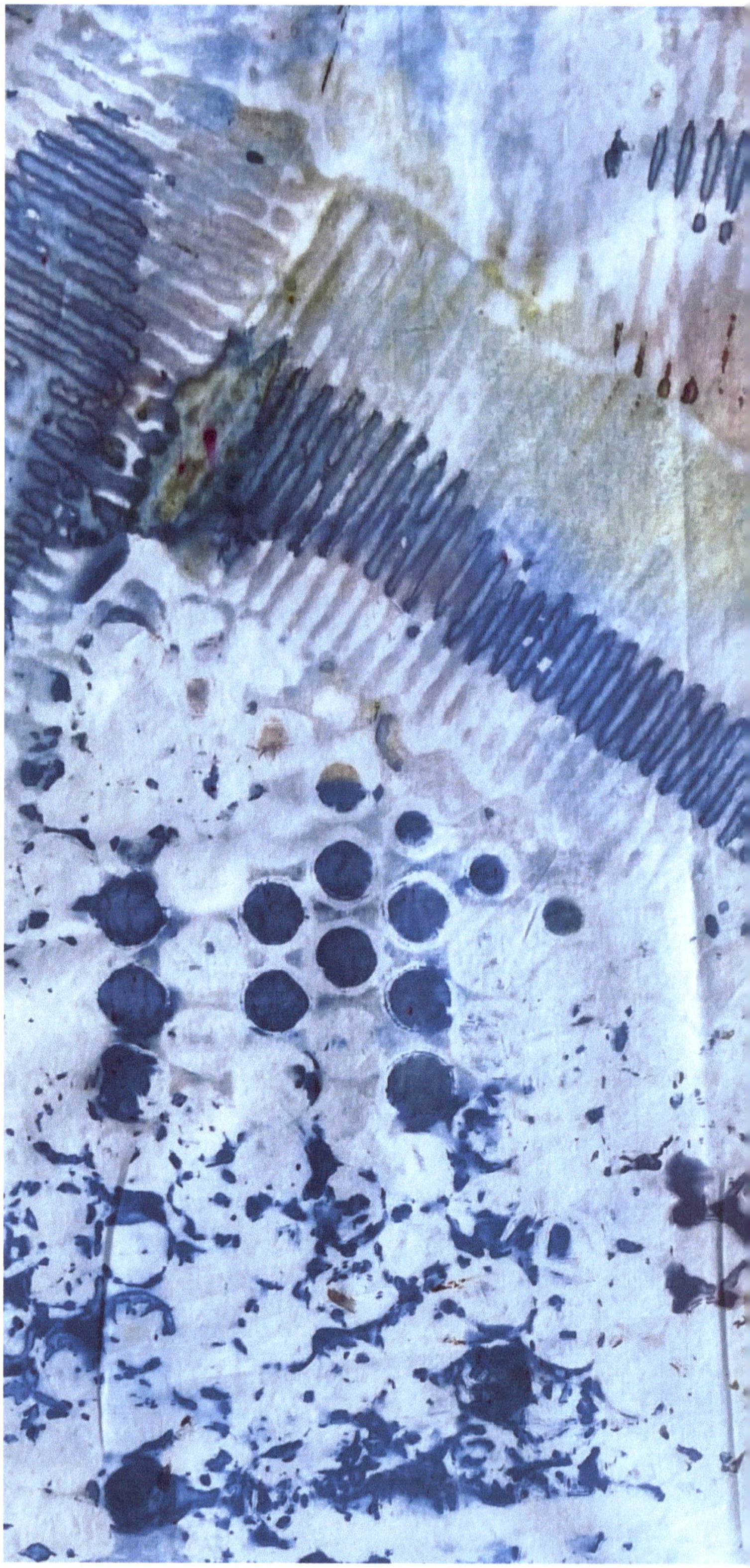

Lines on the print were created by corrugated cardboard.

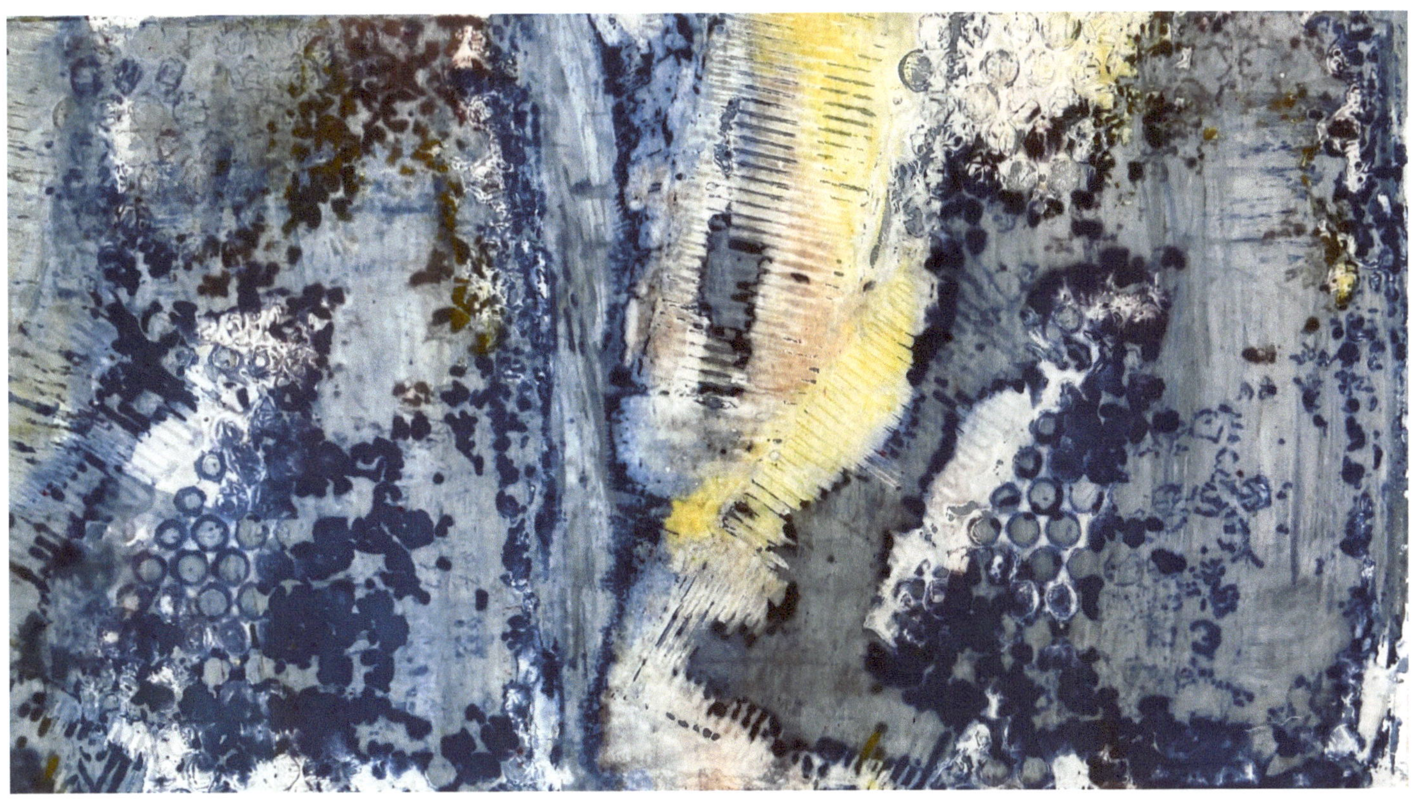

A print pulled from the screen shown on page 53. You can see the texture left behind by bubble wrap.

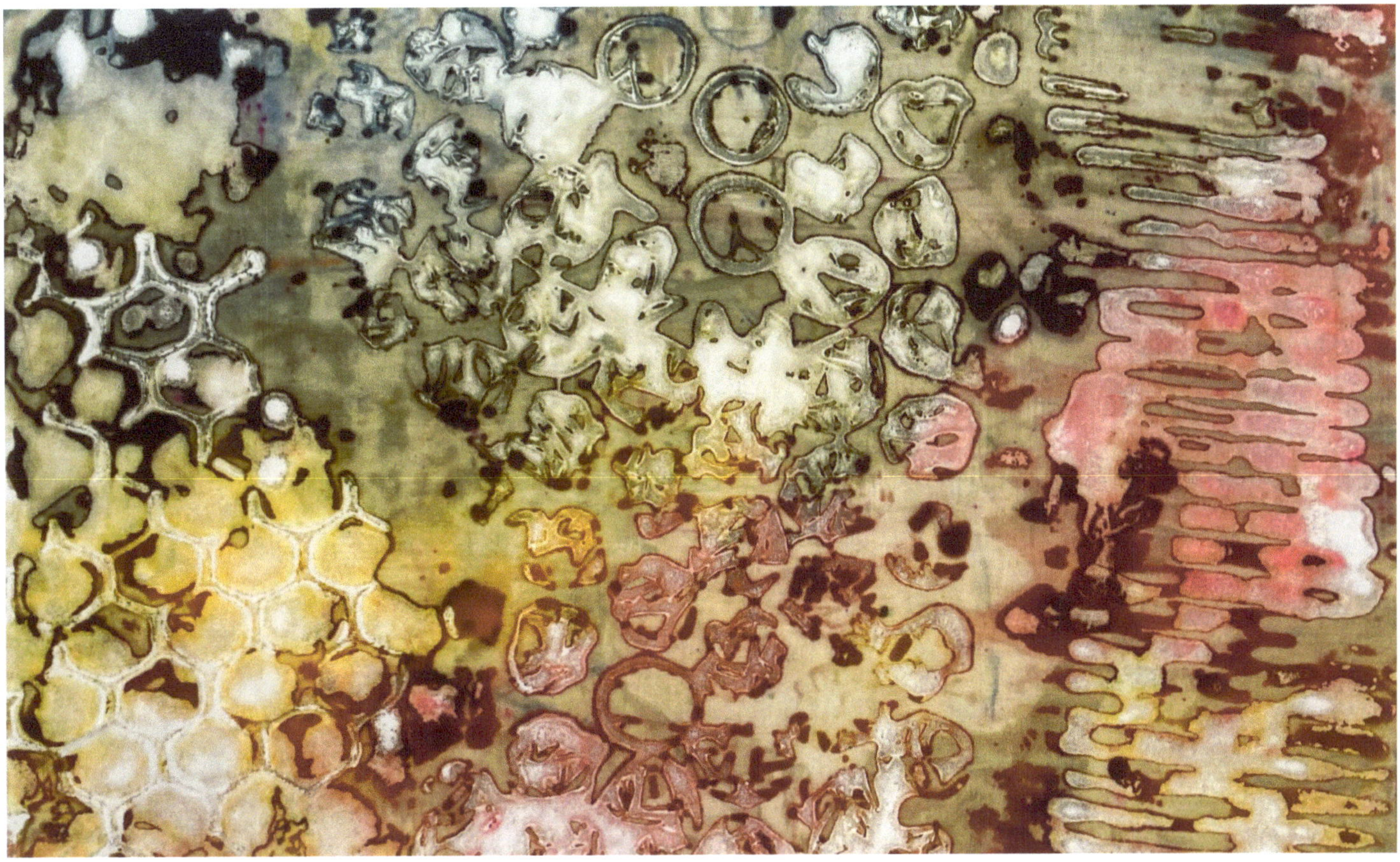

As the design starts to deconstruct, the textures created by cardboard and bubble wrap become more diffuse.

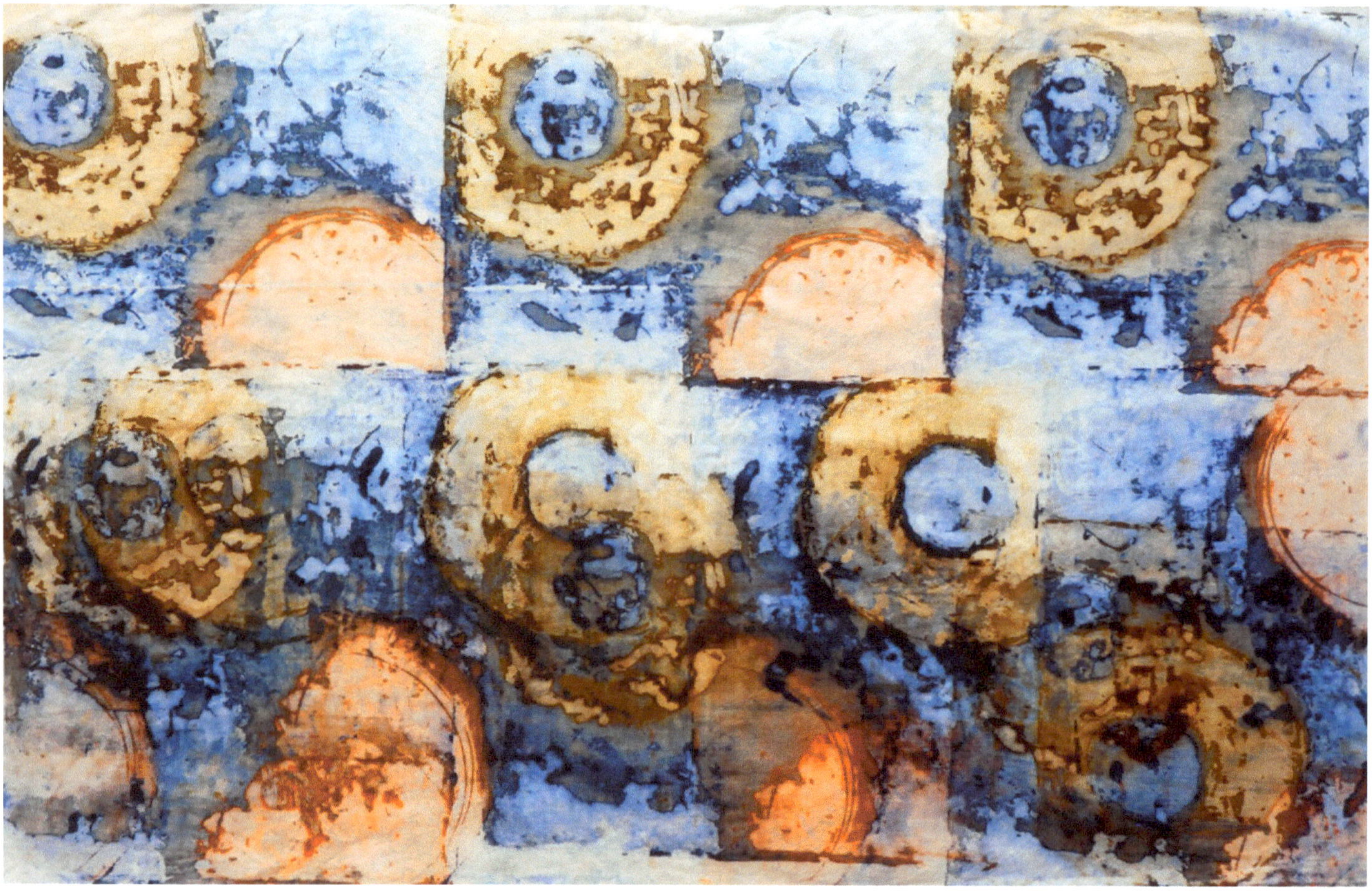

A big circular stamp cut from a car wash sponge was dipped into the dye and pressed onto the screen. The six pulled prints (above) show how the colors of the dyes (Terra Cotta and Indigo) mix to form new shades.

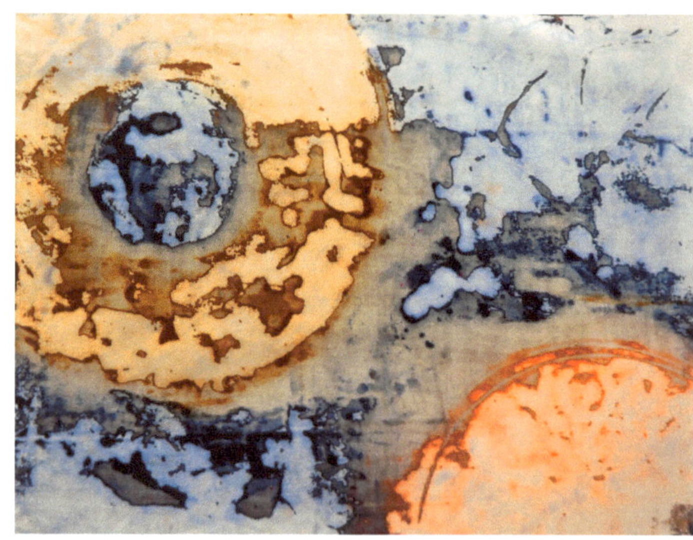

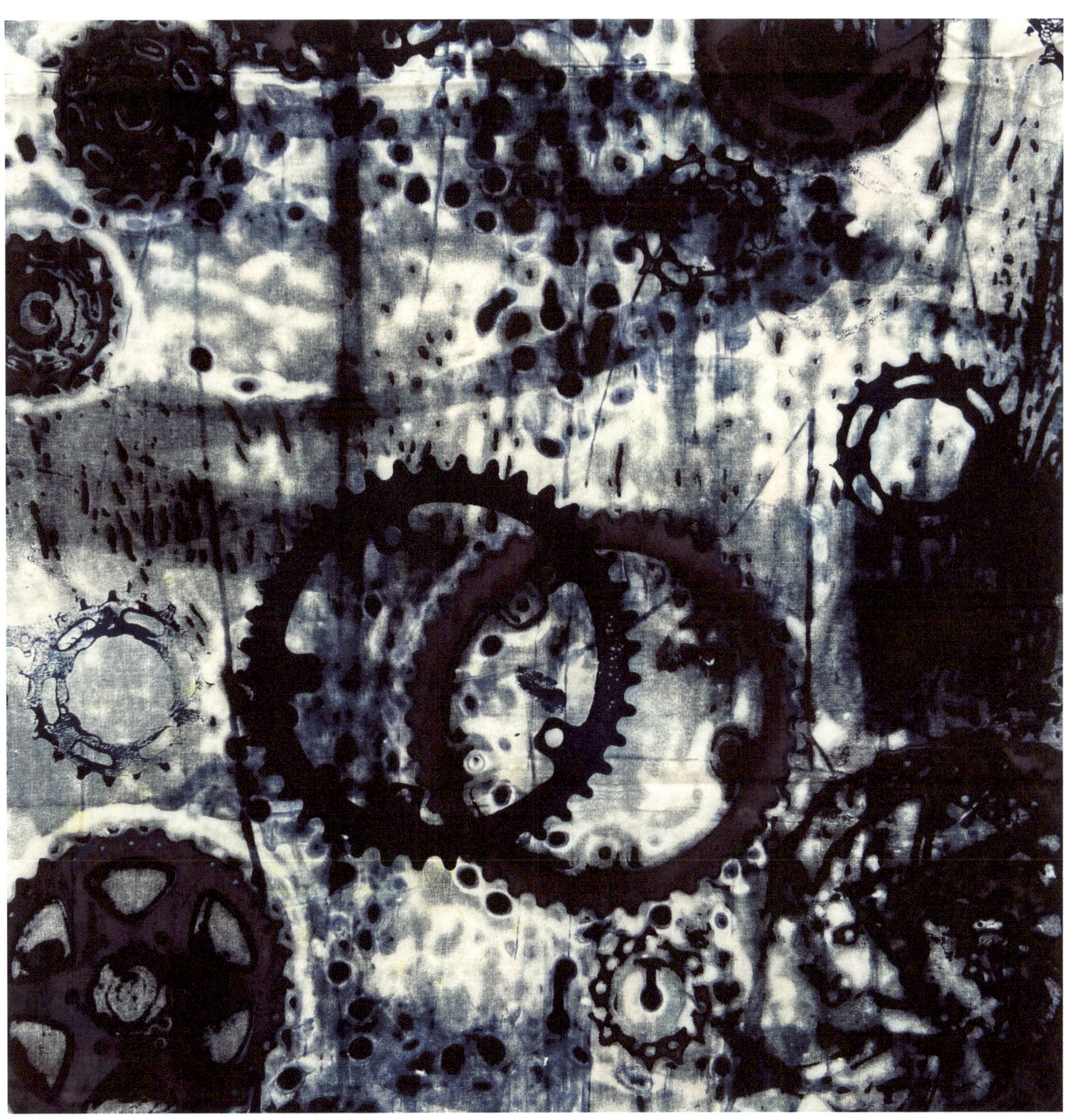

Bike gears were used to create a design for this print. Jet Black thickened dye was applied on the inside of the screen and then the bike gears, painted with thickened Jet Black dye were used as stamps in resist areas, leaving their image behind.

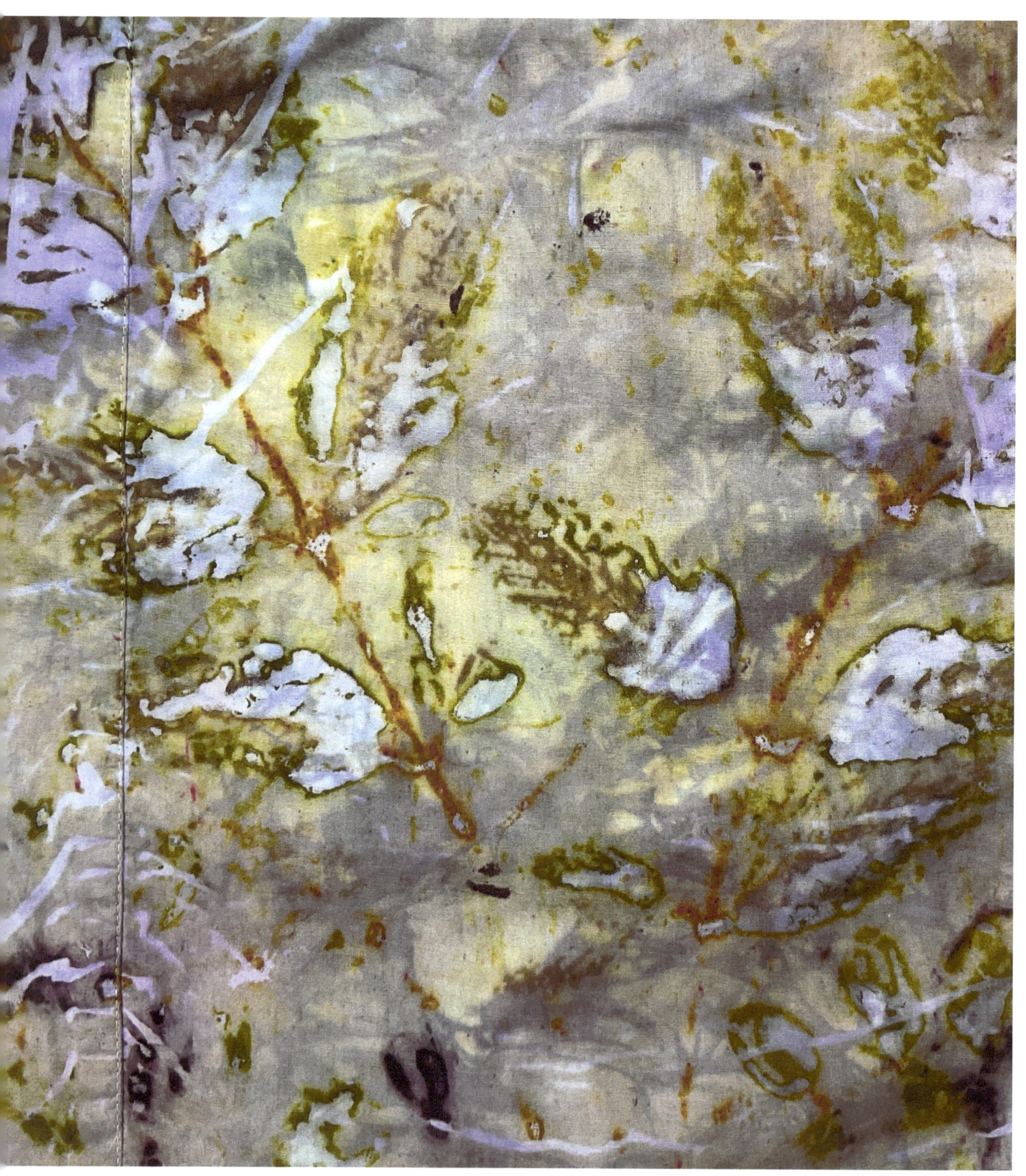

My daughter Rachel used garden plants to create texture in this print. As the screen was almost dry, she added lines with an extruder to look like stems.

USING GRASSES

Lay down an old towel and then cover it with a layer of plastic. Paint the top side of the grasses with thickened dye.

Lay the grass down with painted side up on the plastic.

After arranging the grasses, add a few extra pieces of grass to create a resist.

Lay your screen on top of the grasses with the front side down.

On the back of the screen, paint on thickened dyes in the colors of your "meadow." Add a bit of blue for the sky, straw and gold colors for the field.

Squish the dyes down around the grasses with a squeegee or credit card.

Very important: Lift the bundle of plastic, grasses and screen and carry it out into the sun.

Turn the bundle over so the plastic is on the top. Remove the plastic BUT LEAVE THE GRASSES on the surface of your screen.

Allow the screen to start drying in the sun, approximately 30 minutes.

Keep checking until you see the dye is drying and holding the shape of the grass. If you start to pull off the grass and the dye underneath is runny, then it needs more drying time.

As you pull off the textures, you can print another piece of fabric by using the colored grasses as stamps and monoprinting.

Some of the grass will stick to the screen and will become a resist when you pull your prints.

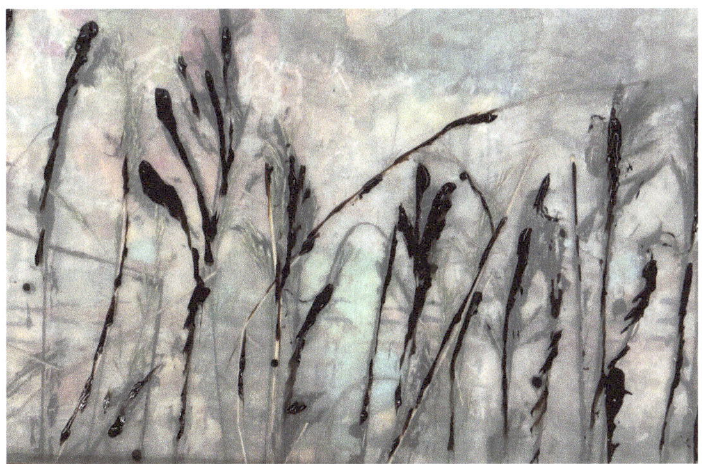

Grasses can make wonderful textures in prints. Start by painting them with dye and laying them painted side up on the plastic sheeting.

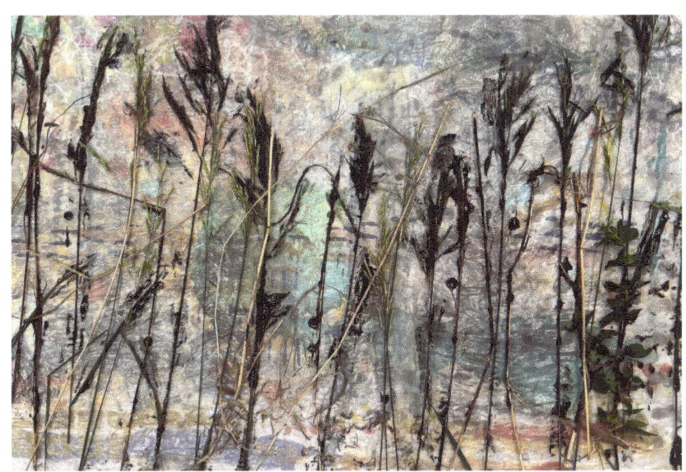

Add additional, unpainted grasses to act as a resist.

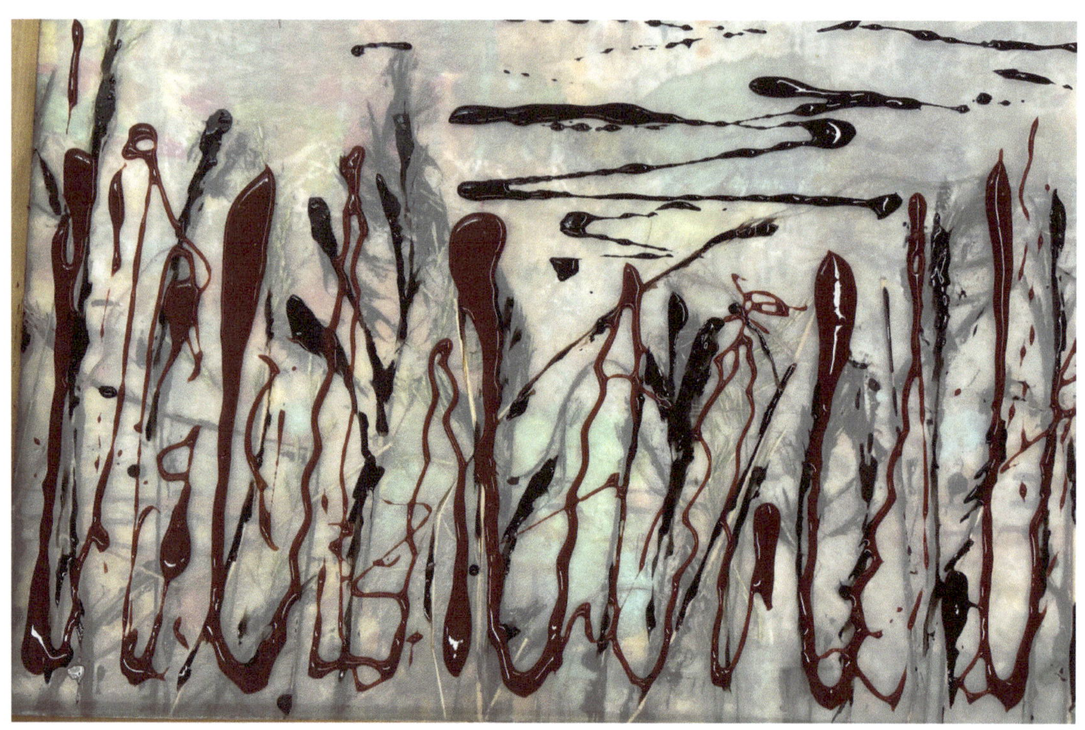

Print paste (thickened dye) is drizzled onto the screen.

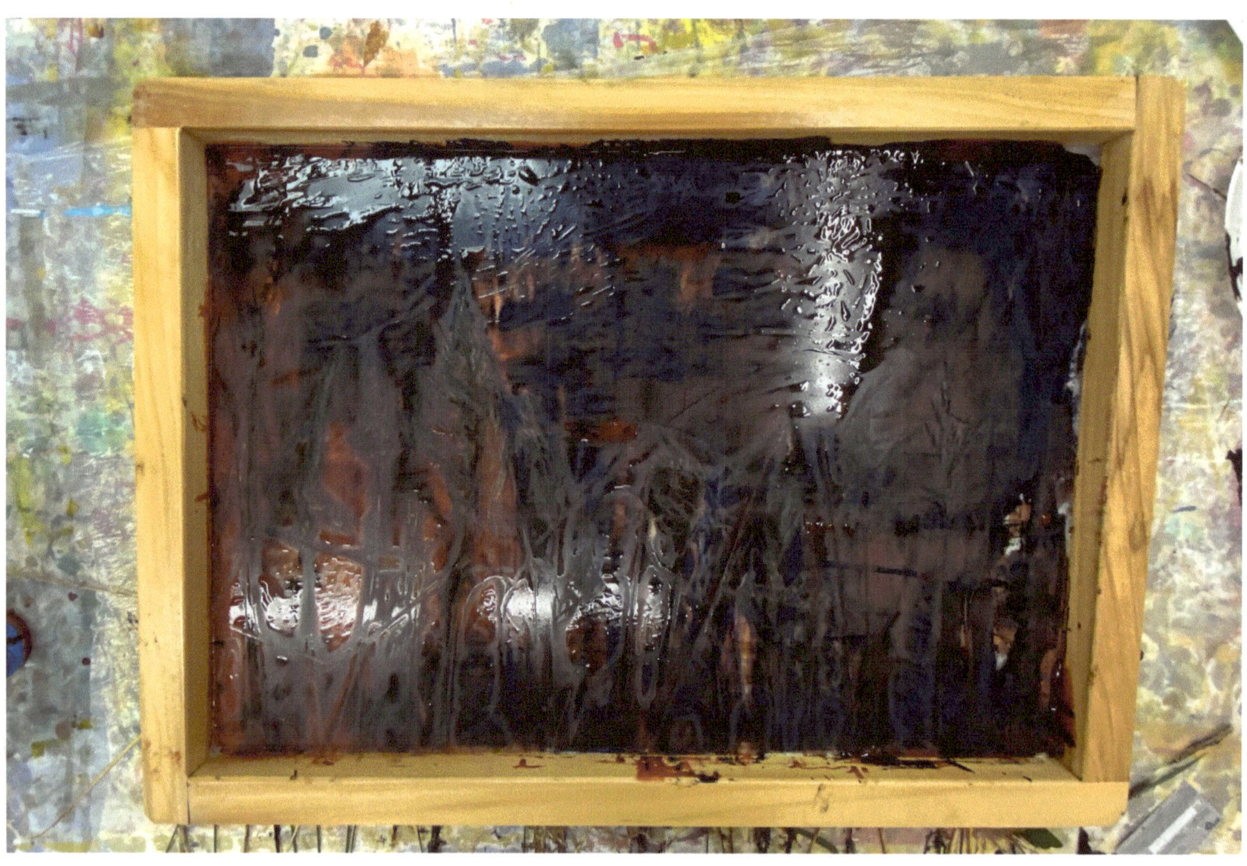

The layer of print paste is squished down into the grasses that are under the screen to create texture.

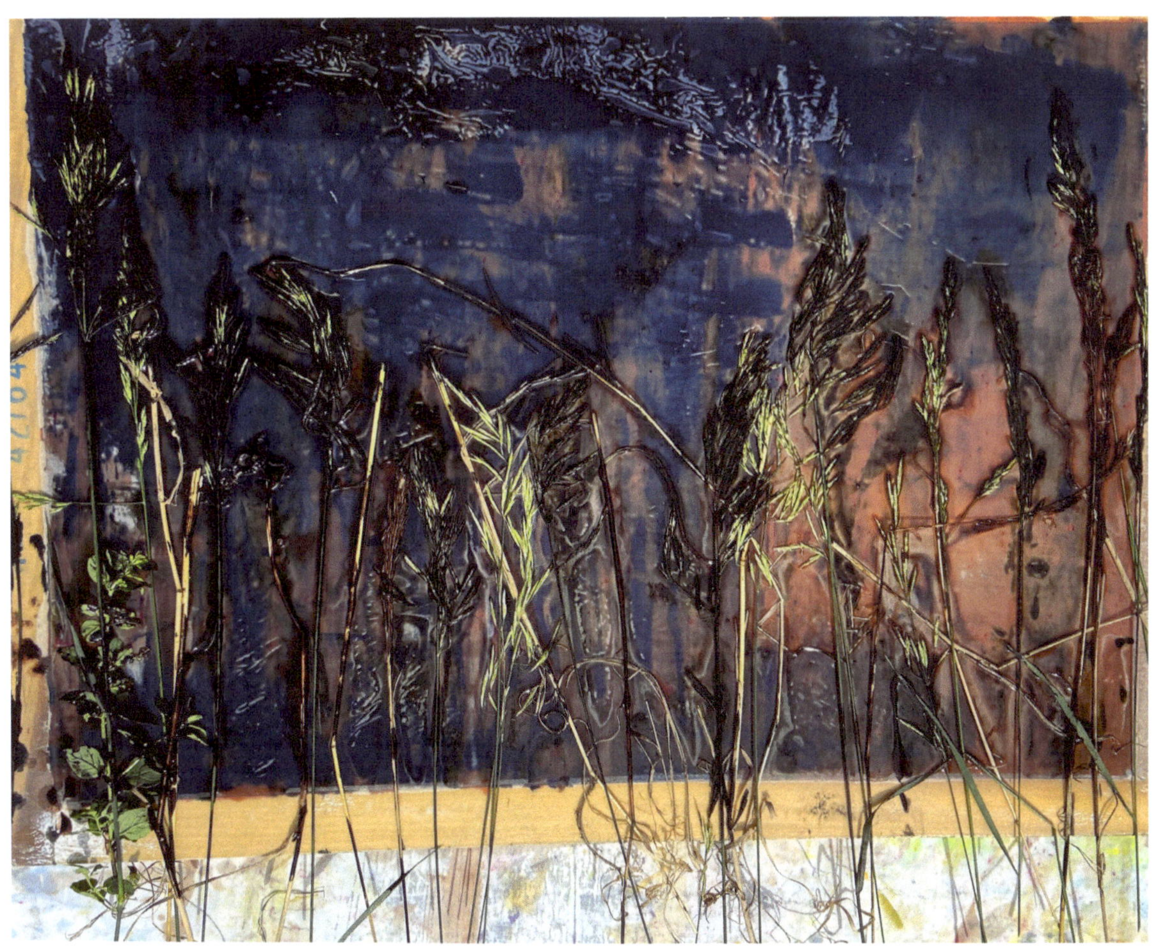

The screen is turned over (with the grasses on top) to dry.

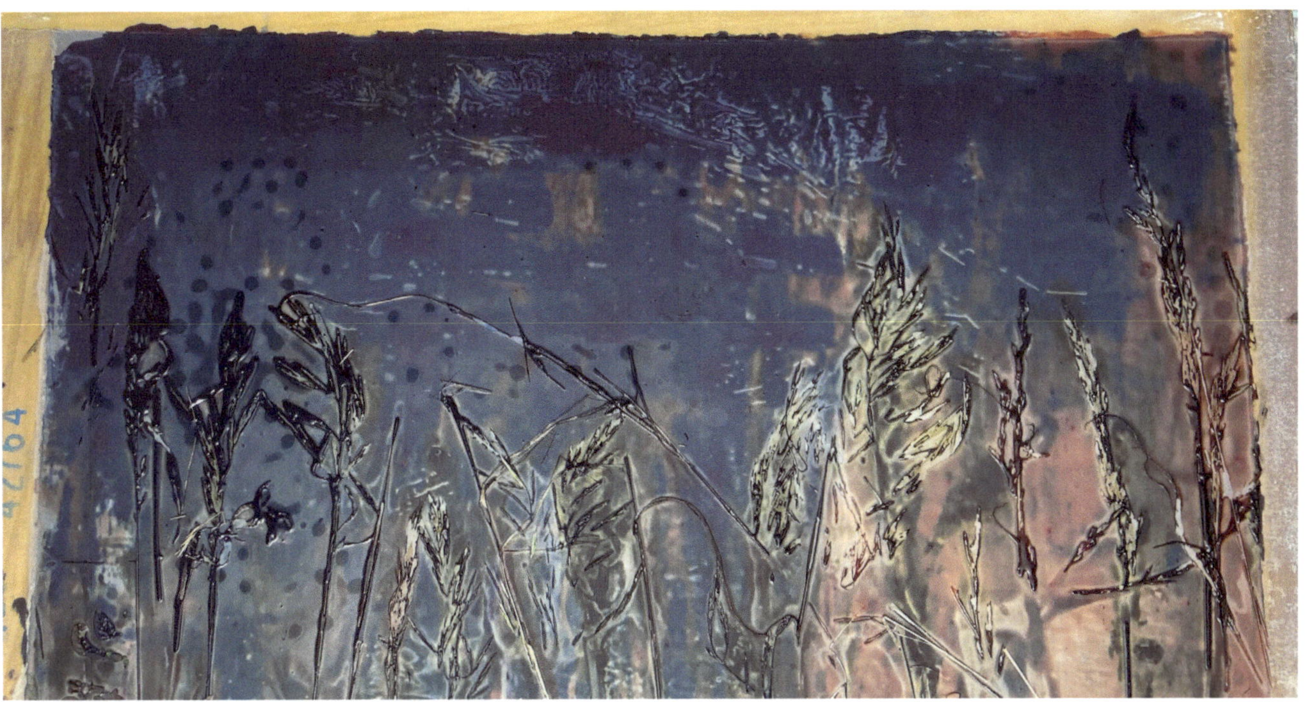

The screen with dried dye is ready to print. Note the texture that is left behind when the grasses are removed. Prints from this screen are shown on pages 62 and 63.

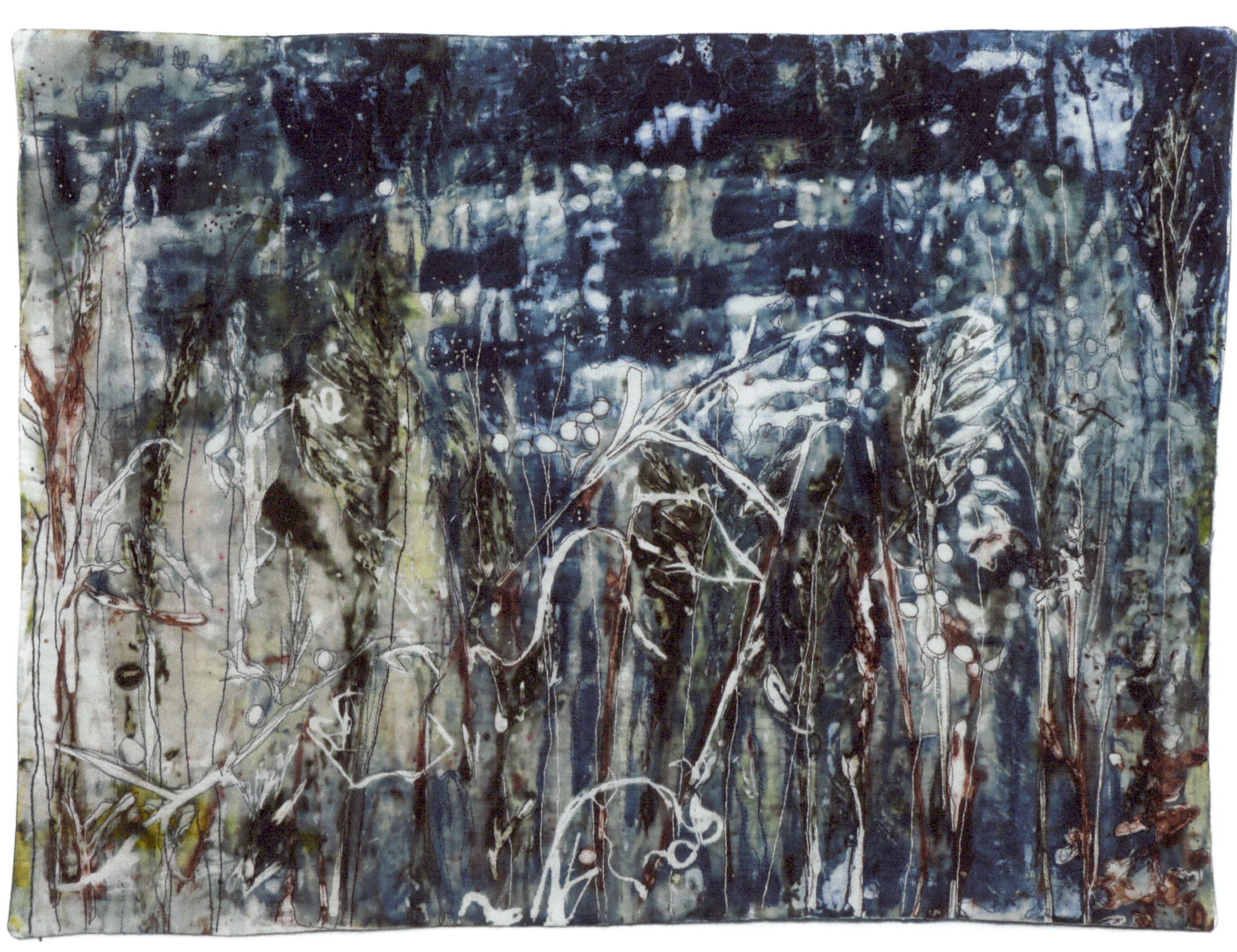

Prints from the same screen (shown on page 61) result in two different looks. One has much more blue and the second pull of the same screen (shown at right) includes more shades of green.

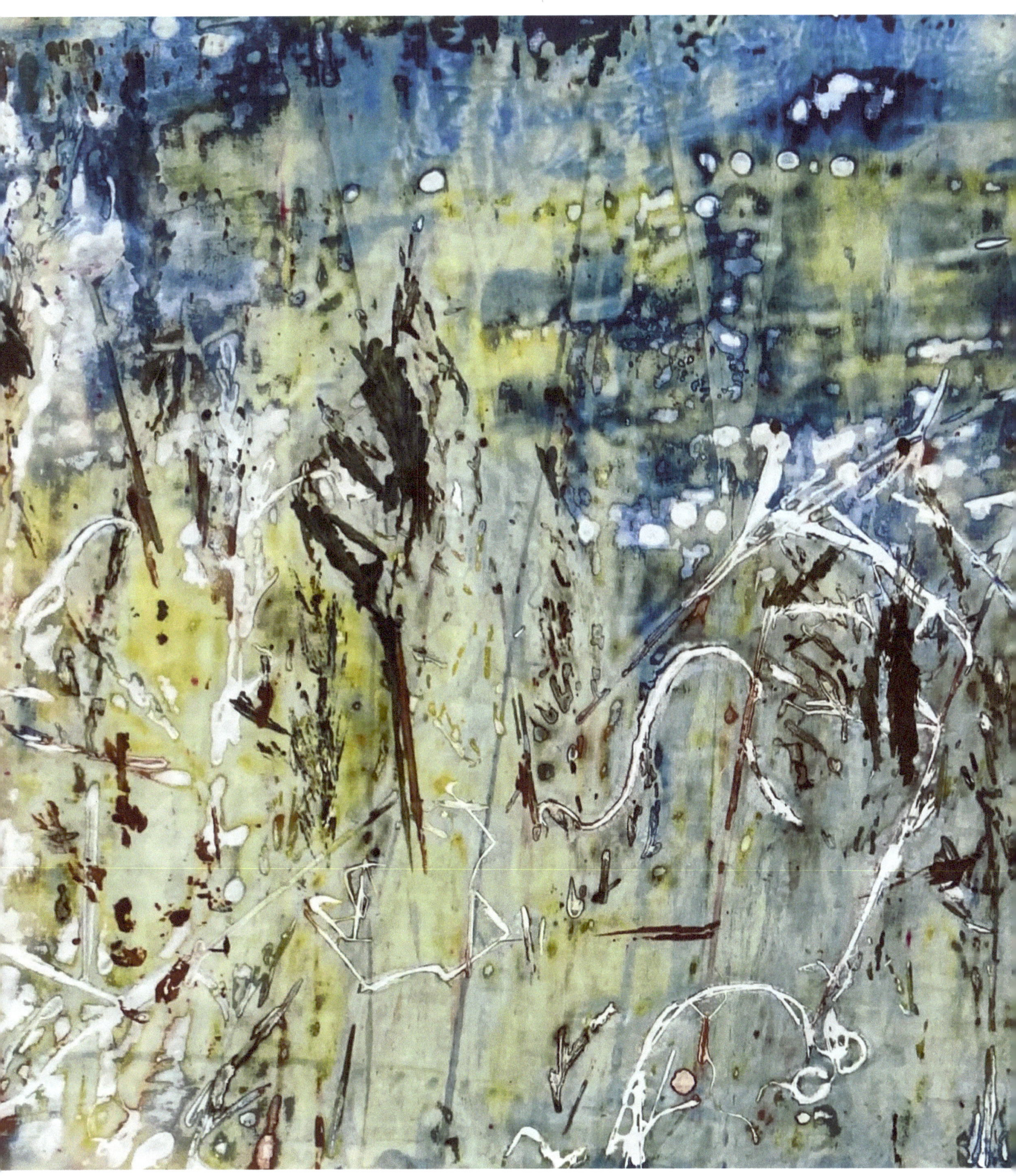

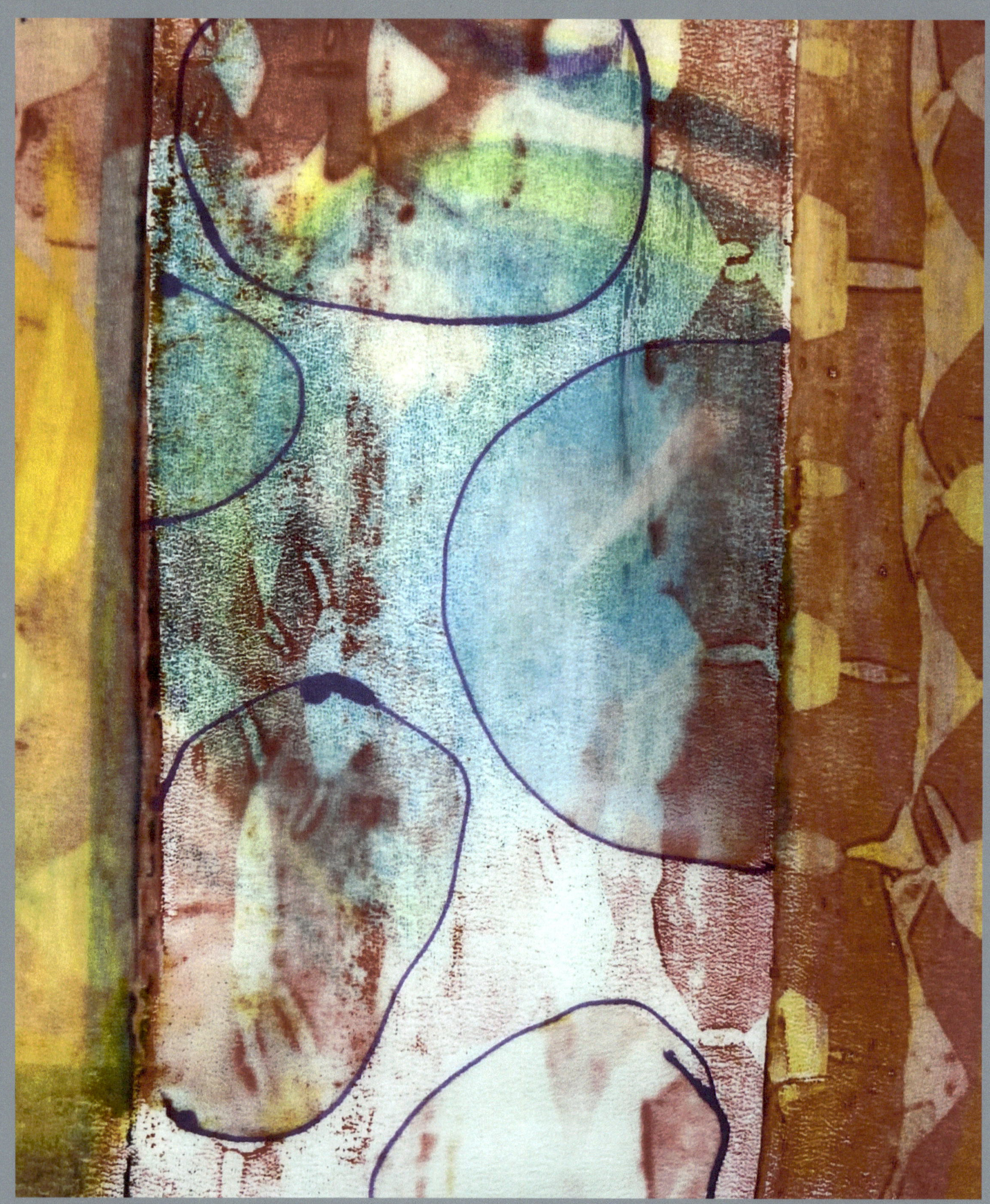

Artist Kerr Grabowski used an extruder to paint dye in defined lines on this screen-printed fabric.

chapter 9

Bottles & Extruders
for Line Work and Writing

There is a beauty in a simple line and in edges created.

Lines formed when using a bottle to "write" with thickened dye on the screen usually act as a resist for the first several pulls.

You can use clear alginate with every pull to keep the consistency in color of the prints.

You can also use the mud and every print will have a darker background, or you can use thickened dye (colored print paste) to create a background that's another color.

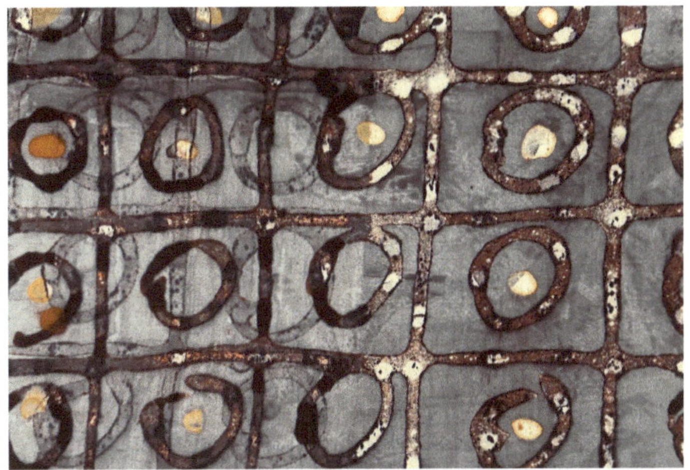

Jet Black dye was used to paint a grid on the screen. Brick color dye was added to the circle centers.

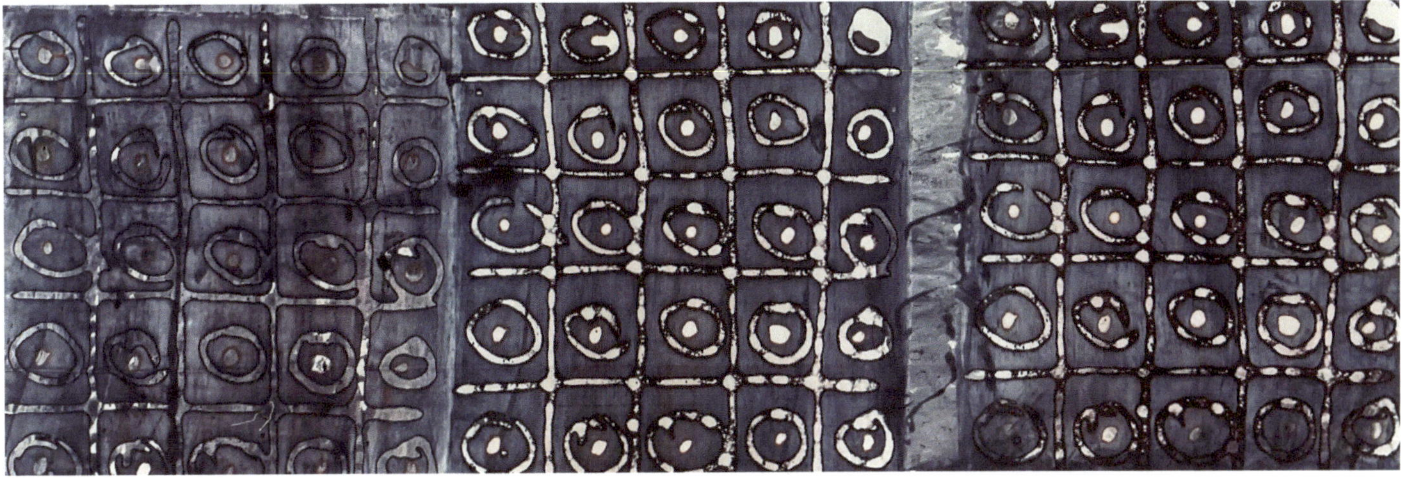

This series of three prints was pulled from a screen that featured a black grid and circle pattern painted on with an extruder.

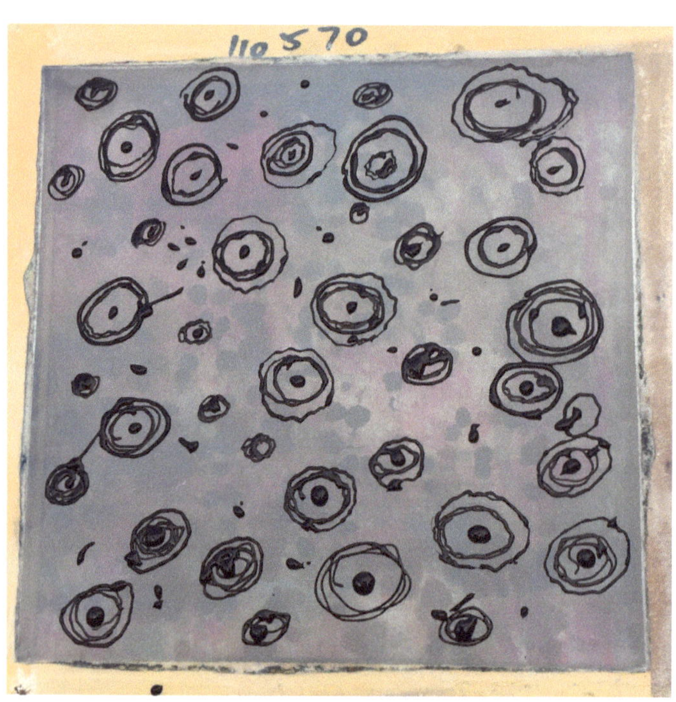

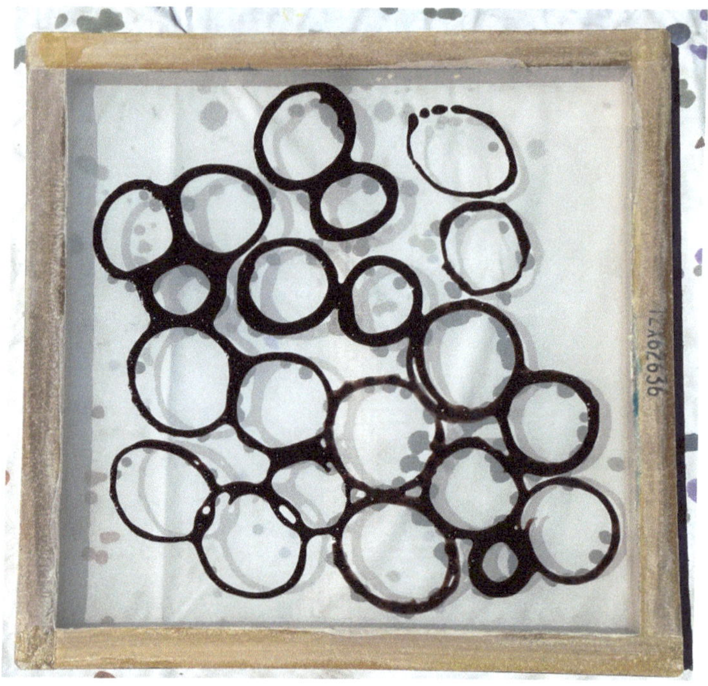

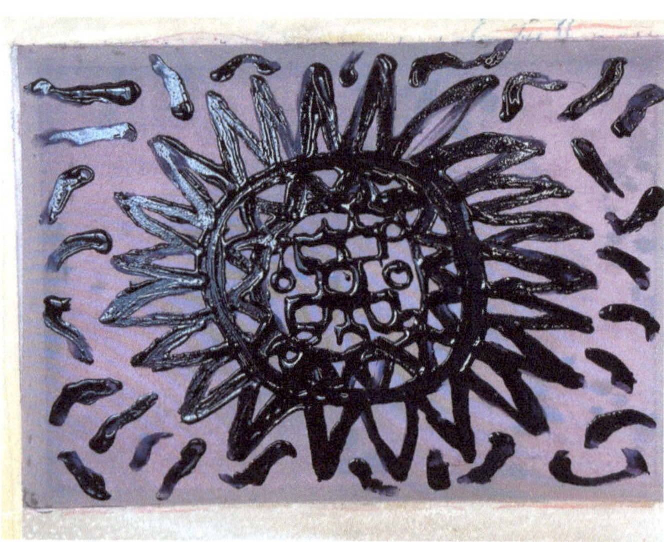

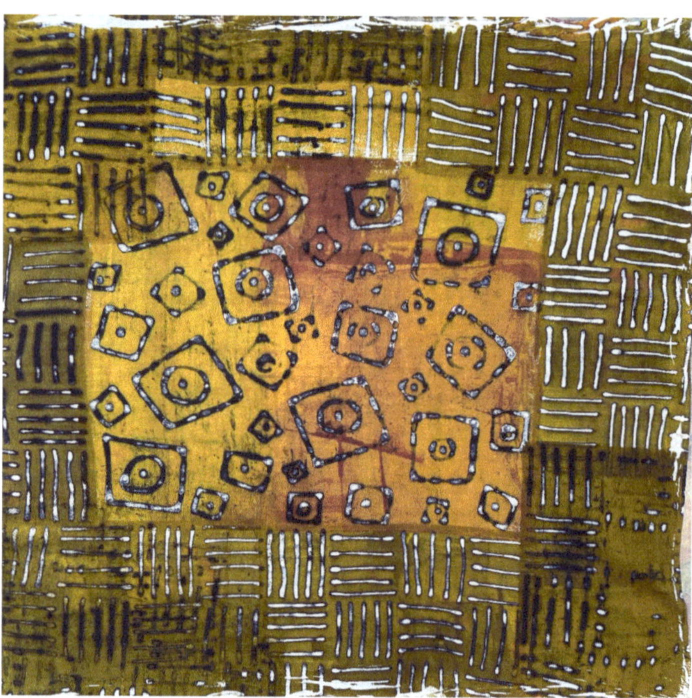

Bottles and extruders can be used to "draw" fine designs on the screen with thickened dye. Bottom left: Artist Jeanne Gray filled her screen with line work before pulling a print. Bottom right: Dishtowel by Mary Rowan Quinn.

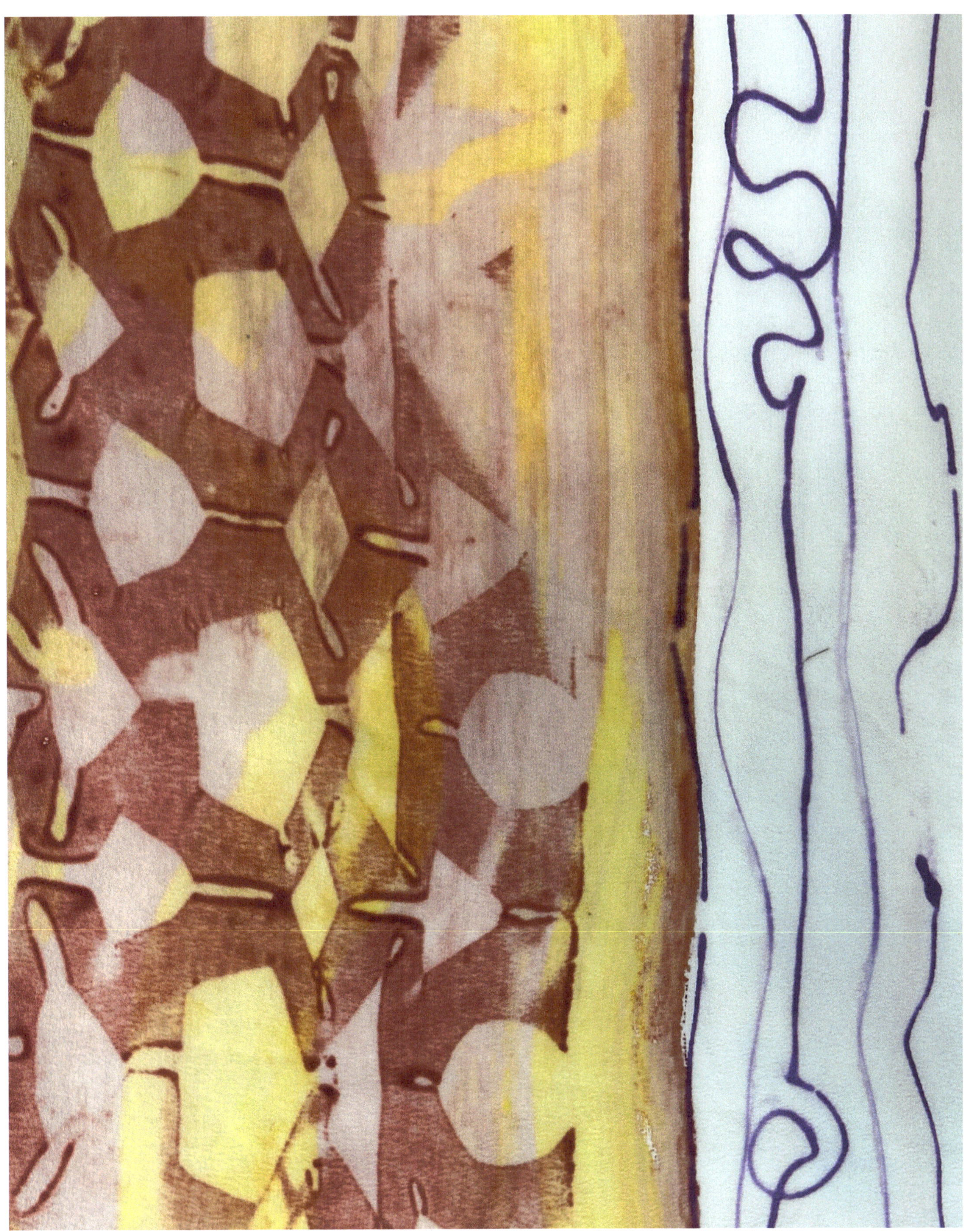

On this piece of printed silk, Kerr Grabowski drew squiggly lines with dye using an extruder.

WRITING ON THE SCREEN

To write on the screen and avoid having the letters appear backward in the final print, you must put the writing on the INSIDE of the screen.

Use four cans of the same size to lift the screen off the surface of the table. Apply the lines of writing with a bottle, extruder or paintbrush. Keep the screen on the cans to dry in the sun.

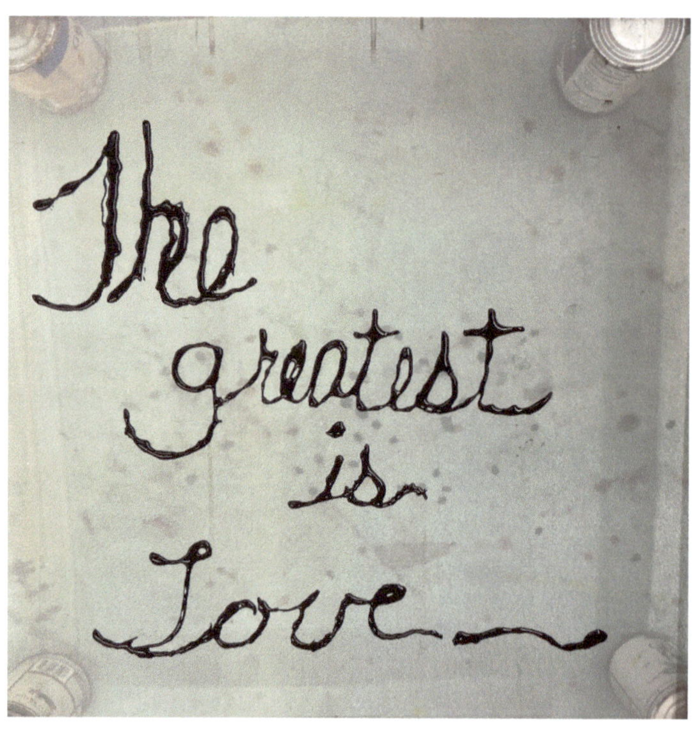

Writing is done on the inside of the screen.

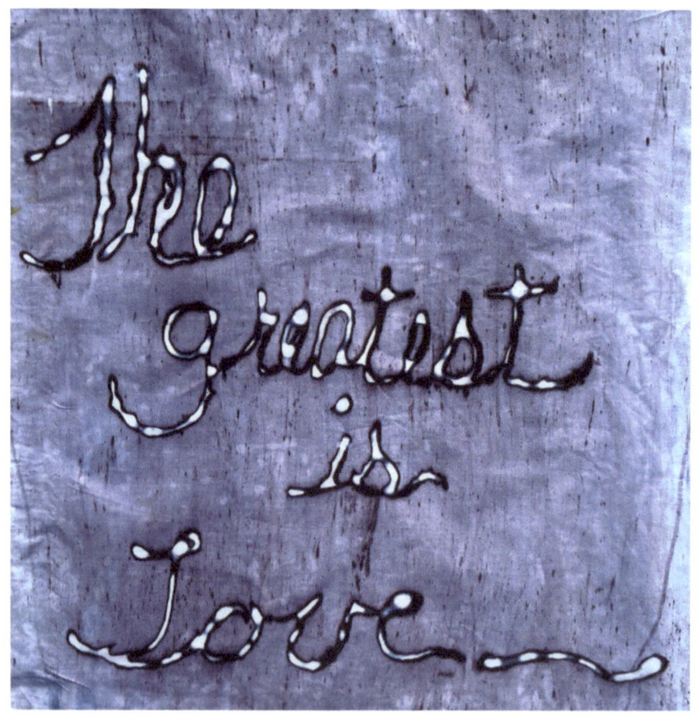

A print from the screen above that was pulled with clear alginate. The gray background appears because the alginate lifts pigment from the black dye.

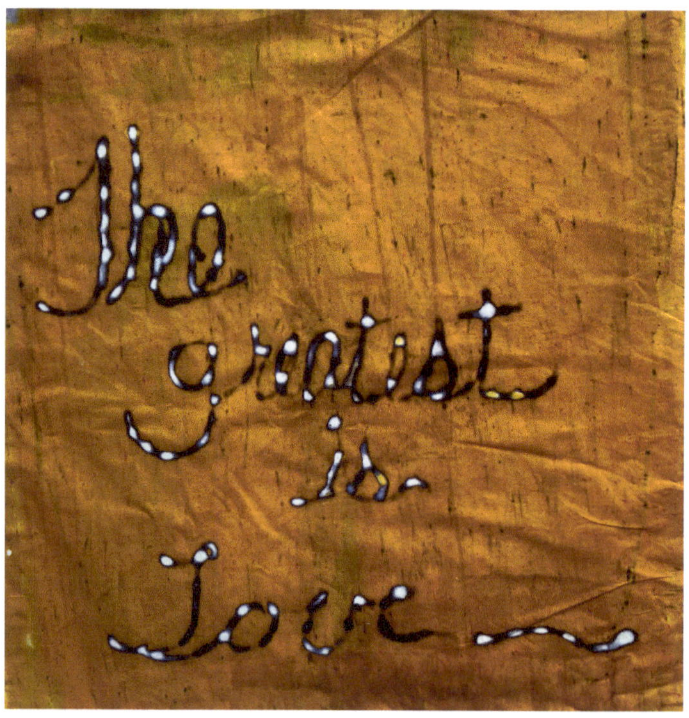

This print was pulled with colored alginate (print paste).

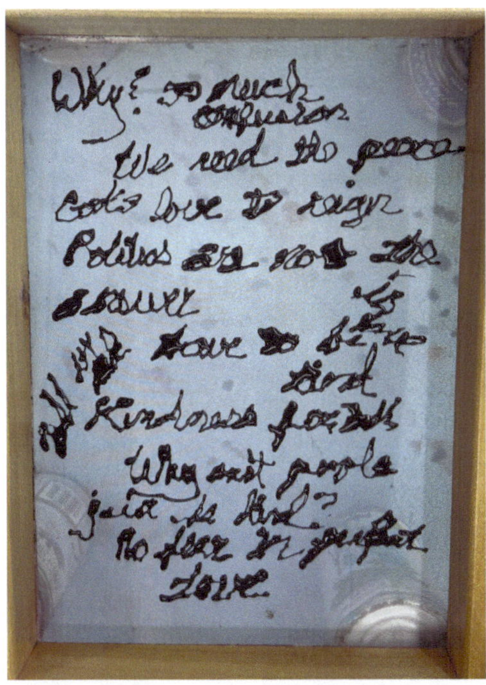

A larger screen can accommodate more lines of text. You must write on the inside of the screen to keep the words from being backwards when the print is pulled.

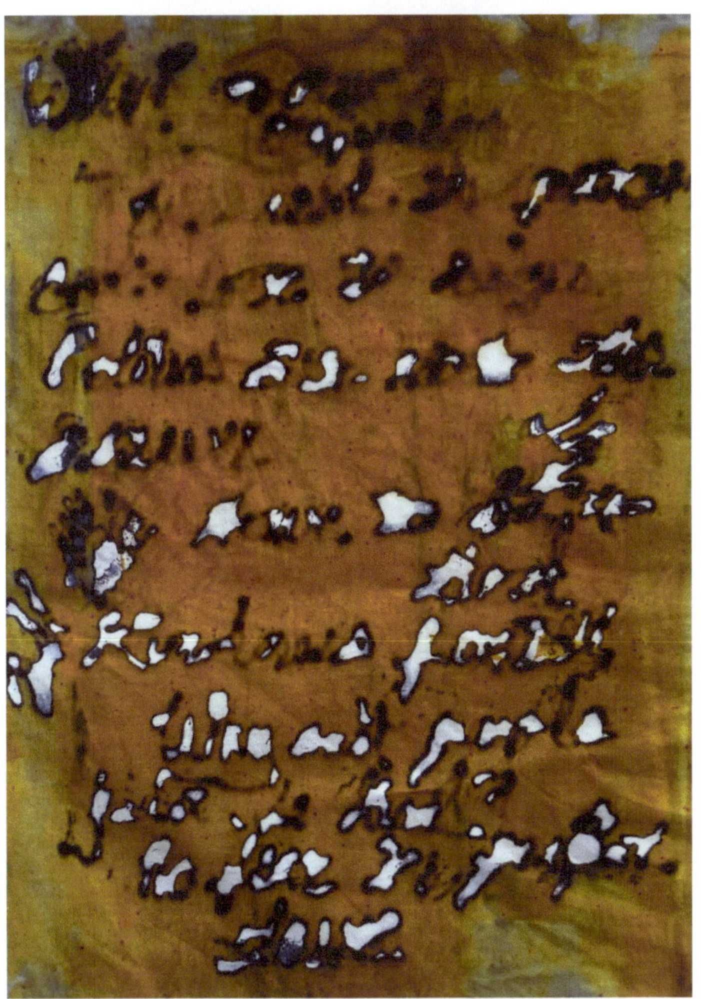

A print pulled from the screen above with colored print paste (alginate).

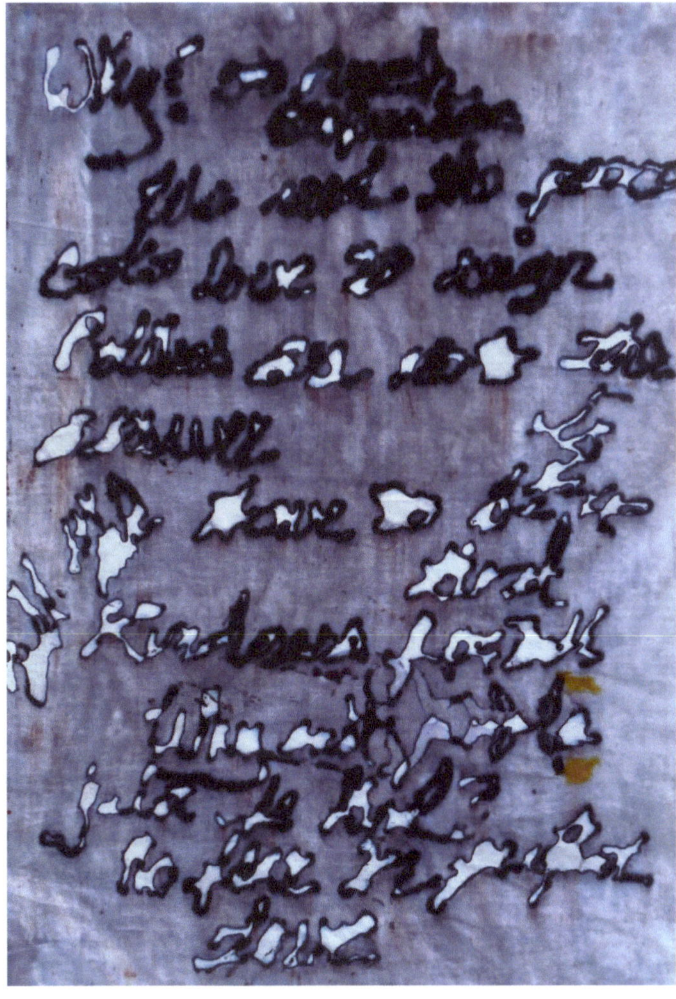

This print was pulled from the screen above with clear alginate.

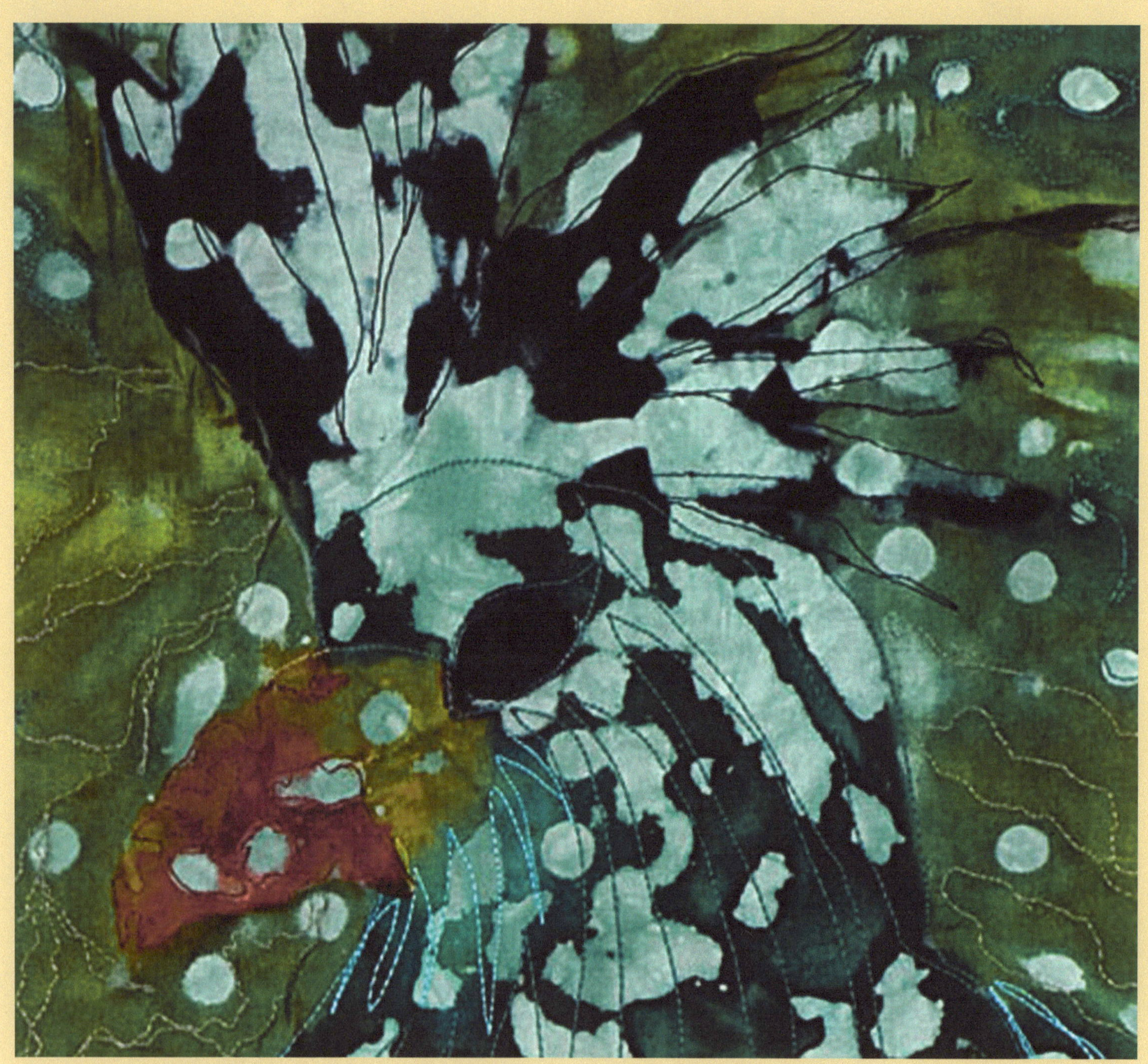

A detail of the stiched art piece "5 O'Clock." A piece of black fabric was appliqued onto the bird's eye.

chapter 10

Resists & Discharge

For more options with printing, try using different resists with both the fabric you plan to print on and the screen itself.

SOY WAX RESIST

You can apply melted soy wax on your fabric before pulling your prints using batik tools, stamps, stencils or freehand images. Roll on using brushes or a small paint roller. After applying the soy wax to your fabric, place it in your freezer for five to 10 minutes. Twist and crinkle the fabric when you remove from the freezer to create the batik-type effect.

Then pull your prints as usual, creating a resisted area and more texture.

You can also add a soy wax pattern to your screen to make a resist before adding your print paste image. This creates a more defined white resist area.

> NOTE:
> *Soy wax is not as heavy as batik wax and not as lightweight as candle wax.*

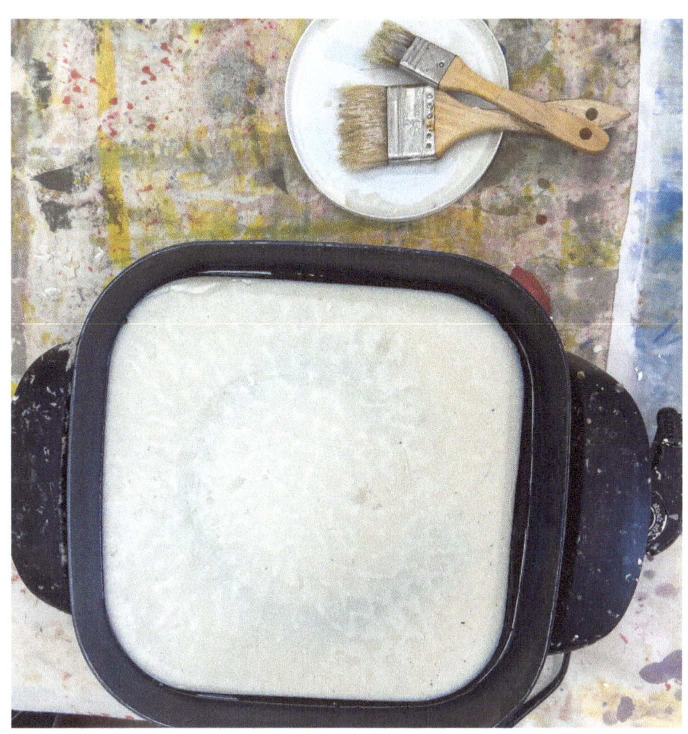

An electric skillet is used to heat soy wax to 200 to 220 degrees.

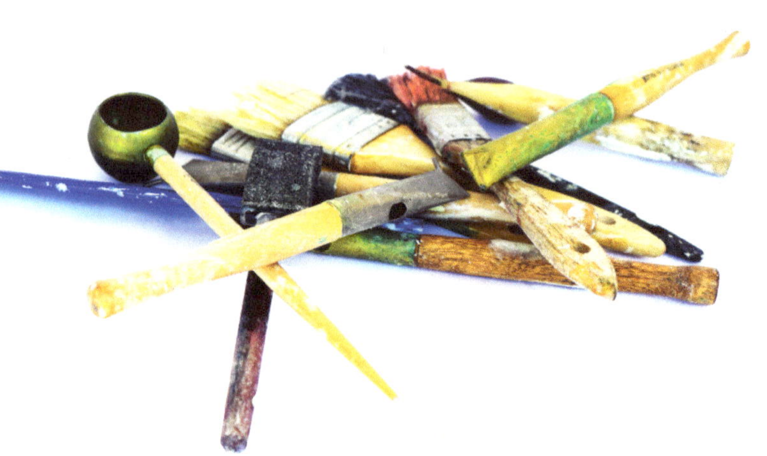

Batik tools and brushes can be used to apply soy wax to your screen.

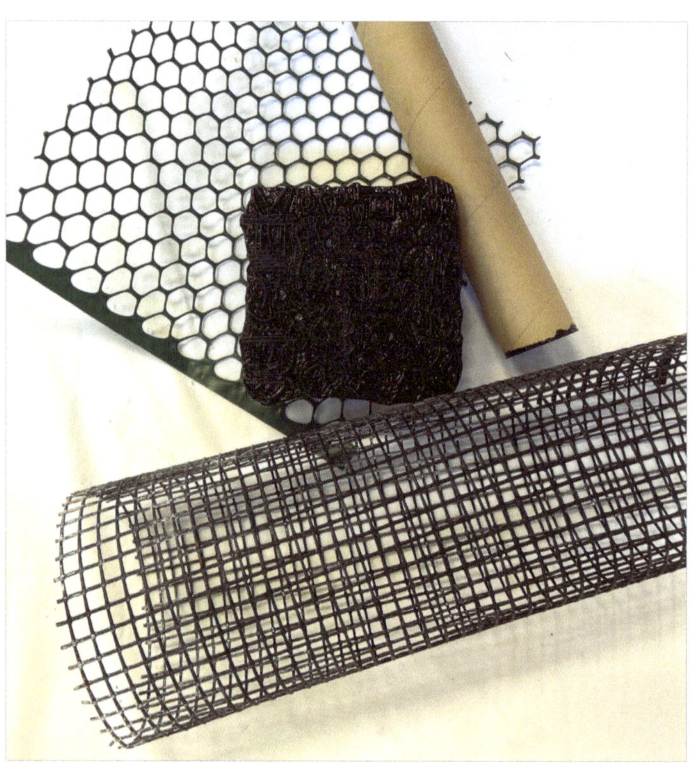

Wire mesh, plastic grids and even paper towel tubes can be used as tools to apply soy wax.

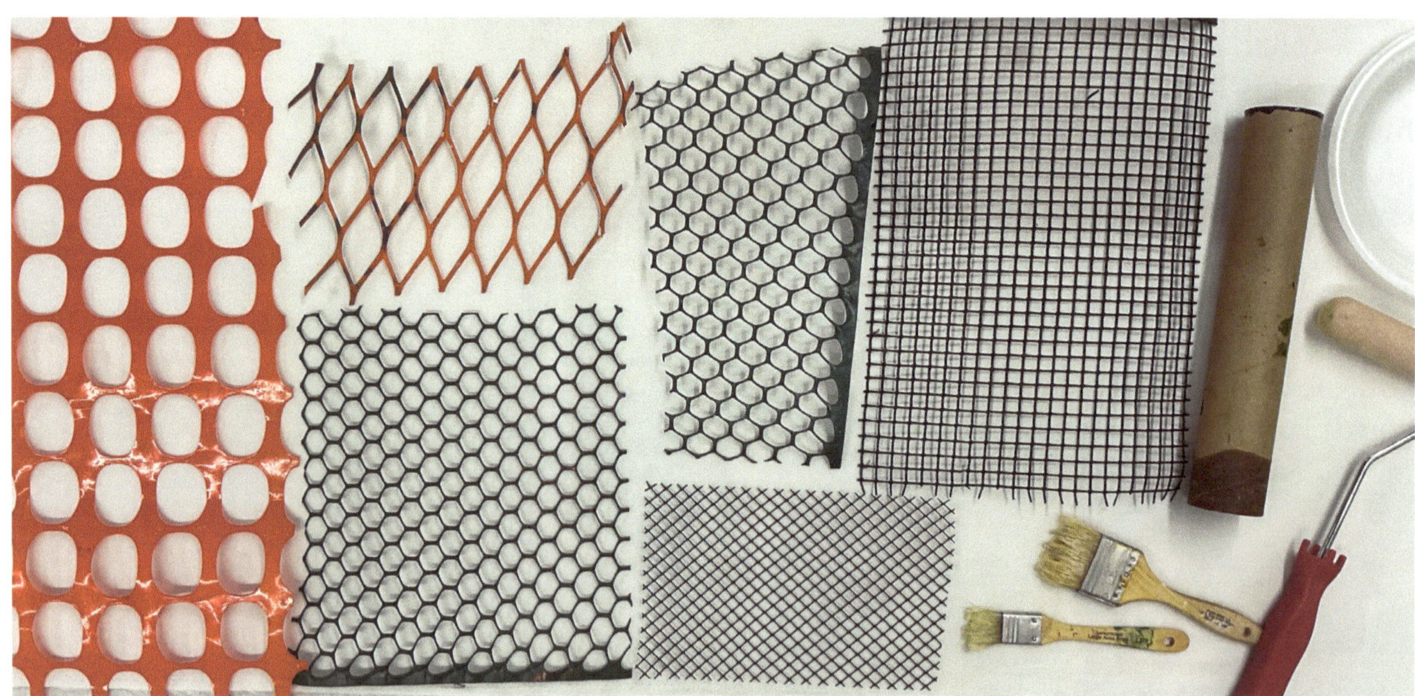

Soy wax can be applied to a screen by using materials like these as stencils. Lay the netting or fencing down on the screen and roll on a layer of soy wax with a roller. When the material is lifted off, the wax design remains as a resist.

  Deconstructed Screen Printing: The Beauty of the Organic Line

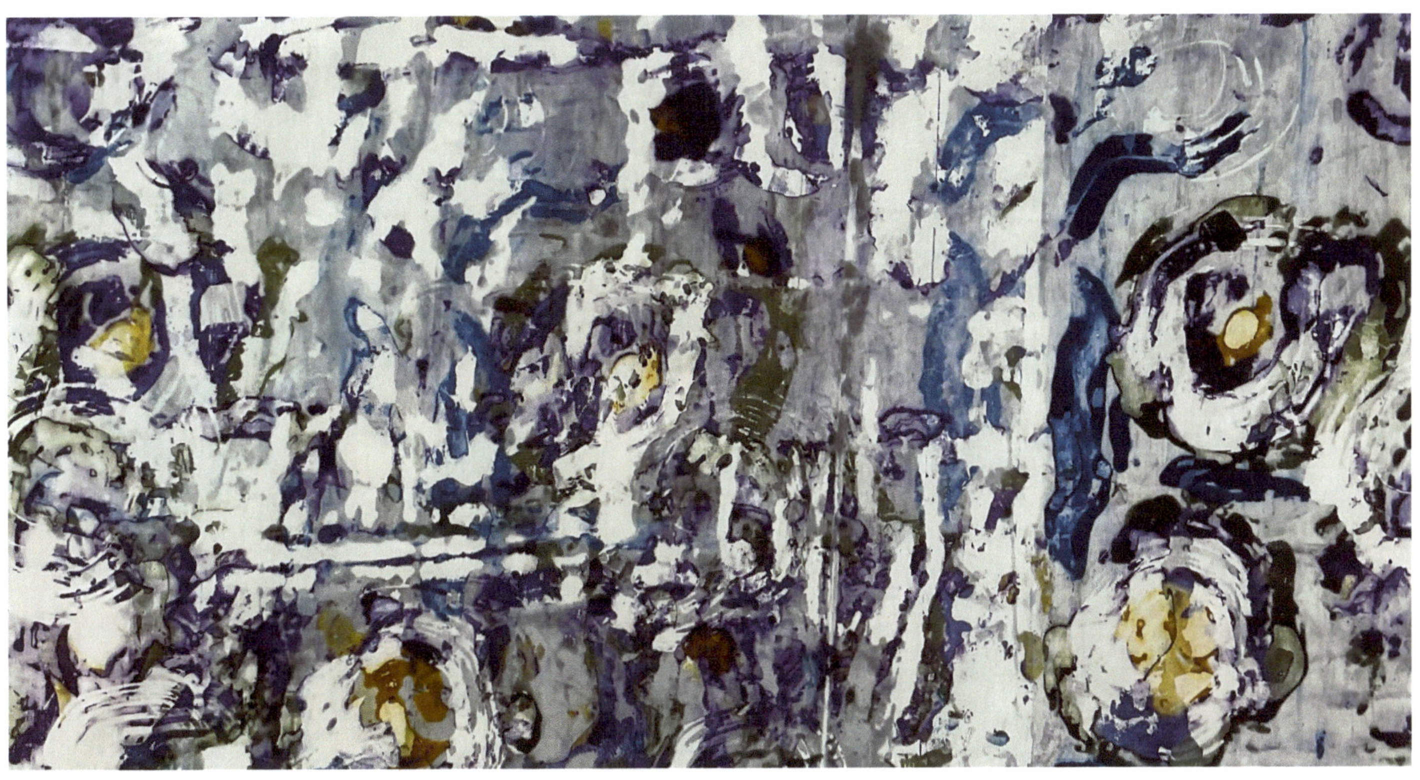

Soy wax applied with a brush creates white markings in this print.

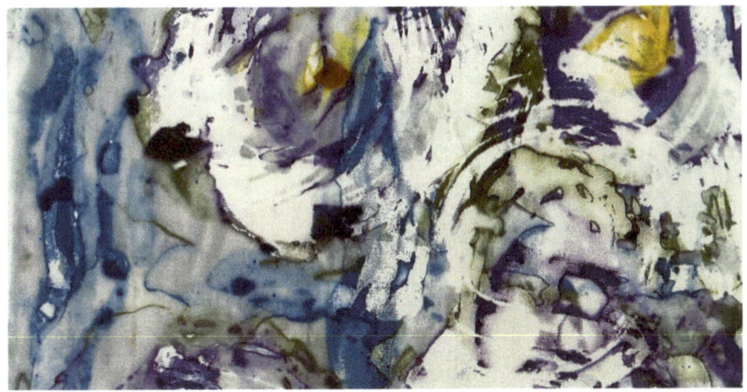

A closer look at the markings left behind when print paste (alginate) is pulled over a screen that has a soy wax resist.

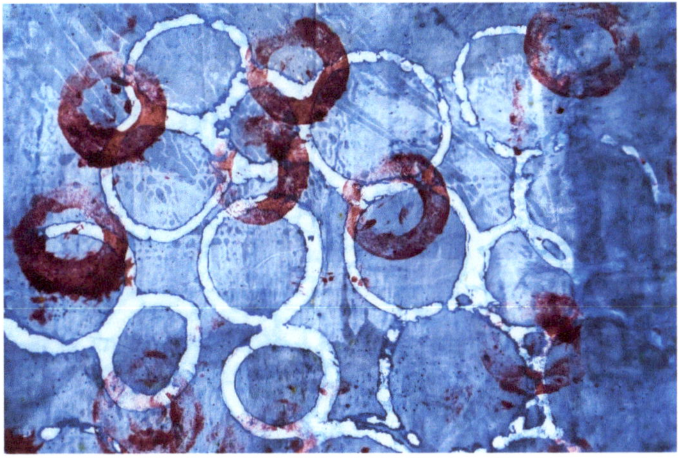

Soy wax applied in a circular pattern leaves behind white circles on the print. The red circles were stamped on with dye once the print was dry.

DYES THAT MAKE A RESIST AND RELEASE SLOWLY

There are some dyes that do not release as quickly as others because of their chemical composition. These dyes create a resist. Some of them include:
- Jet Black (Dharma 250)
- Moss Green (Dharma 134)
- Marigold (Dharma 67)

As an example, in the piece "Five O'Clock," the eye area was painted with Jet Black, which acted as a resist. Therefore, the finished piece had "white" eyes and needed a piece of fabric placed over the white to correct it. (See photo on page 70.)

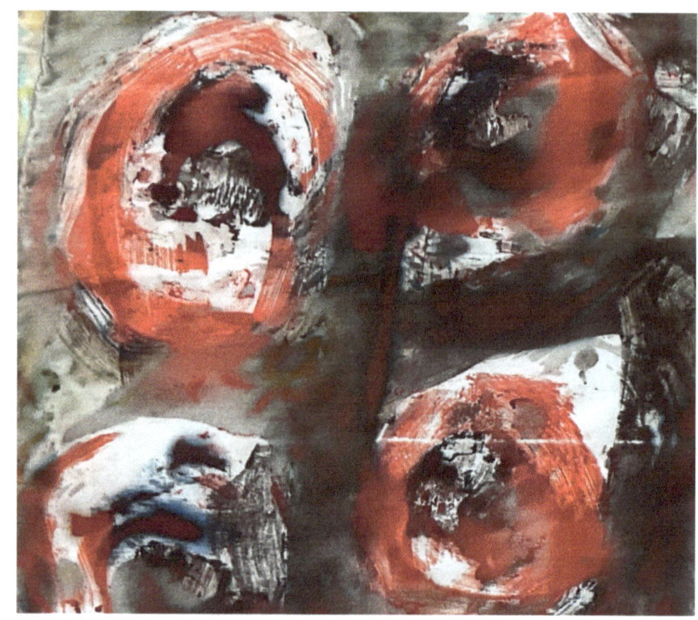

Details of screen prints on a silk scarf.

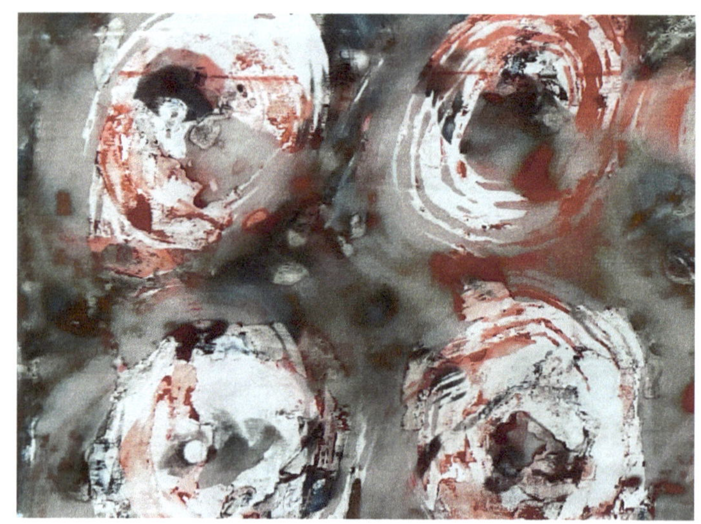

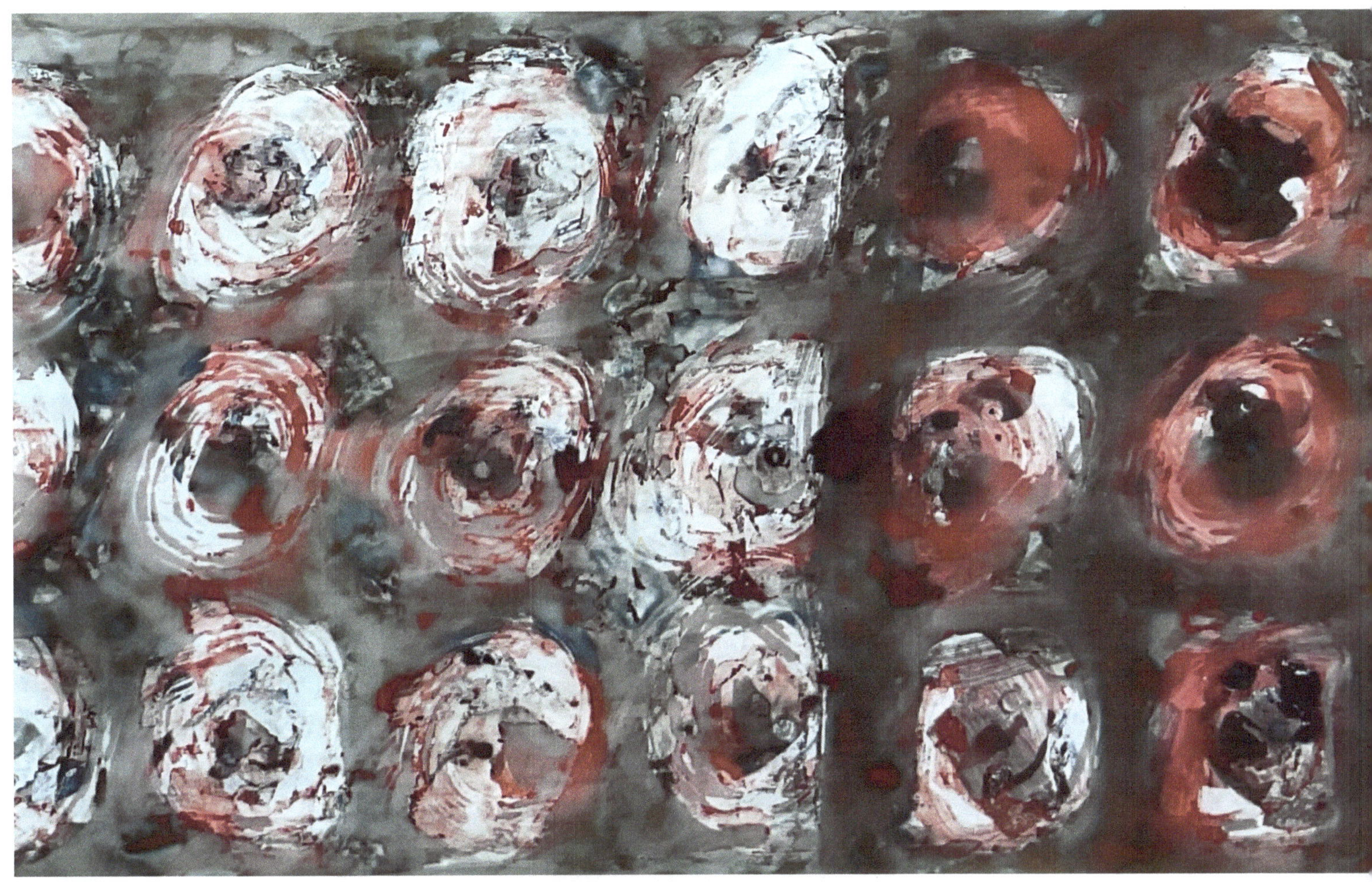

Prints on a silk scarf show how soy wax resist leaves behind white markings.

NOTE:
Soy wax will wash out of your fabrics with hot water and cause no harm to your washing machine or pipes.

PAPER RESIST

Try using shapes cut or torn from paper as a resist by laying them on the front side of your screen.

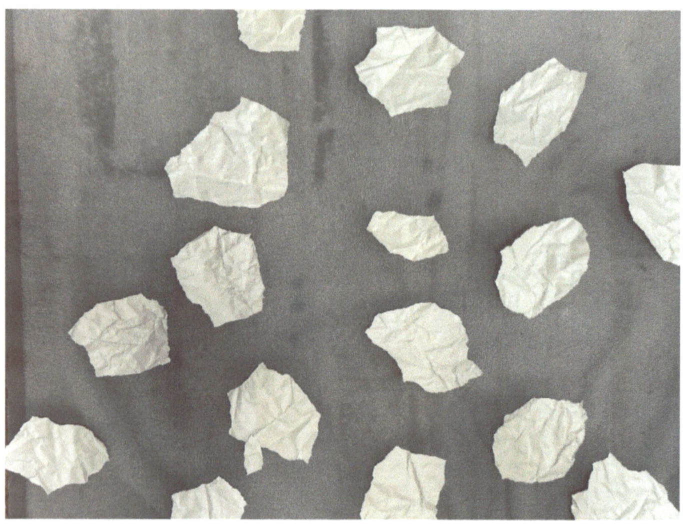

To use paper as a resist, cut or tear shapes from paper and lay them on the screen.

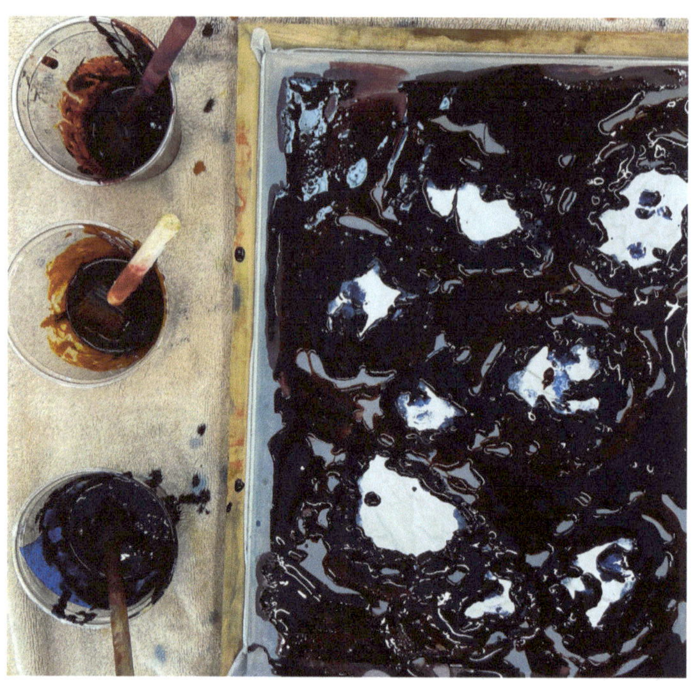

Paint thickened dye around and over the pieces of paper.

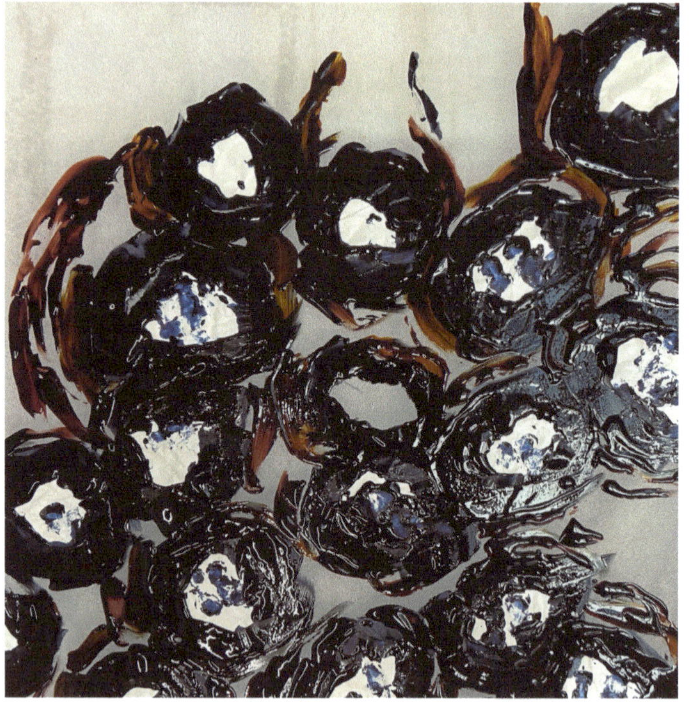

Screen painted with print paste over paper.

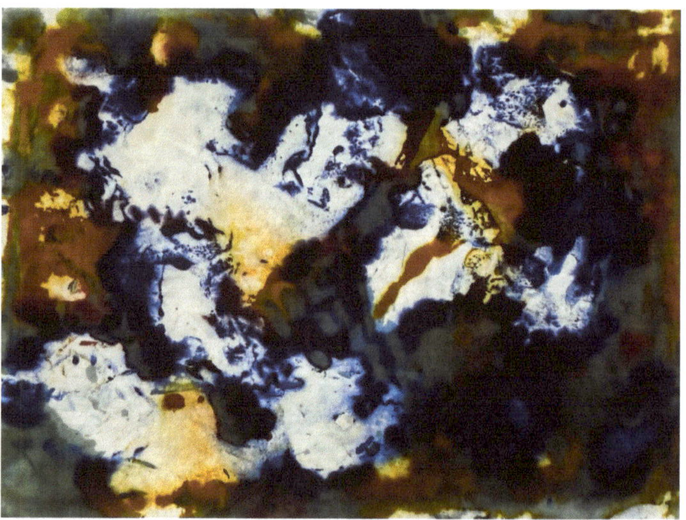

A print from this screen shows white areas where the pieces of paper have acted as a resist.

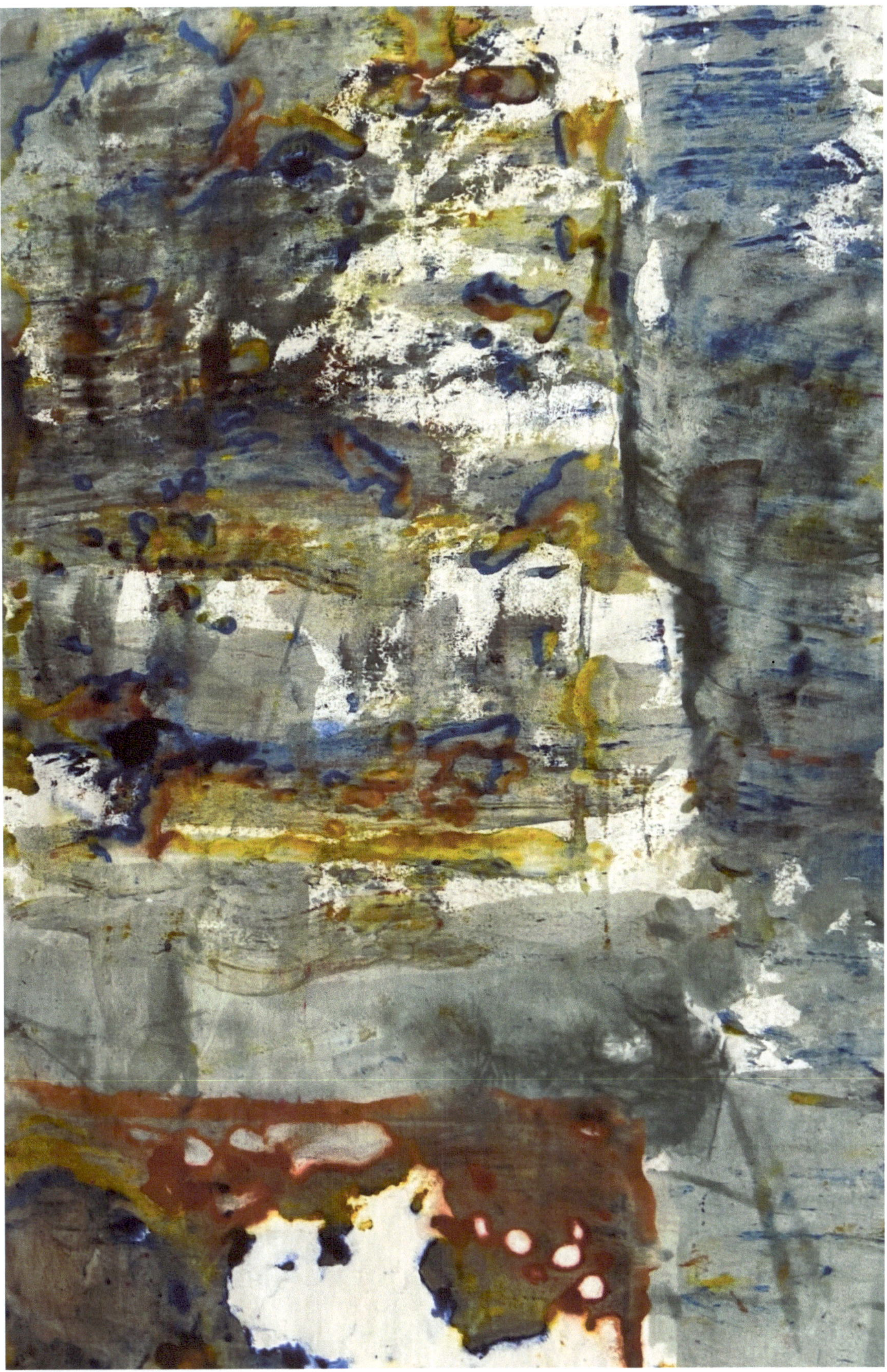

To give this print a more organic look, some of the white areas were filled in by pulling mud over them with a squeegee. The result is a complex design that would be almost impossible to create by just painting on fabric.

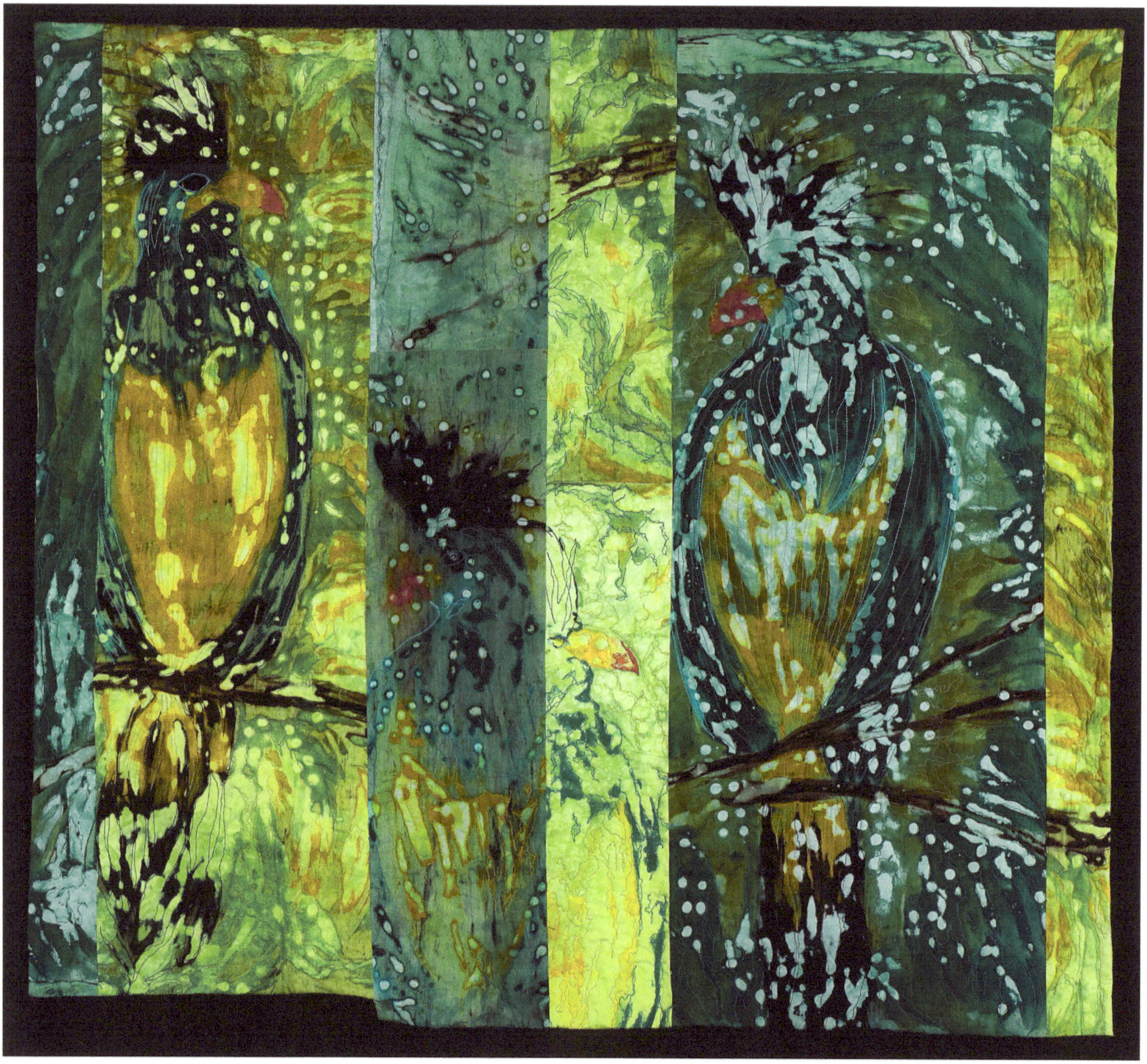

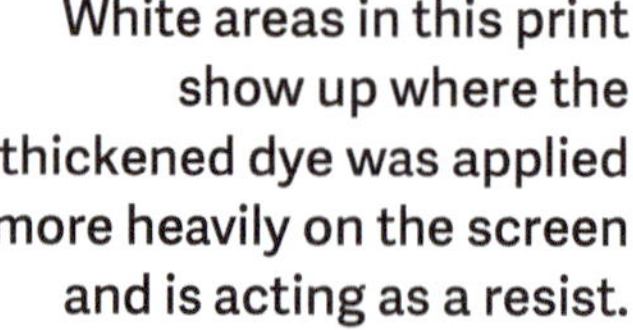

"5 O'Clock" by Susan Brooks

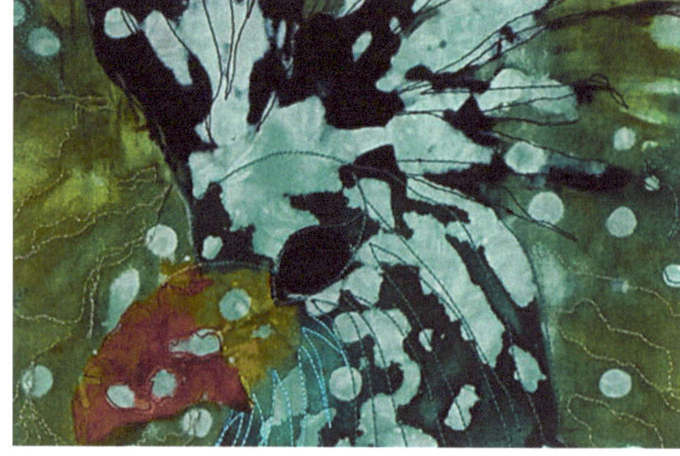

White areas in this print show up where the thickened dye was applied more heavily on the screen and is acting as a resist.

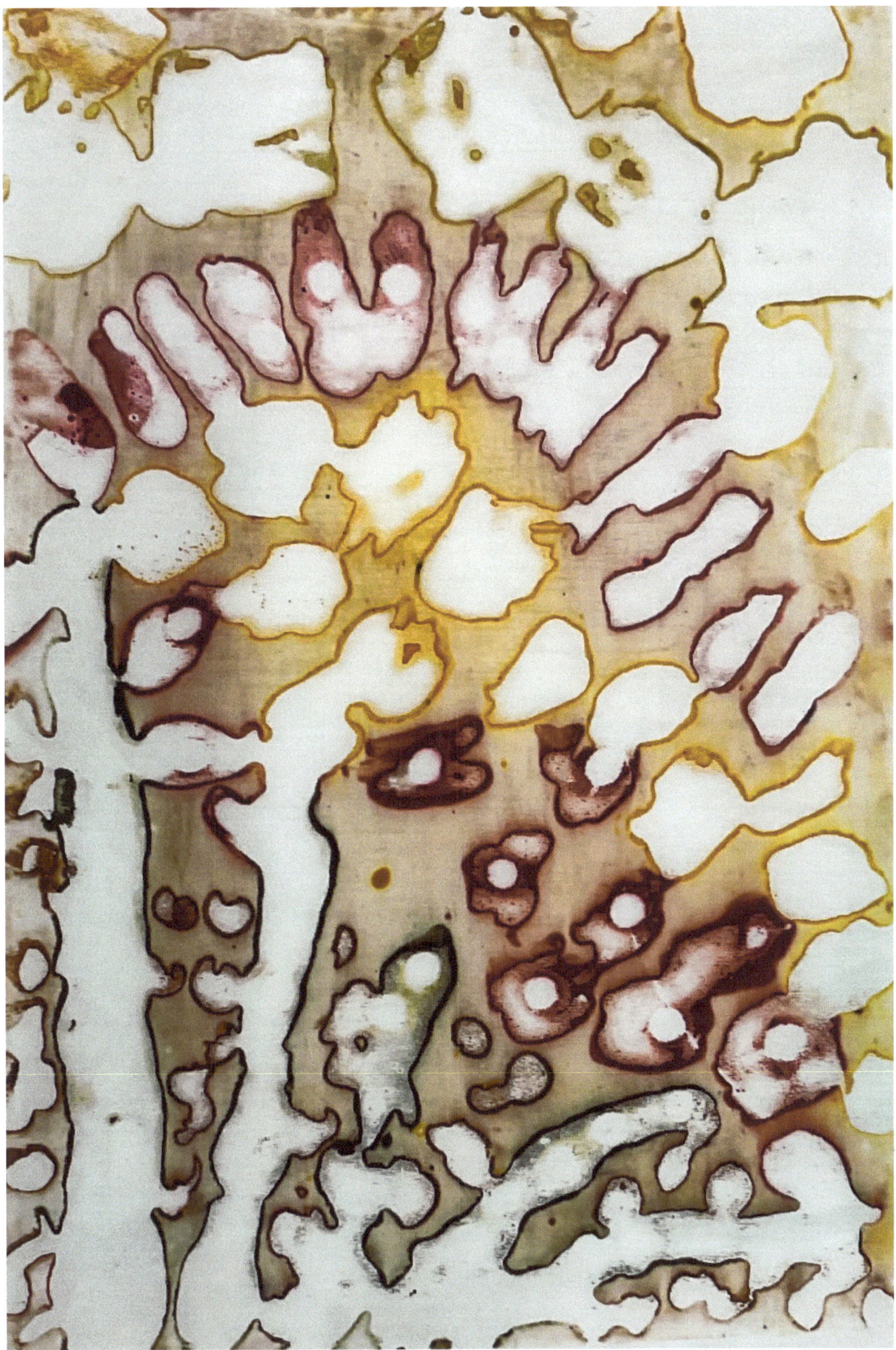

Thick, dried dye creates white areas in this pulled print. As the dye deconstructs, the white areas will pick up more color in subsequent prints.

DISCHARGE

Discharge, or the removal of color, on finished, dried and printed fabrics can add more texture and interest. In the process, consider continuity (i.e. using a circle image as a discharge on a circular image).

Work in a well-ventilated area while discharging with any bleach products.

When using stronger discharge pastes, always wear a professional respirator.

After the color is discharged, which usually takes several minutes to a half hour, immediately wash the fabric in your washing machine using Anti-Chlor to stop the bleaching process that could eat a hole in your fabrics.

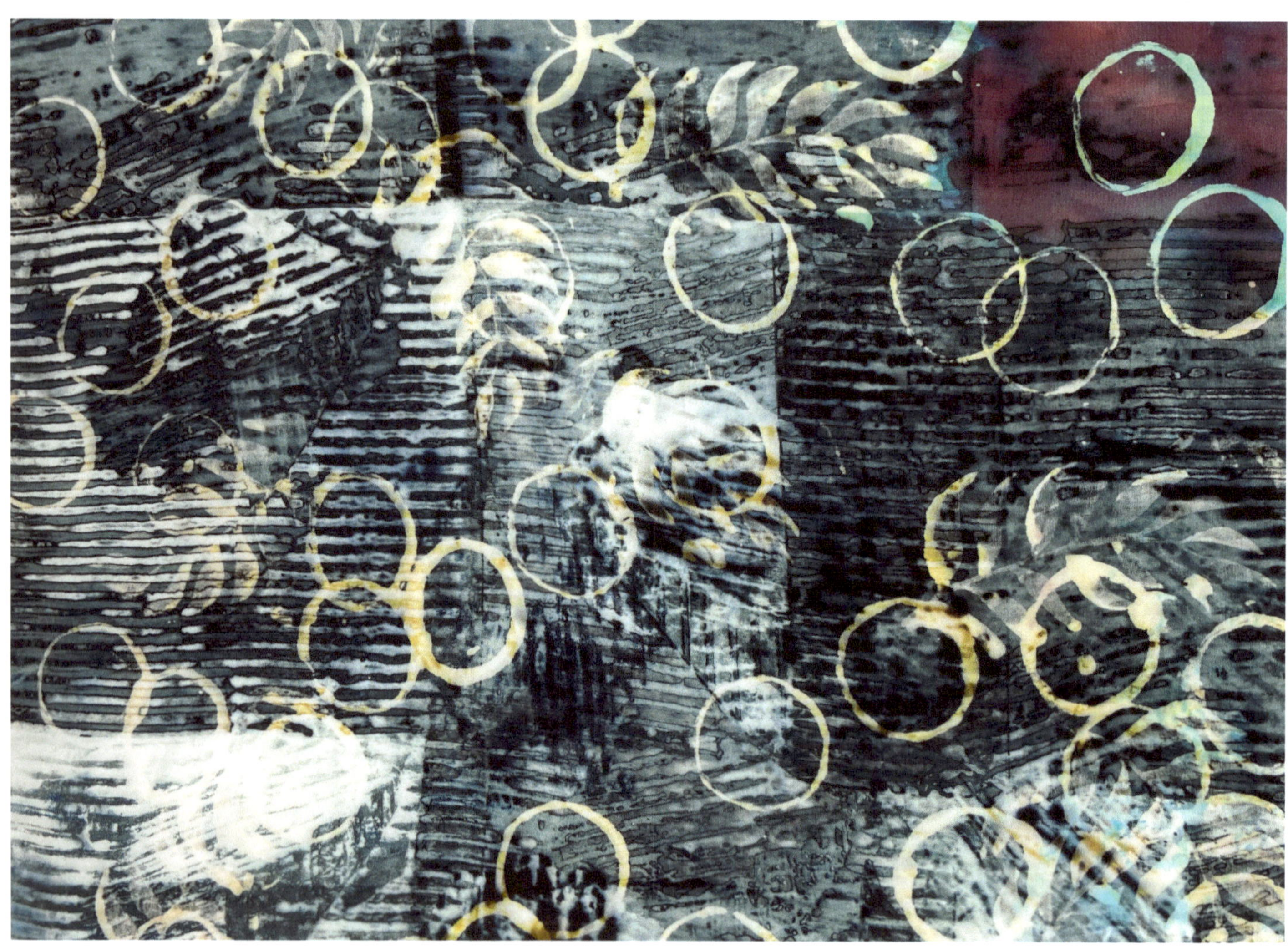

A cardboard paper towel tube was used to stamp toilet bowl cleaner gel onto a print on rayon fabric.

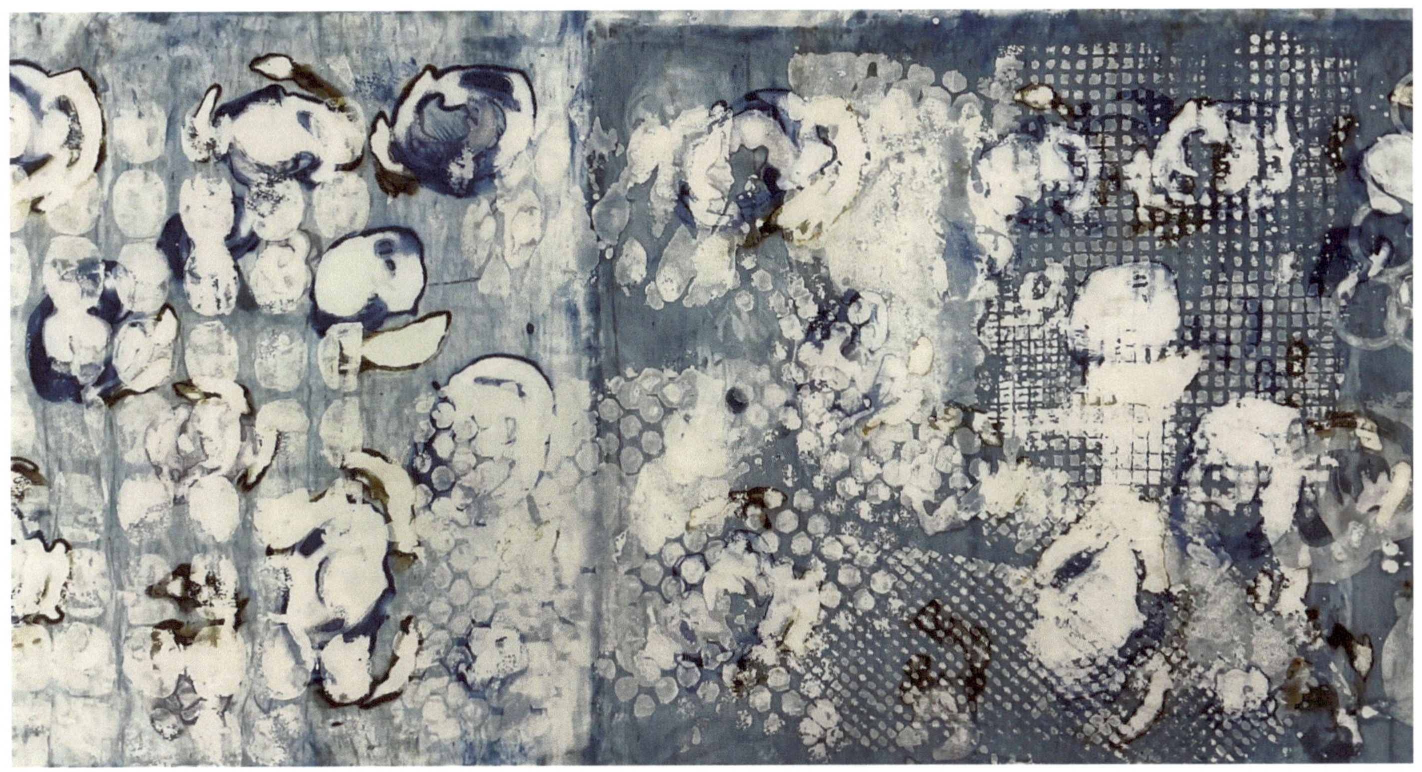

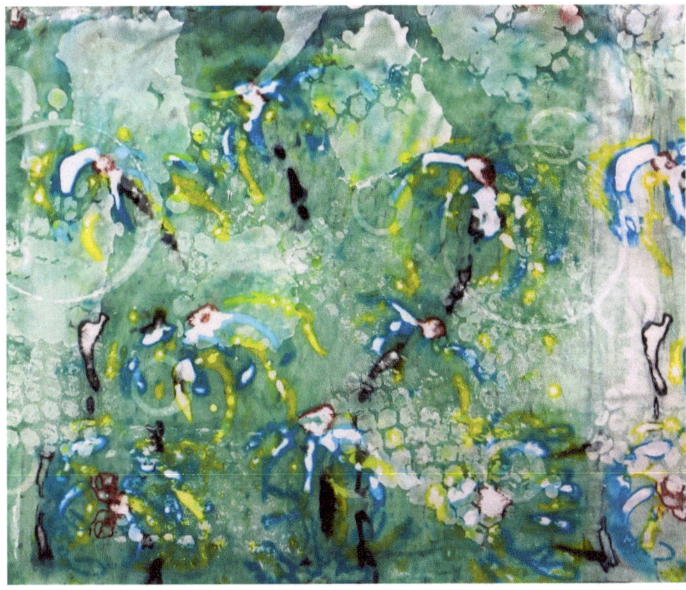

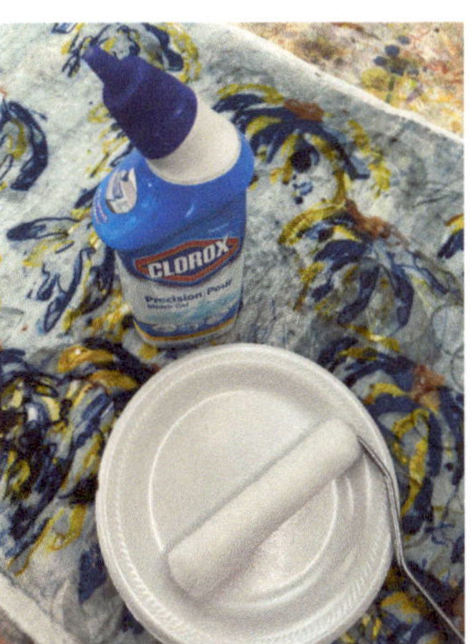

Use a foam roller to apply toilet bowl cleaner with bleach.

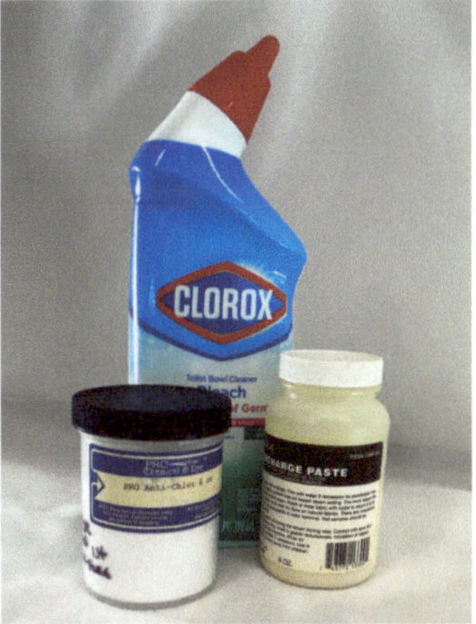

Here are three products you can use to discharge color from your printed fabric.

Top and above: To create this texture, plastic fencing and mesh were laid on printed fabric. Then toilet bowl cleaner gel was rolled over the fencing with a paint roller to discharge color. Above, it's easy to see that the turquoise dye in the prints does not discharge well.

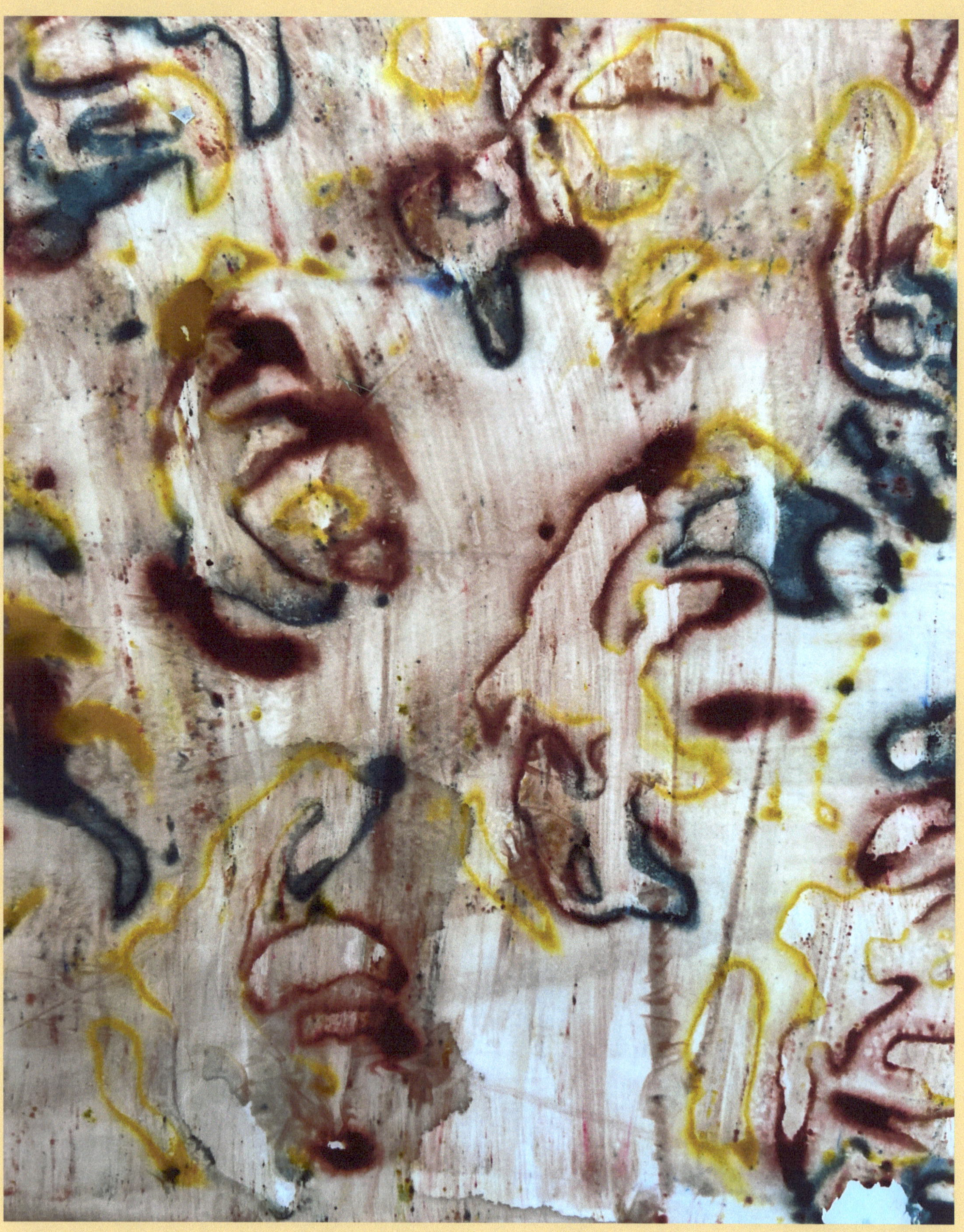

You can achieve a lot of variety in deconstructed screen printing. In this print, clear alginate was used to pull a print on watercolor paper. The original design was painted on in Moss Green and Brick Red.

chapter 11

Printing on Paper

To make frameable art, collage papers, cards or postcards, you can use any of these printing techniques on watercolor papers.

After printing, batch the papers by wrapping them flat in a piece of plastic overnight. Then soak them in a sink filled with water and about ½ teaspoon of Synthrapol and gently rinse until the water is clear of any dye.

Or seal the dyes on the paper using matte medium, spray sealant (Krylon Permanent Protective Matte Finish – 1311) or frame the paper under glass.

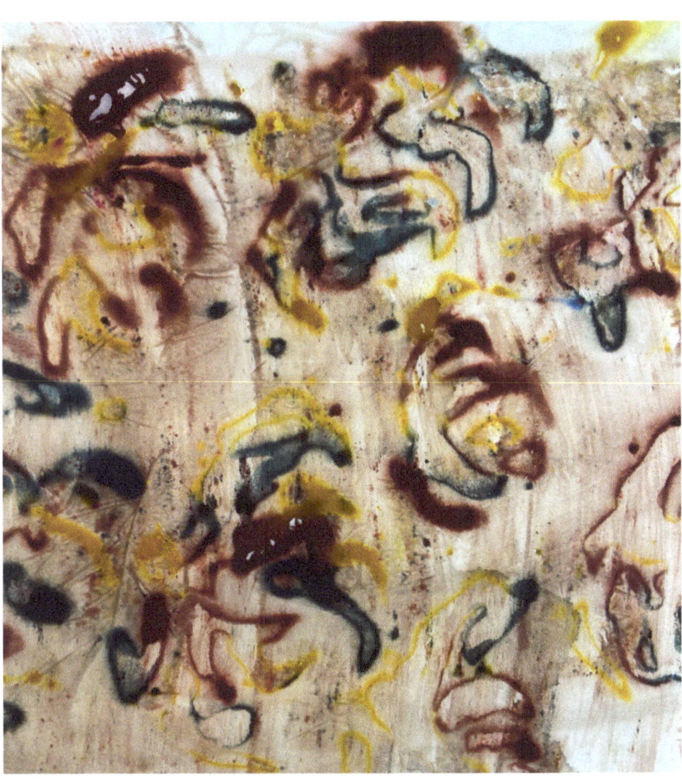

In the second print on Arches Aquarelle watercolor paper, the green mixes while the red and yellow shades separate out.

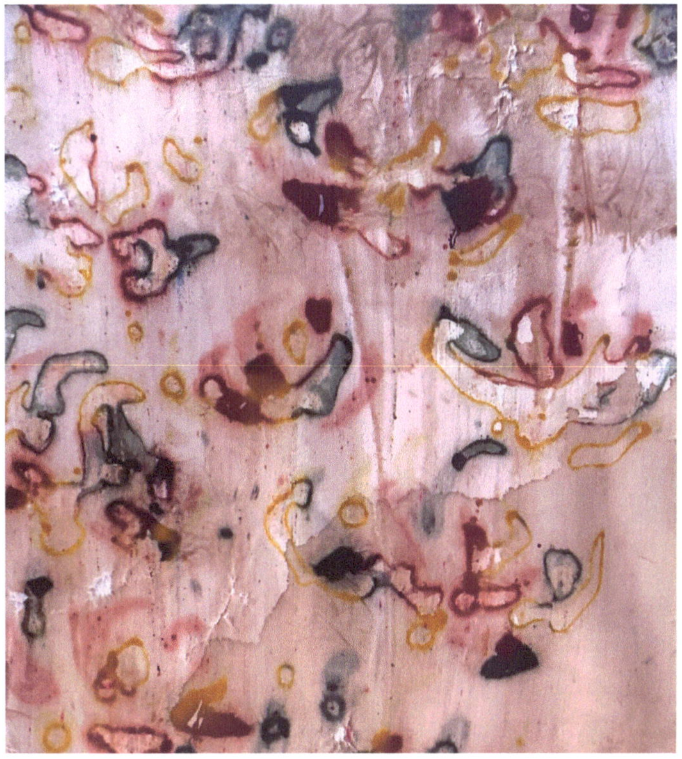

By the third print on paper, the green dye has almost disappeared, and the red dye breaks down into shades of pink.

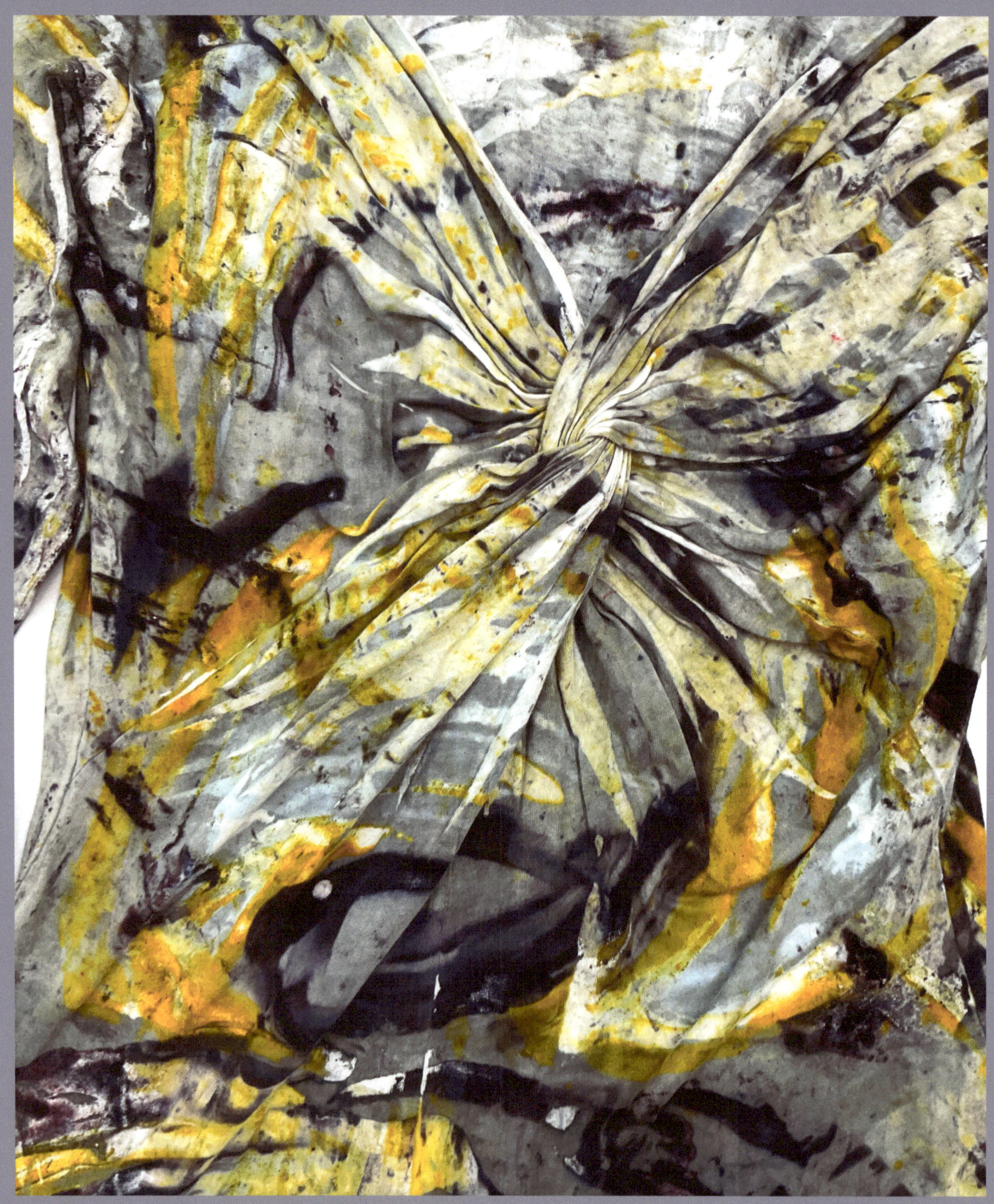

Deconstructed screen printing can be used to create one-of-a-kind wearables and accessories.

Printing on Clothing,
Bags and Purses

Print on clothing made of any natural fiber by laying the clothing down on a cotton sheet and laying your screen on top to pull the print. Smooth out any wrinkles in the clothing, unless you want to create a resist with the wrinkle. Using a gloved hand, "paint" any white areas along the seams and hem with mud to avoid the distraction of the white areas.

NOTE:
You can purchase clothing blanks from various merchants. Experiment with printing on shopping bags, purses and clothing for babies, children or adults.

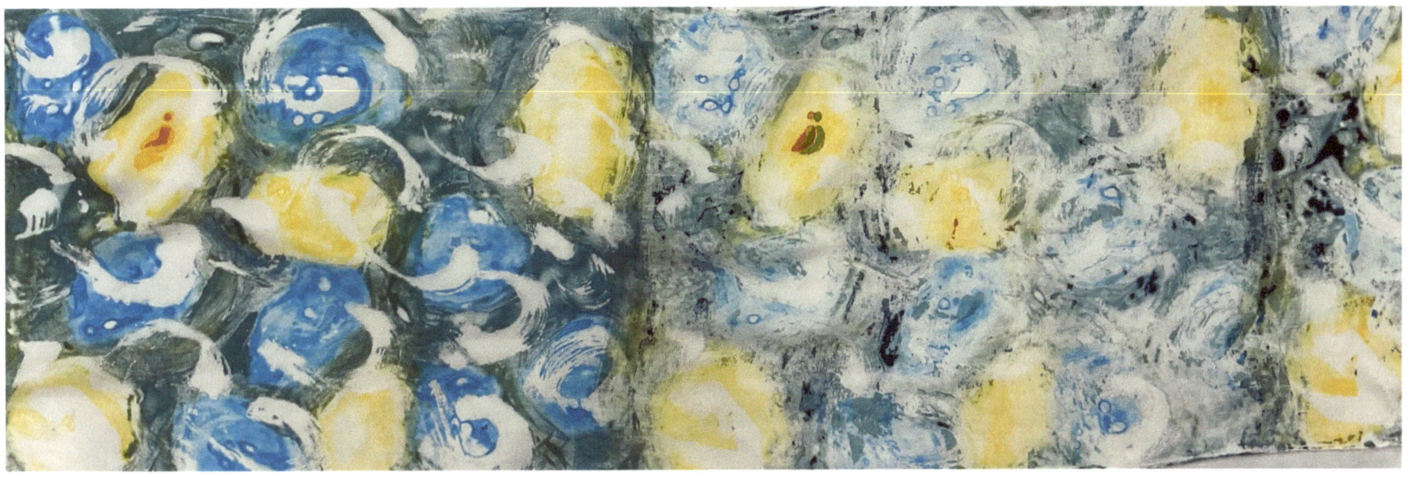

Screen prints cover a silk scarf in beautiful shades of blue, green and yellow. A very large screen is useful when printing scarves or pieces of clothing.

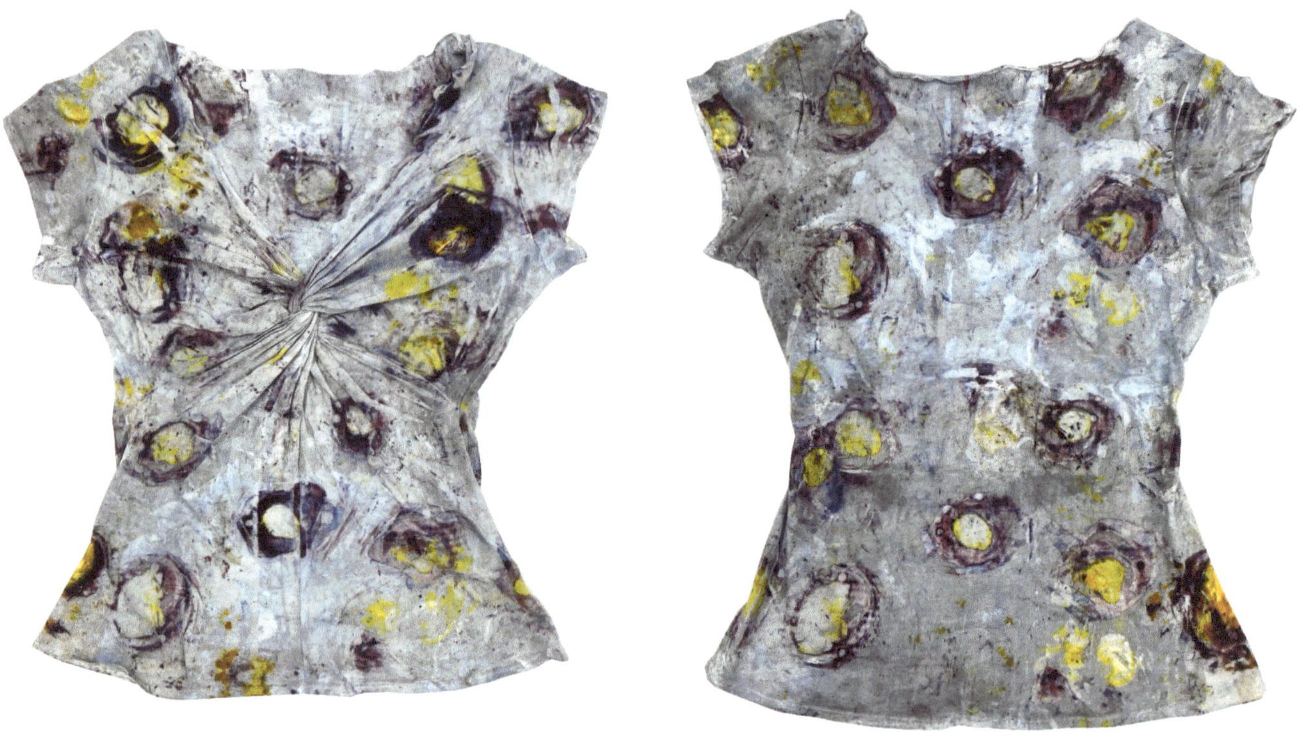

A circular pattern accents this top. When printing on clothing, be sure to smooth out wrinkles as much as possible.

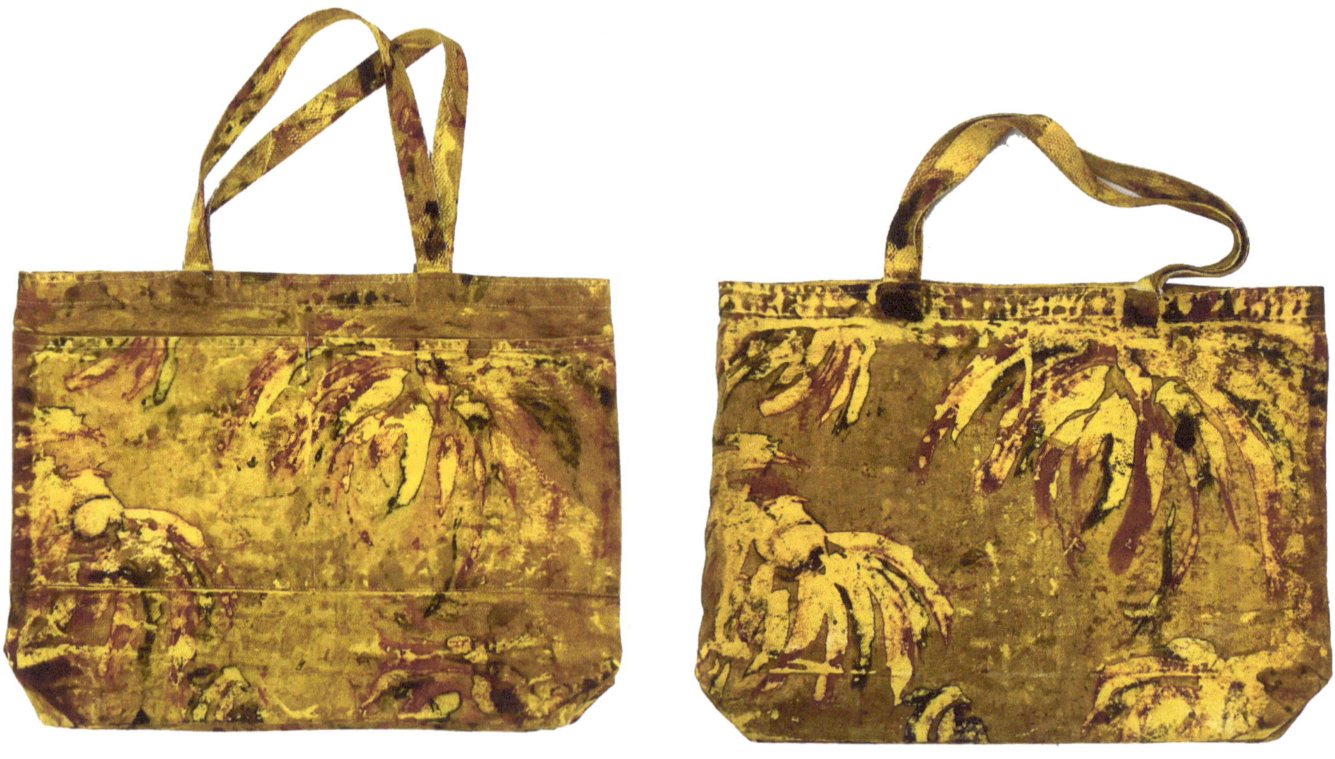

A plain canvas bag was pre-dyed with ¼ strength dye before being printed on.

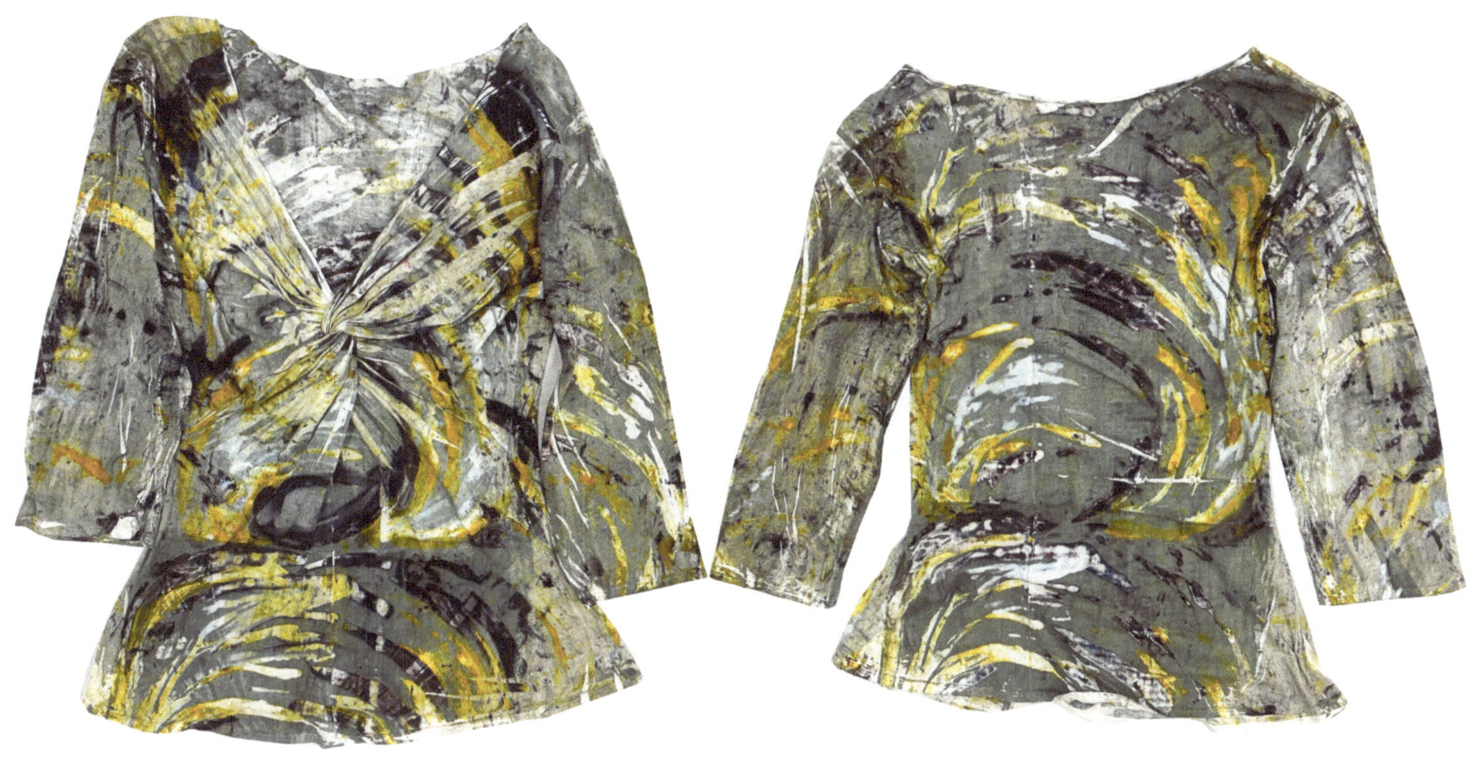

Covering this long-sleeve shirt required several pulled prints for the front, back and each sleeve.

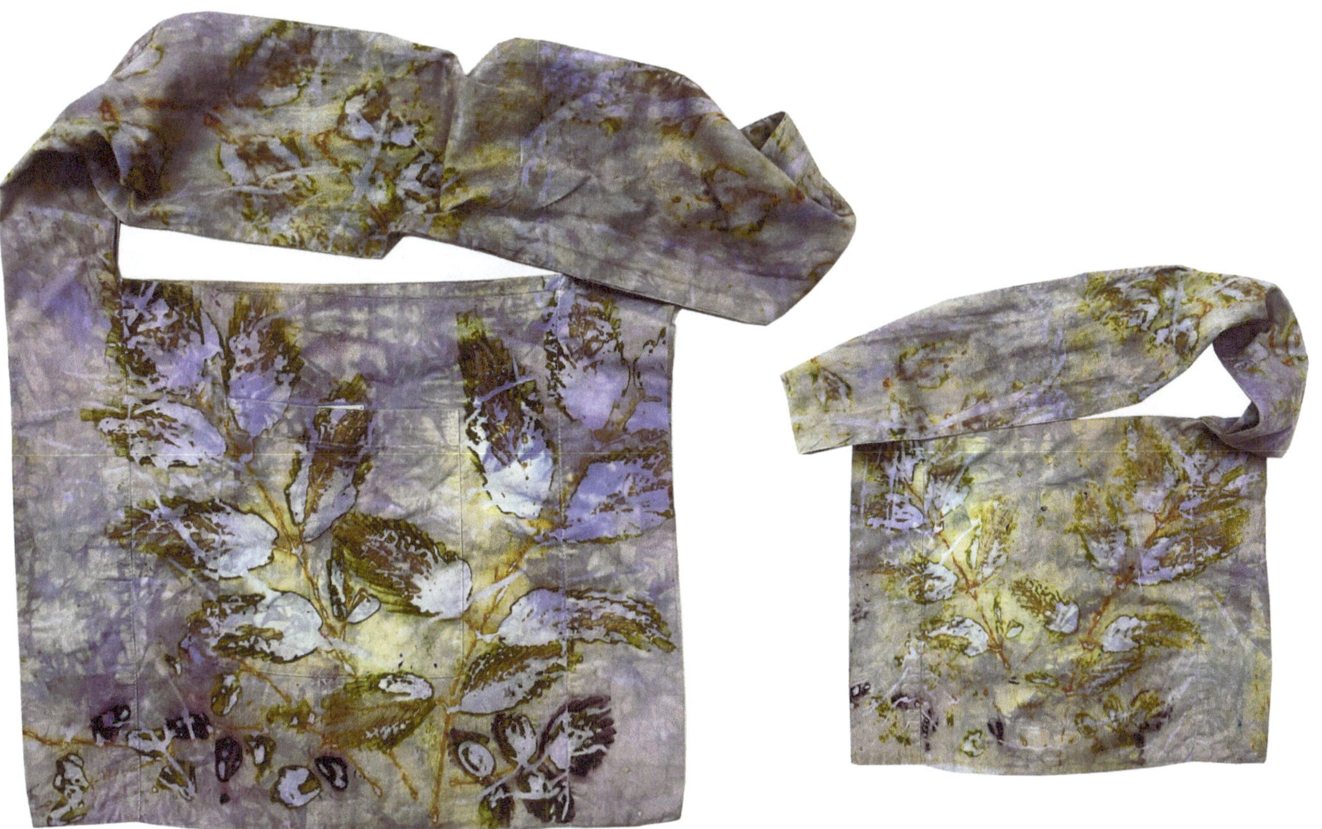

Rachel Zierlein pre-dyed the fabric for this shoulder bag with ¼ strength dye before printing an organic design on it.

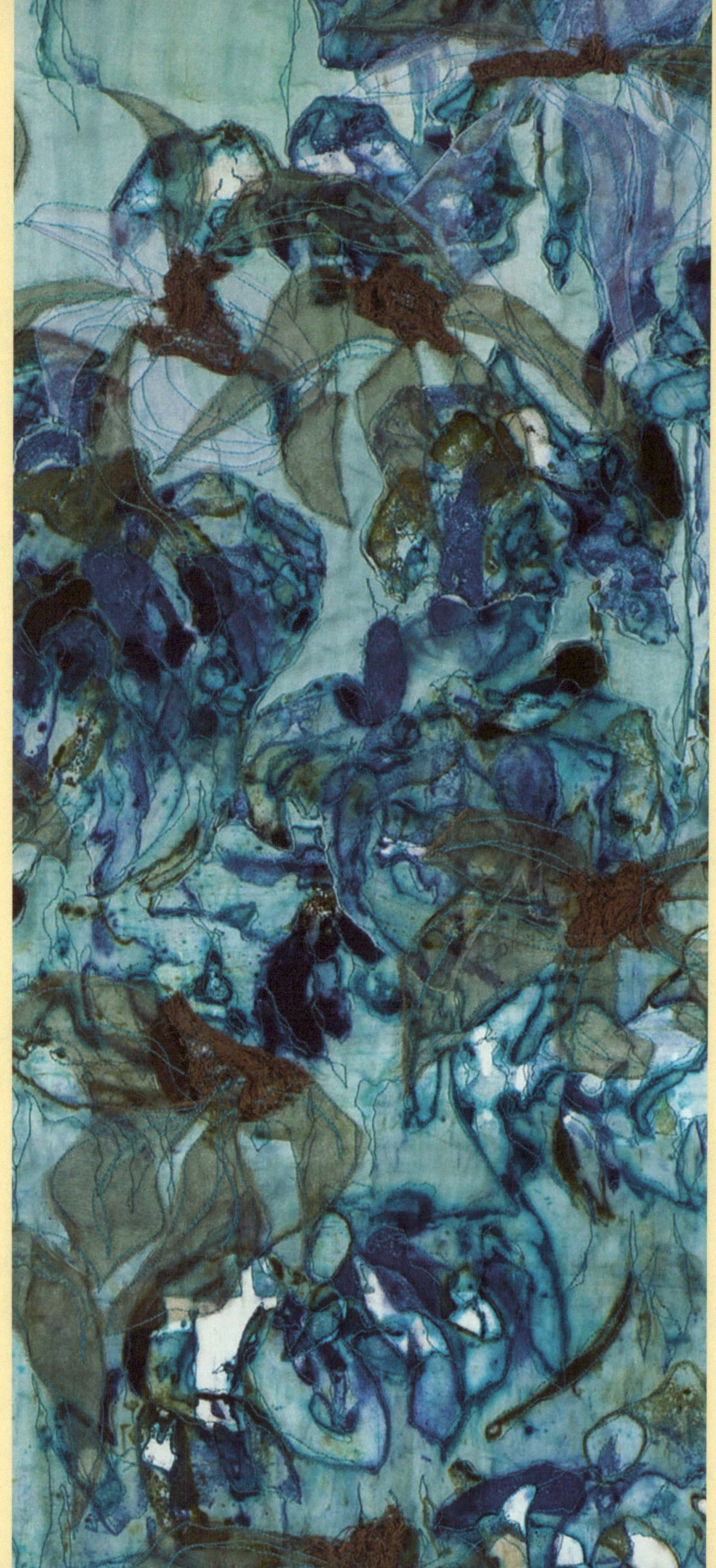

"Marjorie's Garden" (30" x 50") by Susan Brooks, created by overlapping images painted with New Aqua, Indigo and Moss Green dyes.

chapter 13

Batching Fabrics:
Washing or Steaming

To allow the fabric to absorb the maximum amount of dye molecules, the printed fabrics need to be batched. Start by laying out a piece of plastic sheet, then lay the printed fabric flat on the plastic. If the wet, dyed fabric folds on itself, it will transfer the image onto the folded cloth.

Fold the plastic to entirely cover the fabric and then layer another piece of fabric, then plastic on the top and continue layering until all fabrics are covered and wrapped in a bundle of plastic. Leave the bundles to set the dyes for 24 to 48 hours. If they are left in an area below 68 degrees F, keep them warm with a heated blanket or heating pad.

WASHING FABRIC

After the bundles of cotton, silk, linen or wool gauze have set for 24 to 48 hours, they should be washed to remove excess dye. Because wool is sensitive to water temperatures, it will need to be hand-washed in cold water to prevent shrinkage.

Fill washing machine tub with cold water. (Cold water sets the dyes.) While the washing machine is agitating, put fabric into the machine.

Add about 1 capful or 1 teaspoon of Synthrapol (depending on the amount of fabric).

Wash on "wash only" cycle and drain out water. Stop before the "rinse" cycle.

Fill washing machine a second time with hot water and 1 teaspoon Synthrapol. If it is sudsy, you are using too much Synthrapol.

Wash on "wash only" cycle and drain. Stop before the "rinse" cycle.

Wash on "wash only" cycle a third time with hot water and just a bit of Synthrapol. Again, stop before the "rinse" cycle.

> NOTE:
> *Wash out the plastic sheets with the fabric, then the plastic can be reused for years.*

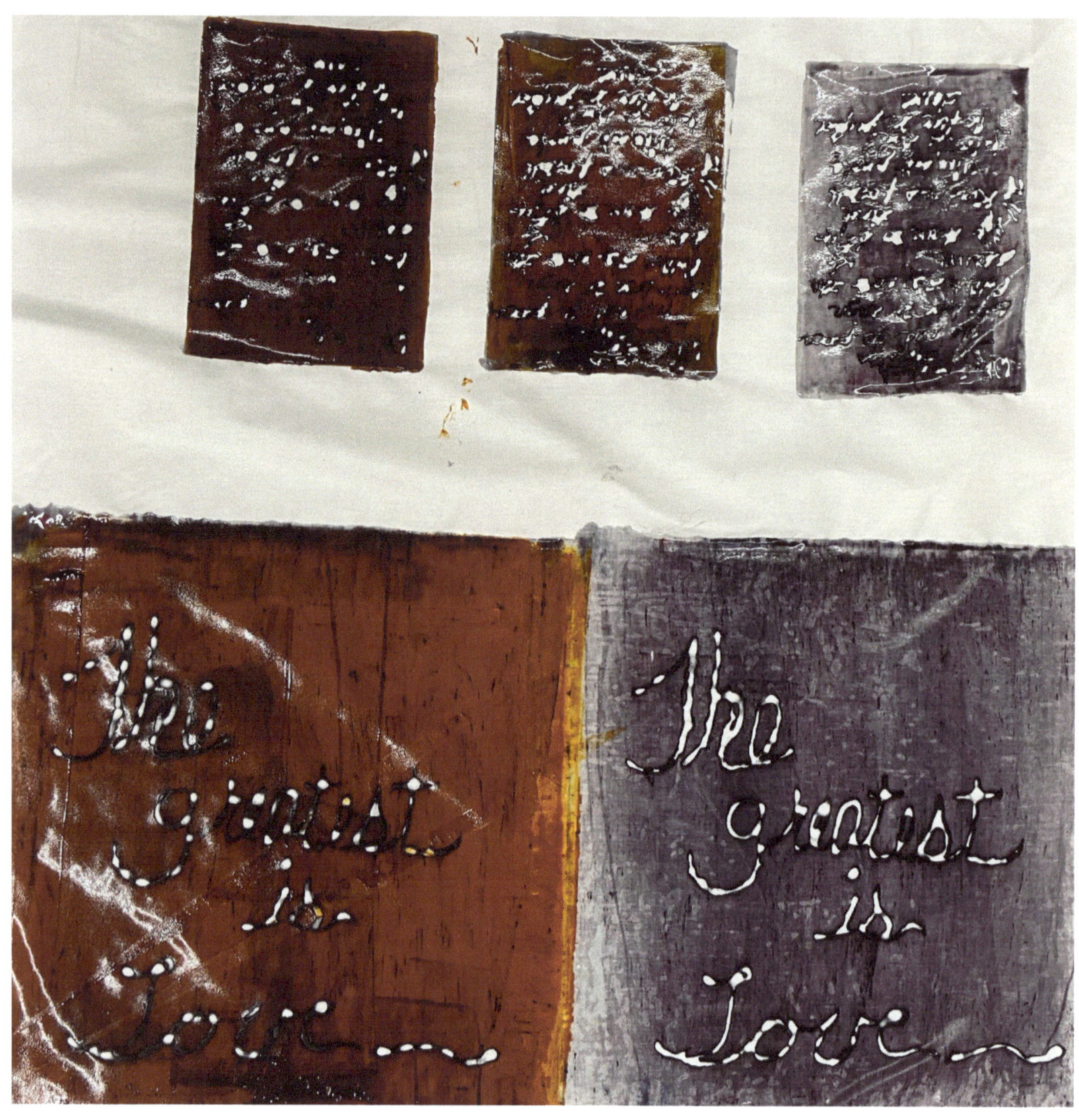

After the prints are pulled, the wet fabric is laid on plastic sheeting to begin the batching process.

On the third cycle, check the color in the water to make sure dye is washed out. Usually, three cycles are enough to wash out all excess dye. If not, run a fourth cycle with hot water and Synthrapol. Let the last cycle run the full wash and rinse cycle.

FOR LOW-WATER WASHING MACHINES

Because you can't stop these machines before the rinse cycle, if you use a low-water usage washing machine, you will need to wash the fabric out by hand, first

   Deconstructed Screen Printing: The Beauty of the Organic Line

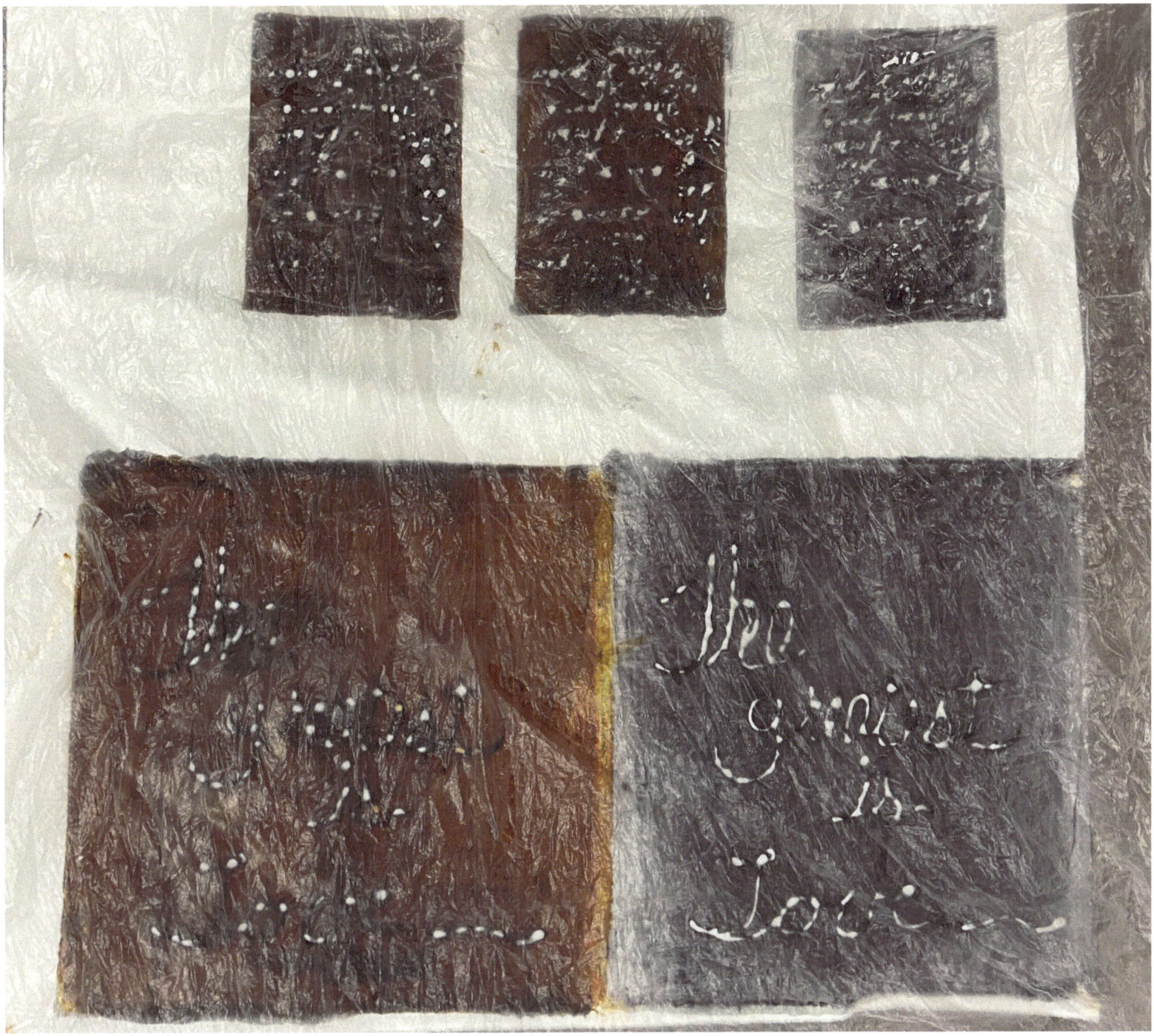

Plastic sheeting is layered over the wet prints.

with cold water and Synthrapol and then with hot water and Synthrapol. You do not need to remove all the dye with the hand washings. Then you can proceed to the final one or two washes in your washing machine using a low-suds Synthrapol.

The bundle of plastic layered with fabric is set on a heating pad. This batching process sets the dyes and ensures saturated colors.

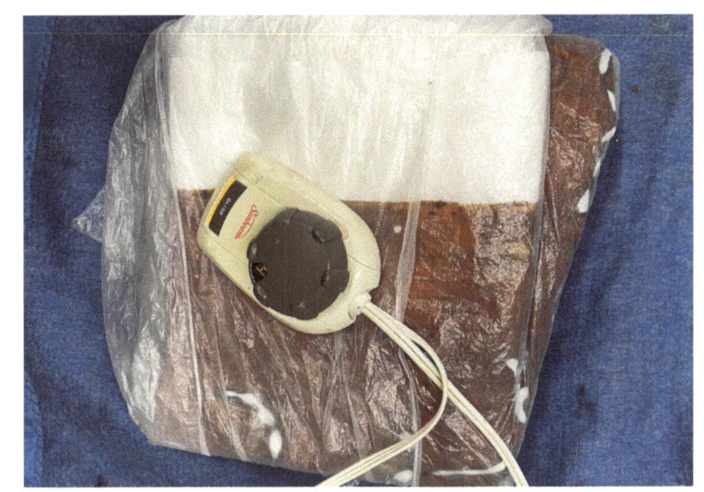

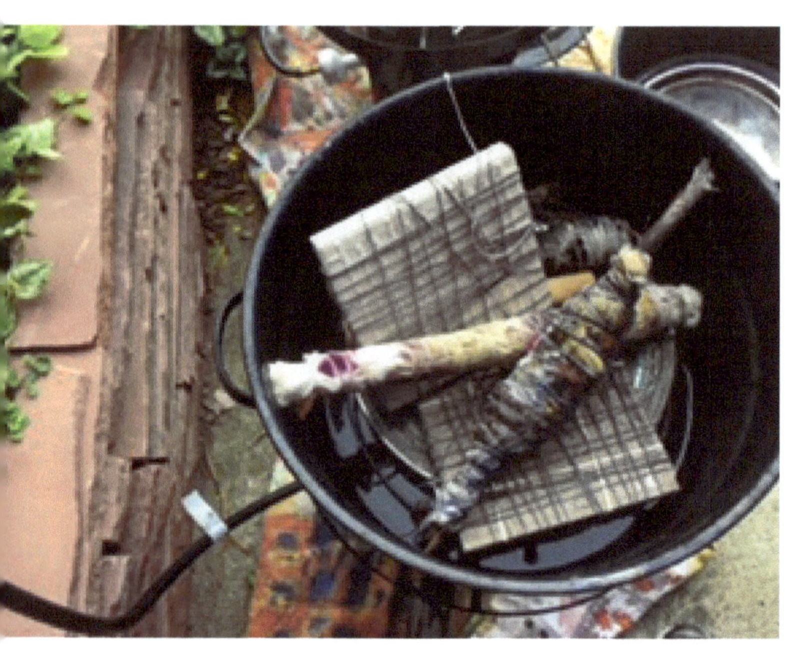

Tied bundles and rolls of fabric are prepared for steaming over an outdoor burner.

THE STEAMING PROCESS

Instead of batching and washing, you can steam fabrics to quickly set the dyes. Steaming can also heighten the color saturation and make pastel colors more vibrant.

Wrap dry fabric in print paper (not newspaper, as it can transfer the ink onto your fabric) or a sheet, making sure that it doesn't touch on itself. Use rubber bands to secure the fabric and paper bundle.

Place the bundle in a steamer that is at full steam. Make sure that no water drops onto or touches the fabric. Steam for 30 minutes. Unwrap and wash out excess dye with washing method described previously.

To build your own stovetop silk steamer, follow these instructions from Dharma Trading:

Building your own steamer to steam a small amount of fabric is somewhat time-consuming but not difficult. Once it's complete, you can use it to subject the dyed fabric to a steam-filled environment without having water drip on the fabric.

1. Put about 2 inches of water in a large pot (a canning pot is ideal).

2. To keep the fabric out of the water, make a stand using a tin can with both

ends removed. Place an aluminum pie pan or wire rack on top of the can. On top of the pie pan place a dish towel or several layers of newsprint cut into circles to fit. These layers will absorb moisture.

3. After placing the wrapped fabric bundle on the stand. Place a piece of aluminum foil over the bundle and lightly crimp it around the edges of the pie pan.

4. To pad the inside of the large pot lid, cut a stack (³/₈ - to ½-inch) of lid-size circles from newspaper. Put a thick cotton towel over the pot first, then place the paper on the towel and the lid on top.

5. Gather up the sides of the towel and fasten over the top of the lid using a clothespin or safety pins. Place the towel-covered lid on the pot. Make sure the towel won't hang down near the flame or burner.

6. Weight the top of the lid with something heavy. You want pressure to build inside, but steam still needs to escape or it will explode.

7. Stay near the pot during the steaming process to ensure safety. Bring the water to a boil, then turn heat down for an even, constant simmer for 30 minutes.

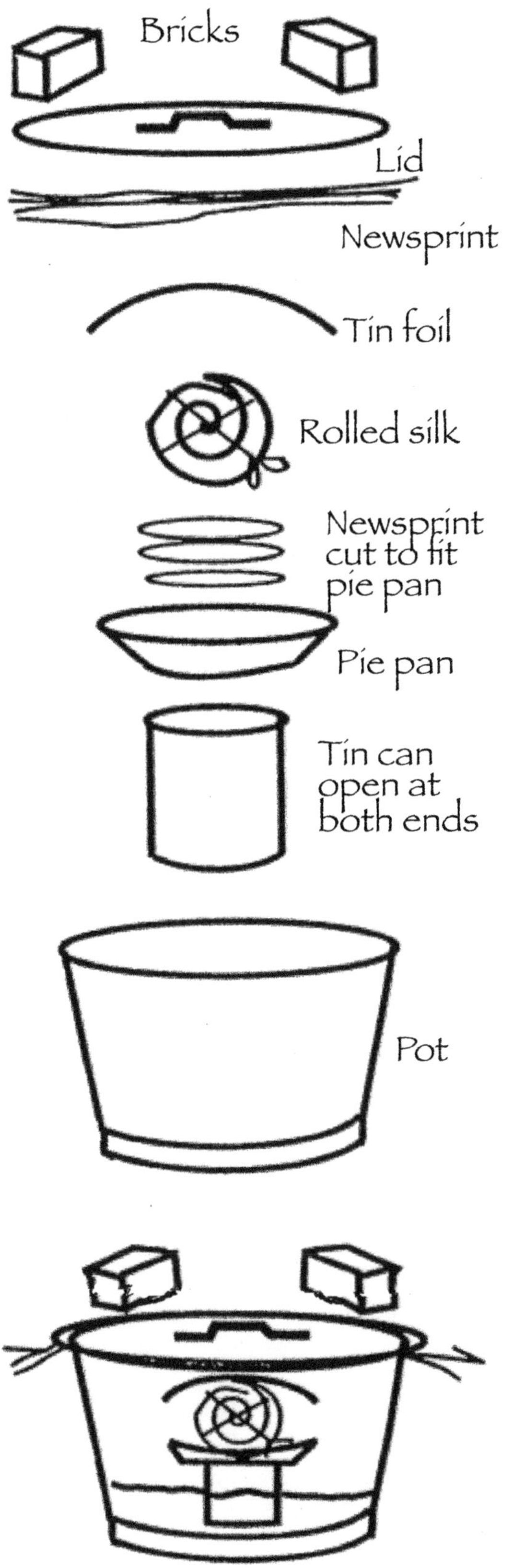

Courtesy of Dharma Trading: www.dharmatrading.com

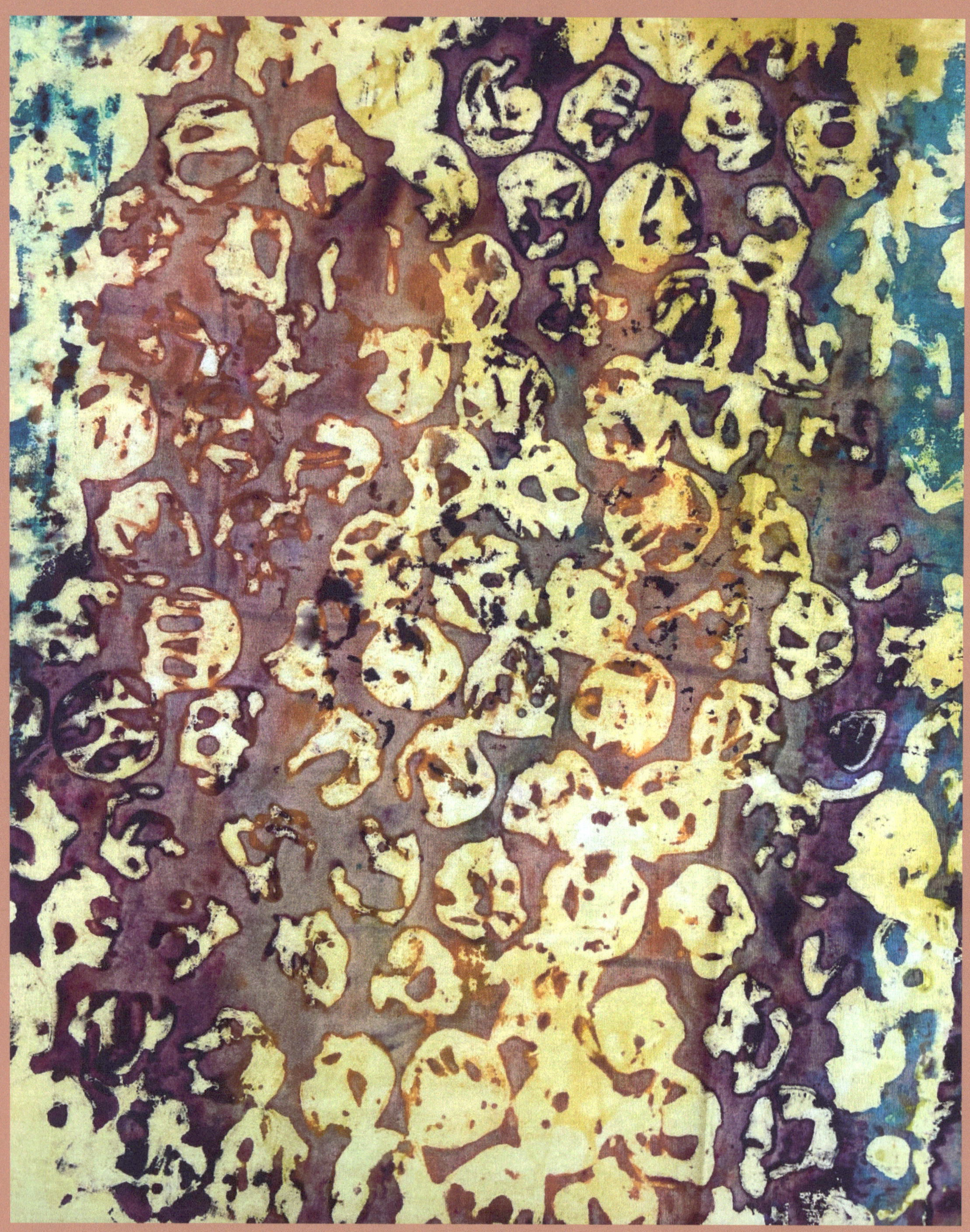

Before pulling this print, the background fabric was pre-dyed with 1/4 strength Palomino Gold dye. Bubble wrap was used under the screen to create texture. The overall design was painted with Terra Cotta, Turquoise and Palomino Gold dye.

chapter 14

Safety Guidelines

The dyes and chemicals used in this deconstructed screen printing process are all stable and, with care, safe.

Always use gloves to prevent the dye and chemicals from absorbing into the skin. Procion dyes will dye any natural materials but will not dye synthetic materials.

Dye powder has small enough particles that, when inhaled, they will become imbedded in the lungs. To avoid this, ALWAYS wear a N95 particulate face mask when mixing dyes. Once the dye particle mixes with water or alginate and is thoroughly moisturized, it is safe to breathe without the mask.

Use a ventilated area and mask while discharging with any bleach product. When using Thiox and other discharge pastes, use a professional respirator mask and only work outdoors.

Any bleach should be washed out in the washing machine using Anti-Chlor and always wear a mask while mixing the Anti-Chlor powder into the water.

NOTE:
Alginate will eat a hole in your silk when steamed.

NOTE:
You can lay down a moist towel or rag to collect any stray dye molecules while mixing dyes.

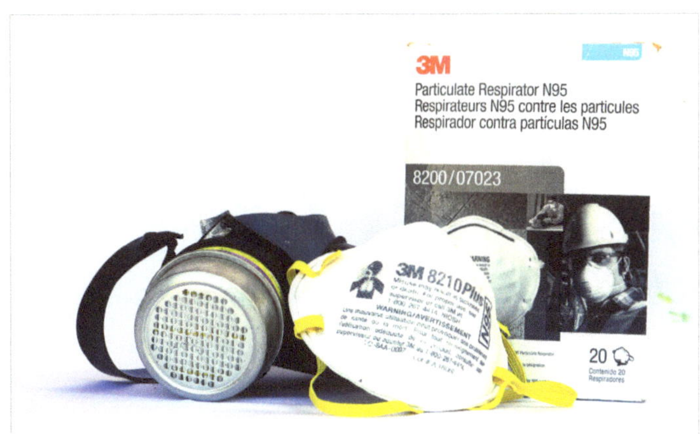

N95 Masks and respirator

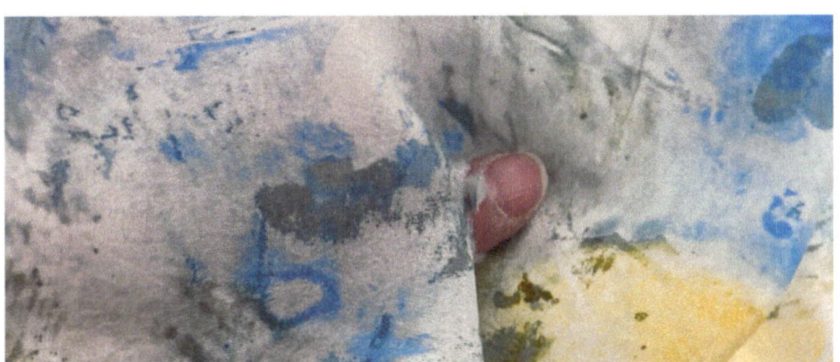

Alginate created a hole in this silk scarf during the steaming process.

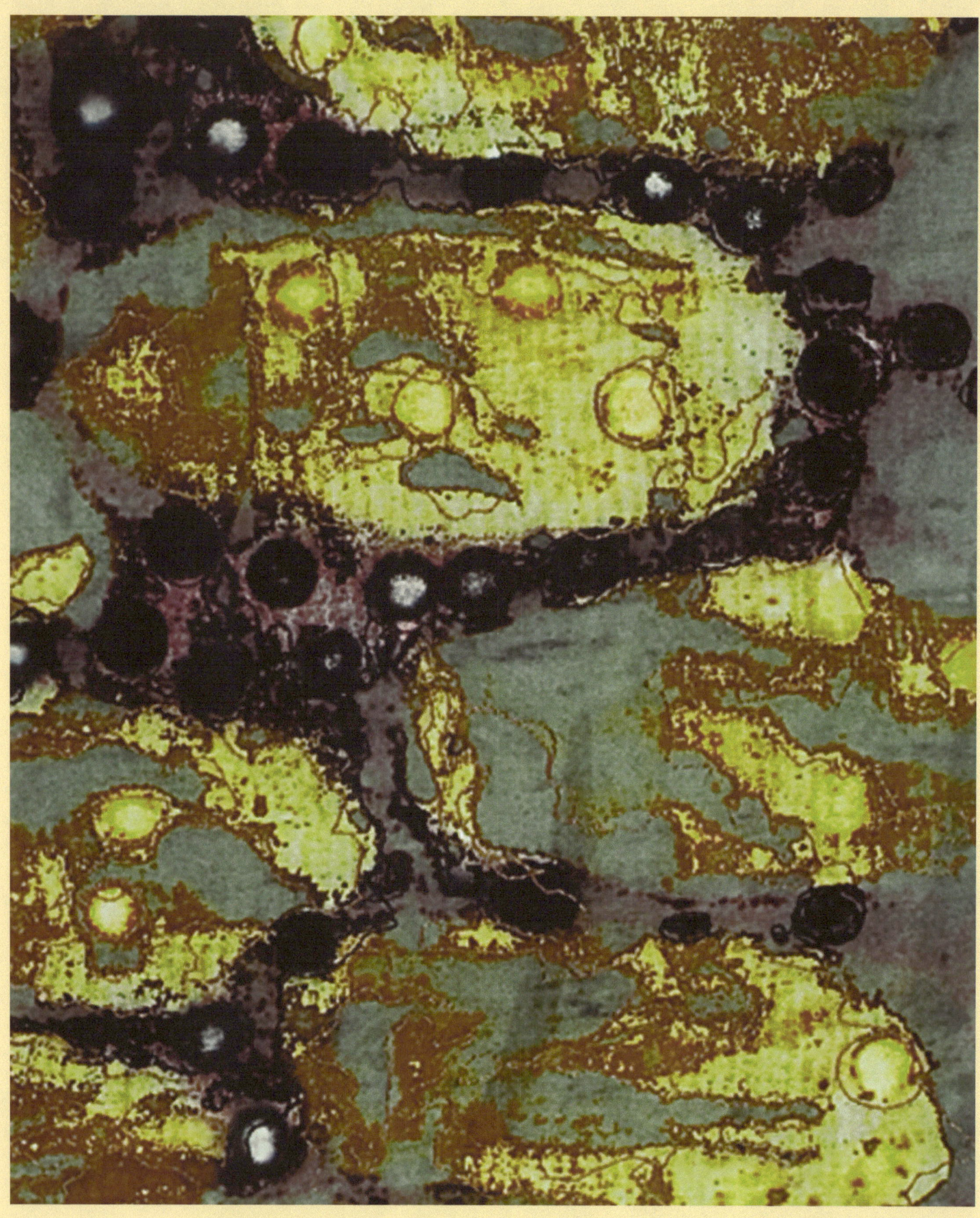

Egg shapes appear in an art piece titled "Little Bird." The design for this piece was painted in Black and Marigold colored dye.

chapter 15

Chemicals

The deconstructed print process requires the use of a few chemicals.

SODA ASH (SODIUM CARBONATE)

Soda ash is a must-have. It increases the pH of the dye solution and forms a permanent bond between the fabric and dyes. Without soda ash, the dyes will wash out. By applying the soda ash into your dye solution, either liquid or thickened, it starts the dyeing process and will break down the dye and cause it to lose its color. Use mixed dye solutions that contain soda ash within 24 hours for best results. However, you use the solution up to three days after mixing, keeping in mind that the color will appear lighter over time.

SODIUM ALGINATE

Sodium alginate is a gelling agent made from seaweed and is used to thicken dyes for printing. It is also used to hold dyes to the fabric, so the dyes and fabric react and make prints.

PROCION MX DYES

These powdered dyes deliver the color for the screen prints. Use caution when using powdered dyes. Always wear an N95 face mask when mixing to prevent the powder

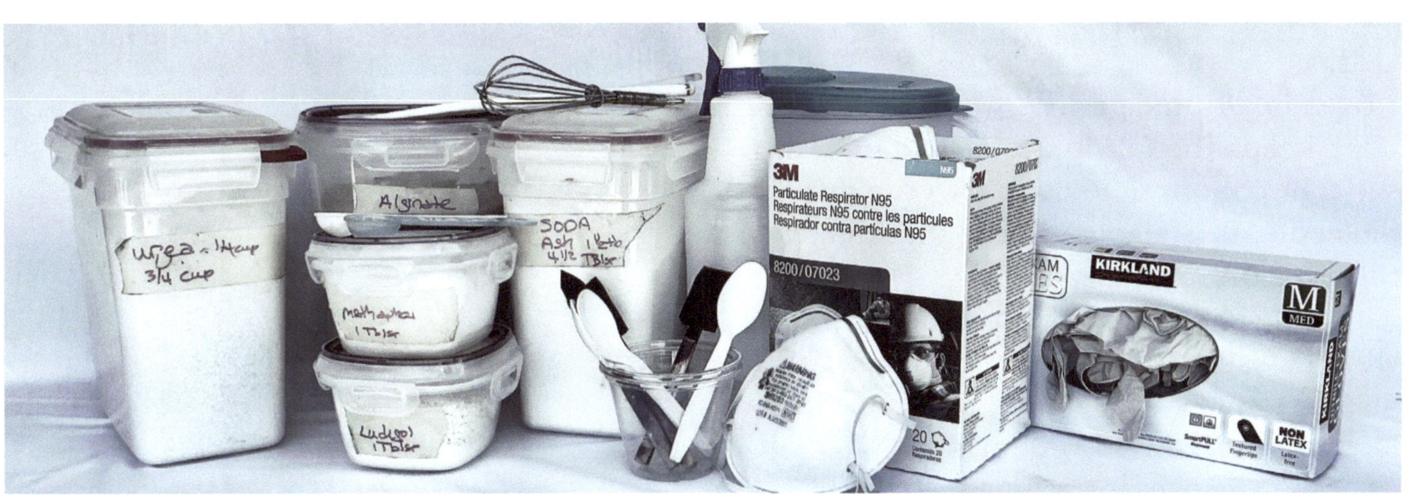

Chemicals used in deconstructed screen printing.

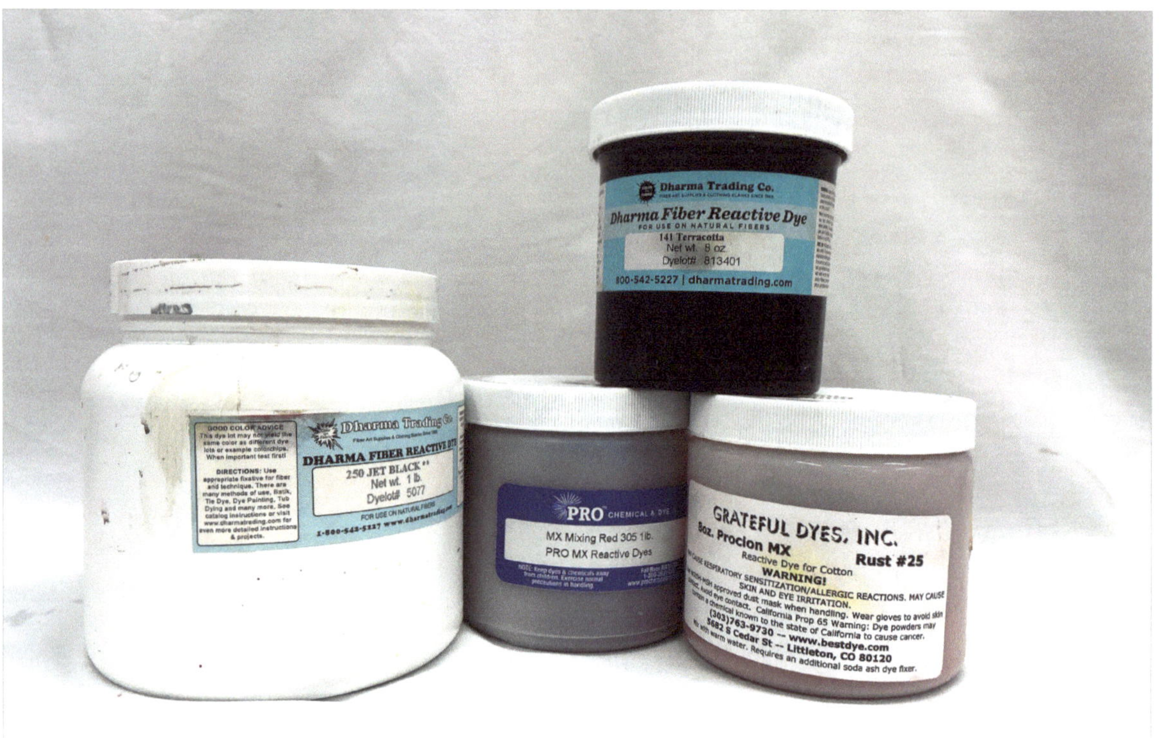

Procion dyes come in powdered form and can be ordered from various suppliers.

from entering the lungs. After thoroughly mixing the dye powder in water or print paste, you can remove your mask.

You can take advantage of flaws in the dyeing process to create new methods. For instance, "ice dyeing" causes the dyes to "crystallize" and separate into various colors, making a beautiful effect.

UREA

Urea is a humectant or water attractor. Urea keeps the fabric wetter and allows the fabric more time to absorb the dye molecule. It is also a solvent that makes the dyes dissolve in water.

It is the chemical substitute for urine, which was historically used in dyeing. It is also a fertilizer and can be purchased at a fertilizer store in 46-0-0 form.

Urea, in its wet form, has a shelf life, and if your alginate/print paste smells like strong ammonia, it will change the

NOTE:
I mix soda ash into my print paste. Because the dyes mixed with soda ash lose their color in two or three days, both in the cups and on the screens, I recharge the cups of dye by adding a bit more dye powder. If I'm leaving the screens to be pulled another day, I don't add the soda ash to the print paste.

pH balance and affect the dyeing process. Only mix the needed amount or refrigerate the unused alginate.

METAPHOS (METAPHOSPHATE)

Metaphos is a water softener. It also creates a "smoother" consistency allowing fluids to flow more evenly. It is used in food products like whipped cream, salad dressings and imitation cheese.

LUDIGOL

Ludigol prevents the inactivity of reactive dyes during batching resulting in brighter colors that stay brighter longer.

SYNTHRAPOL

Synthrapol is used to remove sizing from commercial fabrics because it will interfere with the dyeing process.

It is also a wetting agent reducing the surface tension and allowing the dye molecules to become evenly distributed. Used for washing out printed or dyed fabrics, Synthrapol prevents the darker dyes from transferring to the lighter areas allowing many pieces of dyed fabric to be washed together.

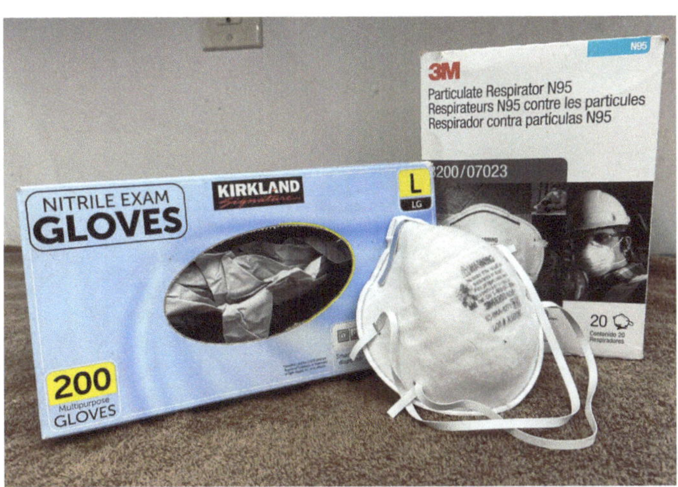

When working with dye in its powder state, always wear a mask and gloves. You may want to keep wearing gloves when using dye to keep your hands clean and to prevent the dye from being absorbed into your skin.

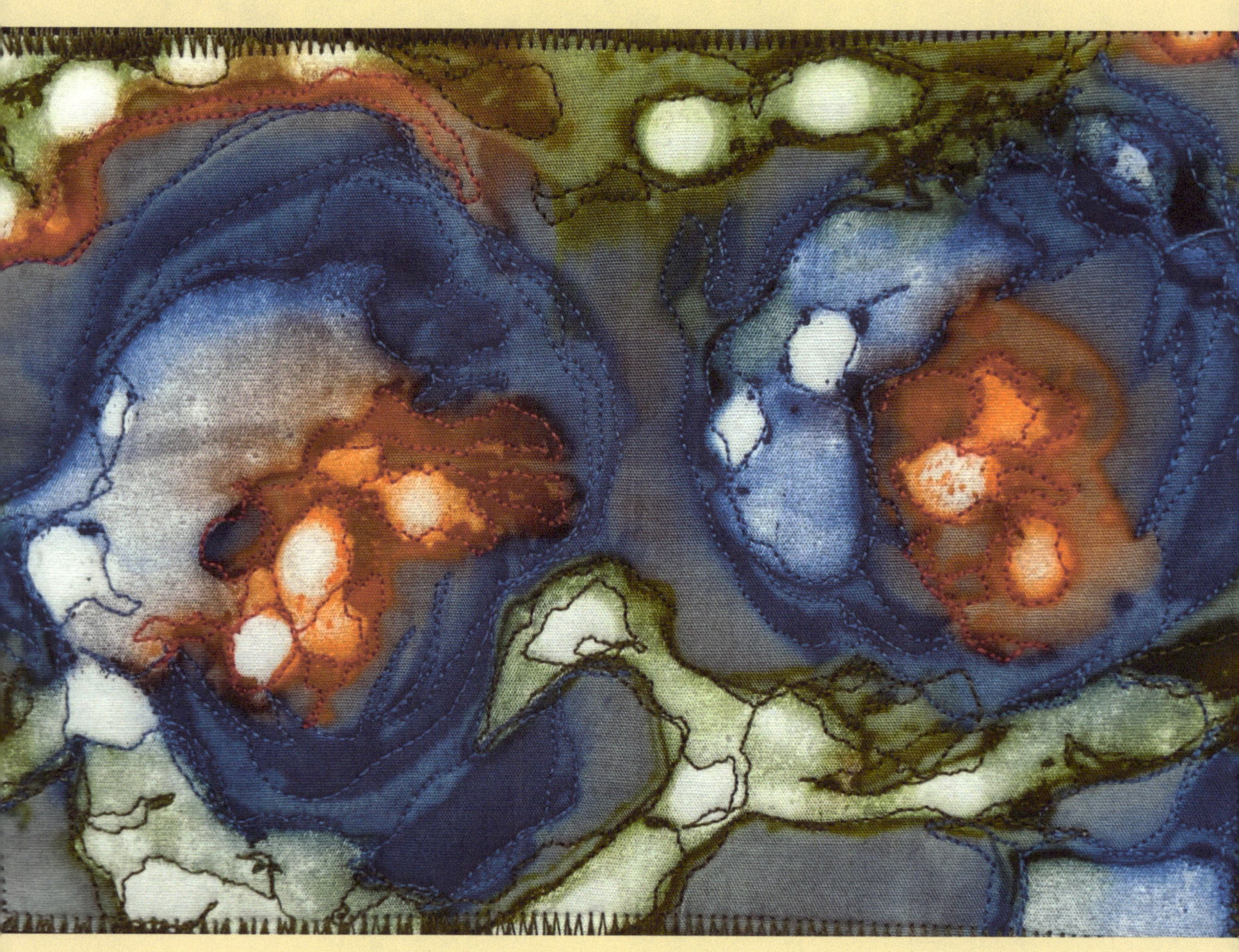

You'll want to use every piece of your printed fabrics! Here a small section of printed fabric was stitched onto a postcard.

chapter 16

Building a Tabletop
Printing Pad

The objective is to construct a flat, smooth, slightly padded surface to provide even contact between the screen and fabric to produce a clear print. (A hard, smooth surface is suitable for printing on paper.)

MATERIALS:

• 1- to 3-inch-thick EPS insulation board measuring 6 feet by 4 feet to cover an entire tabletop, or 4 feet by 3 feet for a medium-sized, more portable tabletop
• Carpet padding (⅜- to ⅝-inch thick) to lay on top of the insulation board
• Roll of 1 mil plastic sheeting. Plastic must be long and wide enough to wrap around the board completely.
• Polyester fabric (optional)
• Duct tape and scissors

DIRECTIONS:

• Cut padding the same size as the insulation board. Cut plastic sheeting large enough to wrap around to the back of the board and overlap about 3 inches.
• Place padding on one side of board, tape padding in place around edges of board, making sure it is smooth.
• With padding side down, center board on the plastic covering, bring plastic around and over edges and to the back. Beginning in the center of one side, tape plastic to the board every 6 inches.
• Complete one side, then repeat on the opposite side, beginning in the center and pulling plastic as tightly as possible. Tape corners last. Plastic must have no wrinkles.
• You may use polyester fabric between padding and plastic to keep surface clean.

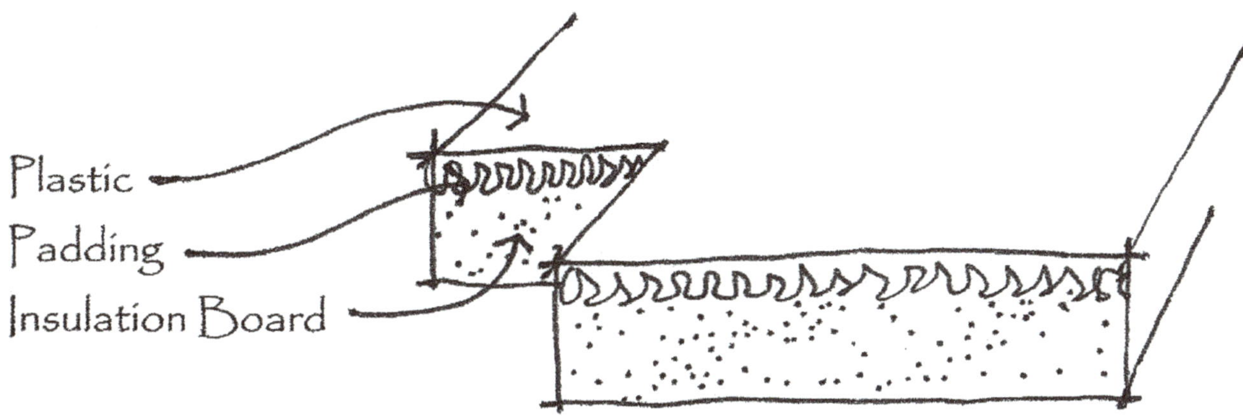

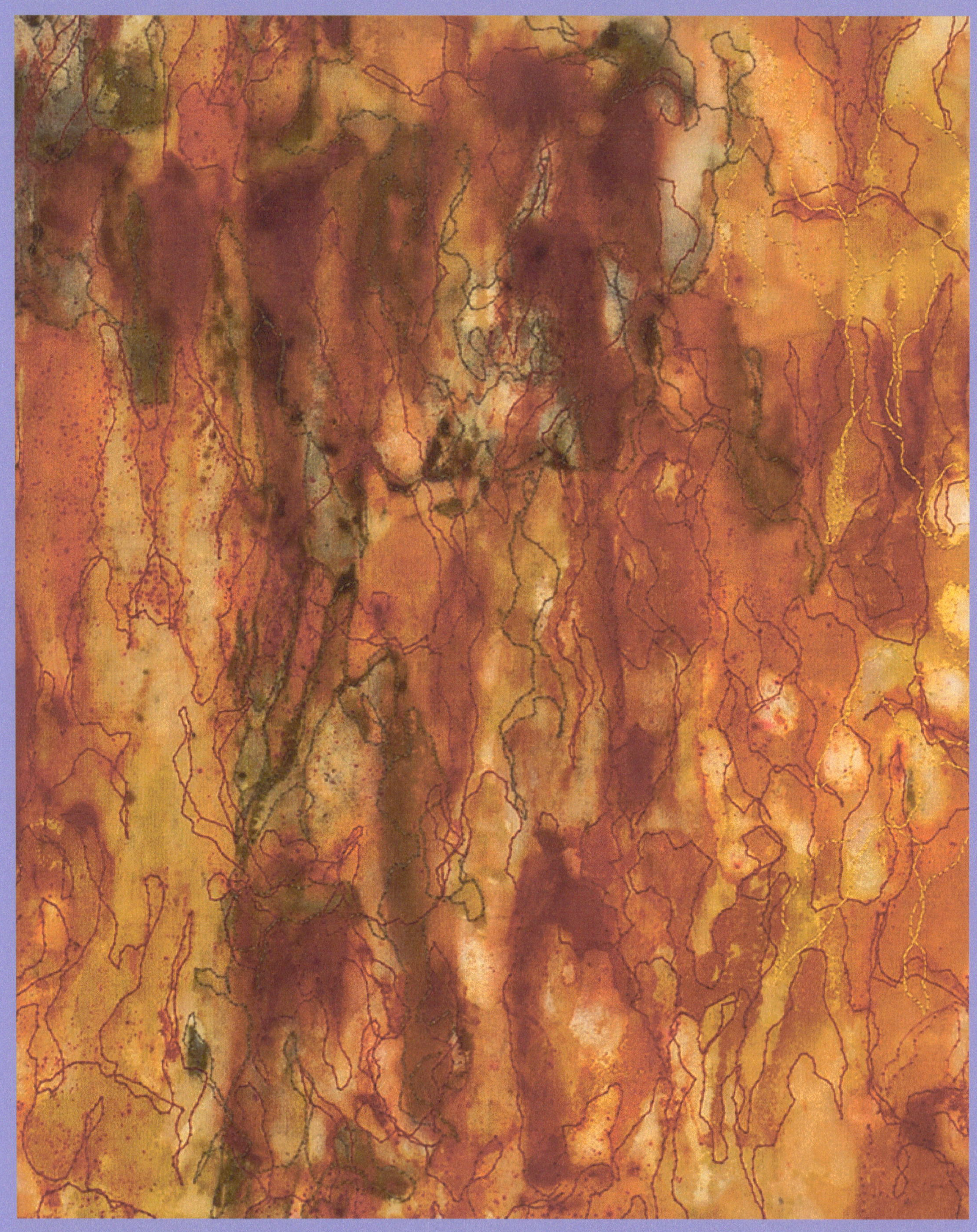

Detail of "Jack Rabbit" (24" x 36") by Susan Brooks, whole cloth artwork inspired by a sunset in the Arizona desert.

Glossary

Alginate: Solution used to create thickened dyes and to pull prints.

Batching: Wrapping fabrics in plastic to keep moist while dye molecules continue to process. Bundles are usually kept wrapped and warm for 24 hours. Cotton fabrics can be kept wrapped indefinitely. Silk cannot be kept past six months.

Deconstructed: An image is painted onto a screen and with every pull is broken down, or deconstructed, until the image is gone from the screen.

Mud: The mixture made from the dyes on the screen and alginate/print paste that creates a new dye color.

Over-dye: Once a piece of fabric is dyed or has a print on the surface, over-dyeing is the processing of a second immersion dye. The process is much like blending paint colors and creating another color on the surface.

Print paste: Alginate that contains dye powder, also called thickened dye.

Pulling a print: Using the clear alginate/print paste or thickened dyes to remoisturize the dyes on a screen and create the printed images.

Well: The area at the bottom of the screen that is taped off to create a space to hold the mud (alginate) until it's pulled.

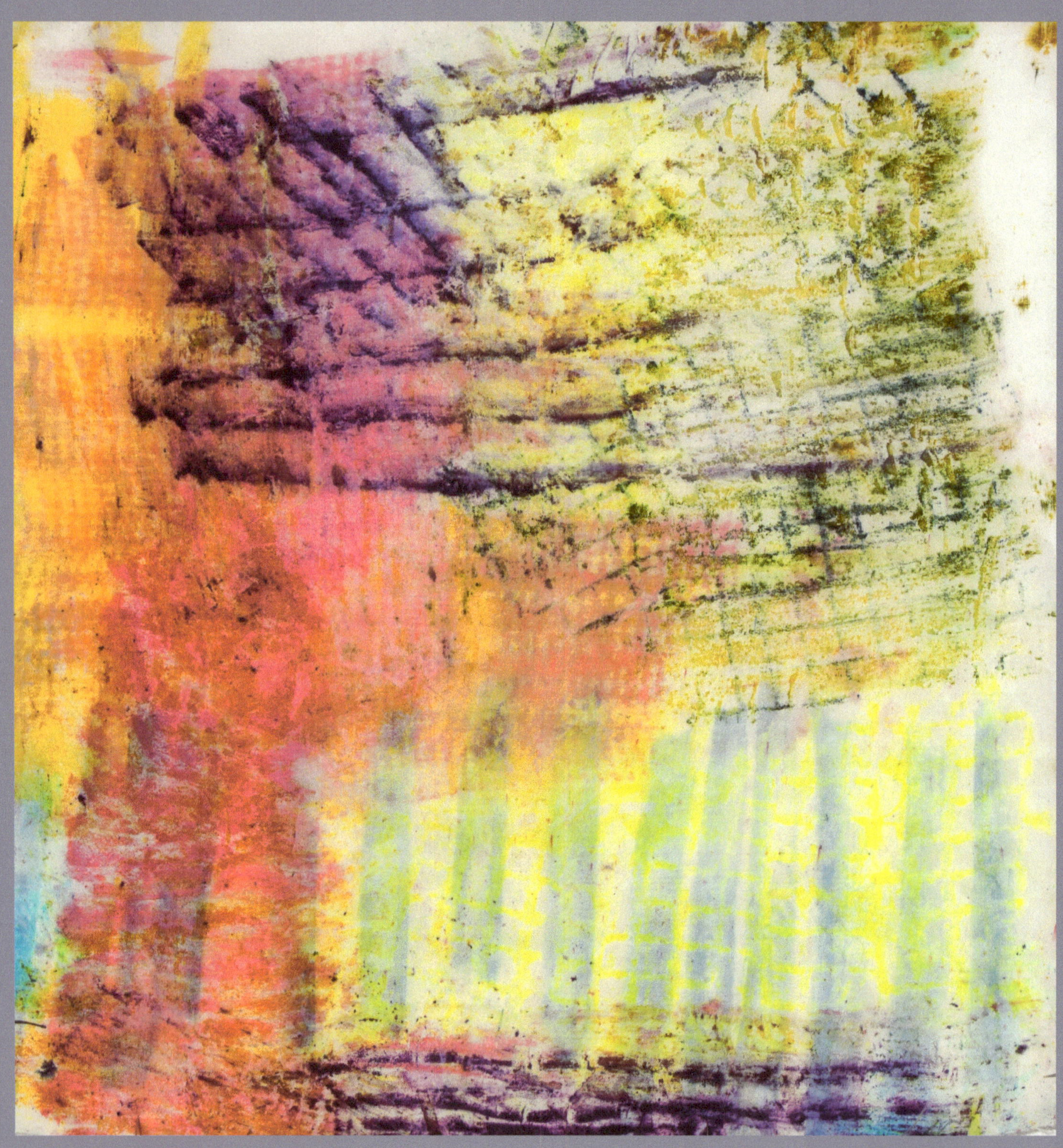

Jane Dunnewold's art piece

Acknowledgments

Many of the techniques taught in this book were originally published in a technical book, *Screen Printing Techniques*, by Albert Kosloff, in 1972.

In 2002, I learned this art form from a wonderful artist and teacher, Kerr Grabowski. Kerr has made the art form uniquely her own, primarily printing on silks to make wearable art.

See her work at www.kerrgrabowski.com.

Jane Dunnewold, another incredible artist and instructor, has also greatly influenced my work. See her work at www.janedunnewold.com.

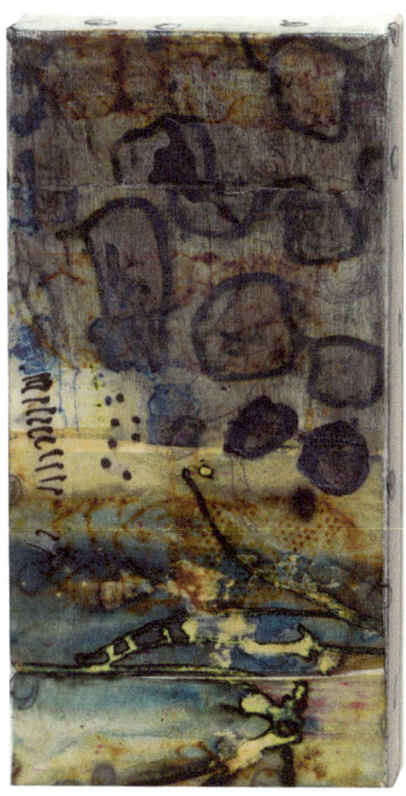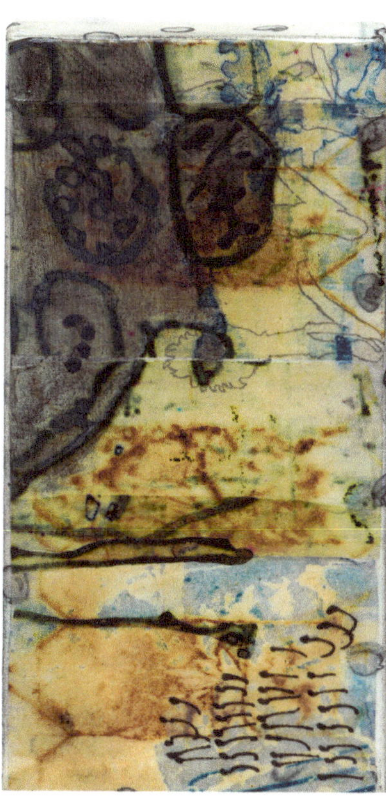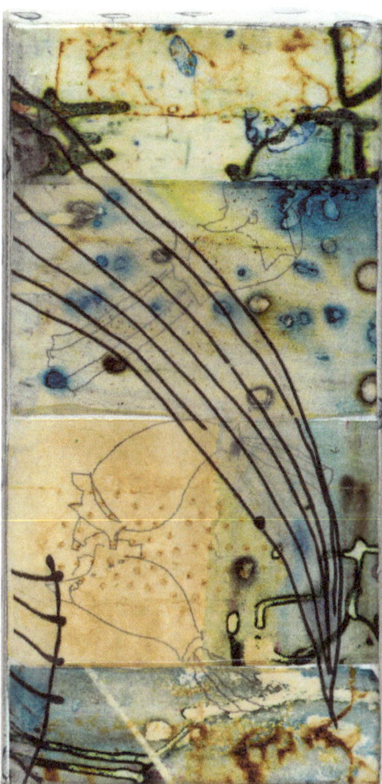

Kerr Grabowski's art piece

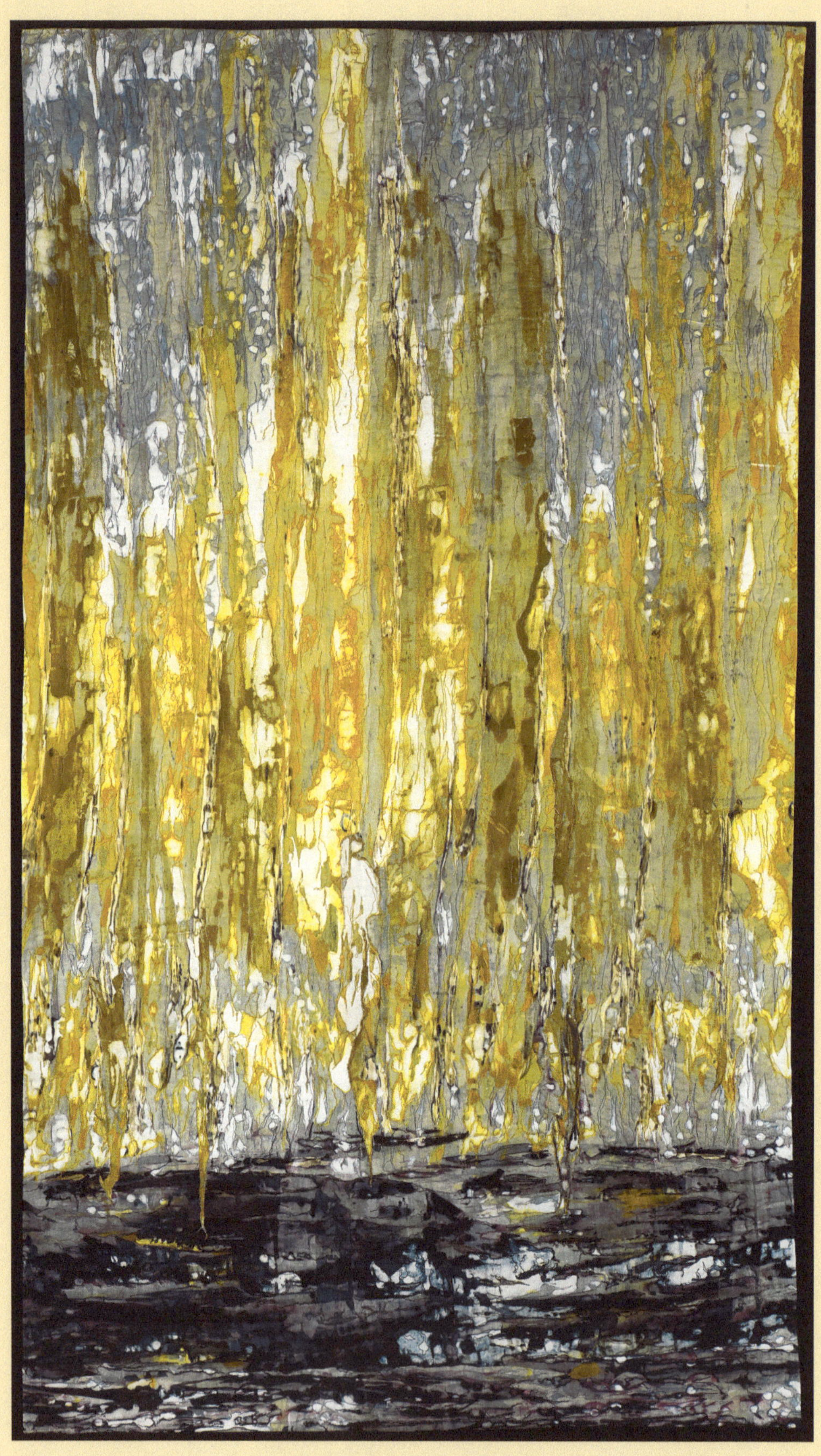

"Remembrance - Heal" (34" x 62") by Susan Brooks, whole cloth artwork of the healing lights in New York City.

FOR DYES, CHEMICALS AND SUPPLIES:

Dharma Trading Company, www.dharmatrading.com

Dick Blick, www.dickblick.com

Grateful Dyes, www.grateful-dyes.com (Grateful Dyes has competitive pricing on dyes, auxiliary chemicals and clothing blanks but limited dye color selection.)

Colorado Wholesale Dye Corp., 5682 S Cedar St., Littleton, CO 80120 303-763-9730, 800-697-1566

Jacquard, www.jacquardproducts.com

PRO Chemical & Dye, www.prochemicalanddye.com

CRAFT STORES:

Hobby Lobby
Michael's
Other local hobby stores in your area

EXTRUDERS:

Vista Apex, www.vistaapex.com

SCREENS:

American Frame Company, 800-651-5150 (They will make screens to your size and seal them with varnish.)
Dick Blick, www.dickblick.com

SQUEEGEES:

The Hyde Store, https://hydestore.com (Hyde 45807 Smoothing Tool White Plastic – 8 inch)

T-PINS:

Hobbylinc, www.hobbylinc.com (1-inch size)
Also available on Amazon.com

PLASTIC AND TEXTURES:

Home Depot
Lowe's
Walmart

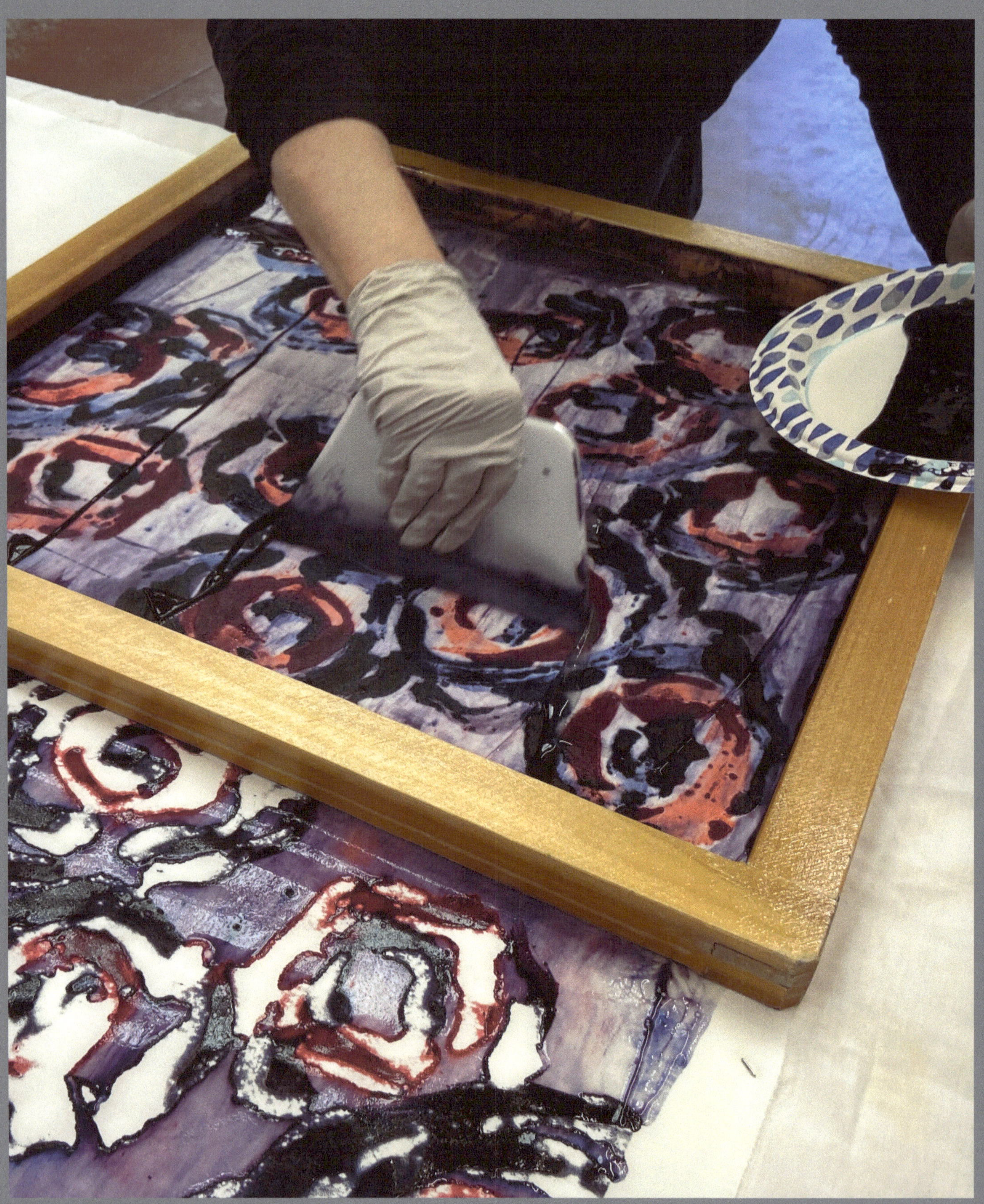

With the deconstructed method, pulling a series of prints always reveals surprising and interesting results.

My Favorite Dye Colors and Mixed Dyes

FROM DHARMA TRADING COMPANY:

Jet Black – #250
Brush Steel - #154
Moss Green - #134
Indigo - #168
Eggplant - #115
Marigold - #67
Palomino Gold - #138
Turquoise - #25
Bronze - #37 (makes a wonderful ice dye)
Brazil Nut - #116
Terra Cotta - # 141

FROM PRO CHEMICAL & DYE COMPANY:

Mixing Red - #305
Mixing Blue - #402c
Brick - # 520
Bronze - #5193
Ecru - # 5223
Winter White - # 010

PROCION MX COLOR FORMULA GUIDE:

Download a PDF guide that provides the formula for dye mixtures from Jacquard: jacquardproducts.com, Procion MX Color Formula Guide (PDF)

HELPFUL RESOURCE ON DYE MIXING AND GRADATING:

Fabric Dye Dictionary by Linda Johansen

FORMULAS FOR TWO OF MY OWN DYE COLORS

Brownish Purple

- 1 teaspoon red
- 1 teaspoon blue
- $\frac{1}{8}$ to $\frac{1}{4}$ teaspoon jet black

New Aqua

- 4 $\frac{1}{2}$ teaspoons turquoise
- $\frac{1}{2}$ teaspoon yellow
- $\frac{1}{2}$ tsp black

About the Author

Creating art using fabrics and papers provides the opportunity to build layers for a sense of protection, safety and security. I create my own fabrics through dyeing, botanical printing, resists and painting and then can add dimension and detail using stitches. I have focused on the elements in plants to imprint the images of leaves and flowers to create another layer of delicate beauty and interest.

Diverse techniques are used to express differing emotions. Deconstructed screen printing is used for a very organic look. The use of painting thickened dyes on plastic has been used for my monoprints of women. The morphing of the dyes can produce a surrealistic effect.

Botanical dyeing, plant-based dyes and prints introduce the beauty of nature into my work. I love stitching and connecting threads to hold the pieces together. The tactile feel and visual beauty of fabric has been a motivation to creativity. As a child, I was fascinated by the possibility of transforming a flat piece of cloth into a uniquely crafted article of clothing. After a journey of making dolls, garments and quilts, I am now driven to experiment with new techniques in dyeing, painting and embellishing fabric.

I enjoy sharing my passion with others by teaching these techniques and broadening my own exploration in fabric art. My aspiration is to tell a story, engage the viewer in a dialogue and challenge them to a deeper emotional experience.

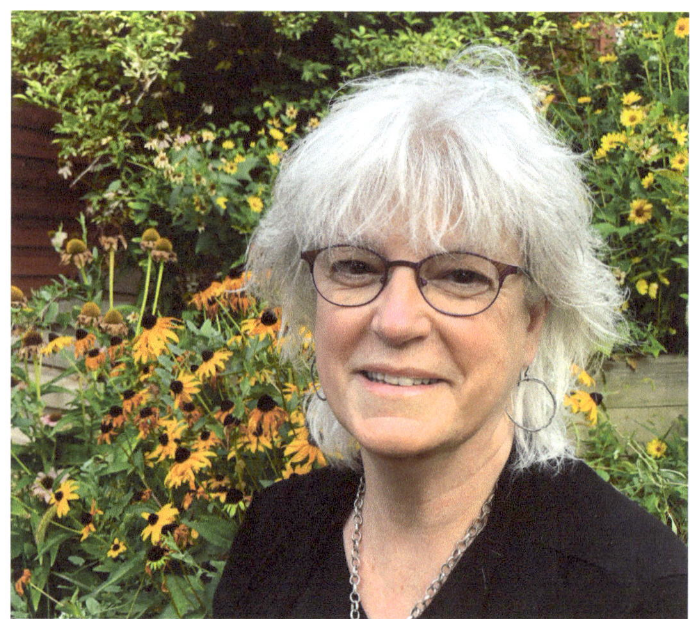

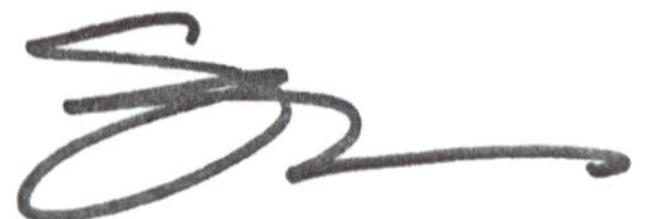

Susan Brooks
Creation's Child
susanbrookstextileartist.com
susanbrooksis@gmail.com

www.ingramcontent.com/pod-product-compliance
Lightning Source LLC
Chambersburg PA
CBHW040044240726
48664CB00004B/1060